THE STORY OF ISLAMIC PHILOSOPHY

THE STORY OF ISLAMIC PHILOSOPHY

Ibn Ṭufayl, Ibn al- ʿArabī, and Others on the Limit between Naturalism and Traditionalism

SALMAN H. BASHIER

STATE UNIVERSITY OF NEW YORK PRESS

To Sara Sviri and David Shulman

Published by State University of New York Press, Albany

Printed in the United States of America

For information, contact State University of New York Press, Albany, NY
www.sunypress.edu

Production Laurie Searl
Marketing Anne M. Valentine

Library of Congress Cataloging-in-Publication Data

Bashier, Salman H., 1964-
The story of Islamic philosophy : Ibn Tufayl, Ibn al-'Arabi, and others on the limit between naturalism and traditionalism / Salman H. Bashier.
p. cm.
Includes index and bibliographical references.
ISBN 978-1-4384-3743-9 (hardcover : alk. paper)
ISBN 978-1-4384-3742-2 (paperback : alk. paper)
1. Islamic philosophy—History. 2. Naturalism. 3. Tradition (Philosophy)
I. Title.
B741.B375 2011
181'.07—dc22

2011006682

10 9 8 7 6 5 4 3 2 1

Contents

Acknowledgments

I would like to thank the Wissenschaftskolleg zu Berlin Institute for Advanced Study. During my fellowship year at the Wissenschaftskolleg (2007–2008) I enjoyed its most generous support and benefited a great deal from the enlightening conversations with fellows and distinguished scholars from all over the world. I also would like to thank the Van Leer Jerusalem Institute for a five-year Polonsky Postdoctoral Fellowship (commencing in 2008) that allowed me also to complete the work on the present book and also to start working on my new project. Among the several friends and intellectuals that I have interacted with during the work on this book I would like to thank especially Sara Sviri and David Shulman, both professors at the Hebrew University of Jerusalem. This book is dedicated to them.

Abbreviations

A	*Alf Layla wa-Layla*
AEL	*Arabic-English Lexicon*
BL	*Book of Letters*
BWA	*The Basic Works of Aristotle*
FUS	*Fuṣūṣ al-Ḥikam*
FUT	*Futūḥāt Makkiyya*
G	*Gilgamesh*
IAI	*Ittiṣāl al-'Aql bi-al-Insān*
INM	*Islamic Naturalism and Mysticism*
KH	*Kitāb al-Ḥurūf*
MHQ	*The Meaning of the Holy Qur'an*
SD	*The Self-Disclosure of God*
TCD	*The Collected Dialogues of Plato*
THA	*Ḥayy Ibn Yaqẓān*
THY	*Ibn Ṭufayl's Ḥayy Ibn Yaqẓān*

Introduction

The story of Islamic philosophy is the story of the development of the human intellect from the rationalistic phase, represented in this study by Fārābī (d.950)[1], to an illuminative phase represented by Ibn Ṭufayl (d.1185) and Ibn al-ʿArabī (d.1240).[2] Illuminative philosophy is based on a model of mystical illumination that found its best expression in Plato's *Seventh Letter* and that is illustrated in *Mishkāt al-Anwār (Niche of Lights)* by Ghazālī (d. 1111) and *al-Ishārāt wa-al-Tanbīhāt (Allusions and Intimations)* and the mystical recitals of Ibn Sīnā (d. 1037)[3] The central tenet of this model is that following a rigorous and thorough exercise of the rational faculty, the human reason reaches a certain limit and is flooded with light. The thinker whose reason is brought to this *liminal* situation becomes aware of the limitations of his rational faculty and the possibility of obtaining knowledge by means of mystical illumination rather than mere rational conceptualization. This epistemological awareness is then extended to a comprehensive, liminal depiction of the ontological status of the world. Things in the world acquire an intermediary nature, and the world as a whole itself becomes a liminal entity between Truth (*ḥaqq*) and its existential manifestations (*khalq*).

In this book, I use Ibn Ṭufayl's work and the work of other Islamic thinkers to present the main principles of illuminative or liminal philosophy, while emphasizing its special capacity at articulating a synthetic vision of the naturalistic (or philosophical) and the traditionalistic (or religious) accounts of the epistemological and the ontological orders of reality. Ibn Ṭufayl was known for his encyclopedic scholarship and his generous sponsorship of intellectual research, which is confirmed by the detailed account that Ibn Rushd (d. 1198)[4] provides for the meeting that Ibn Ṭufayl arranged between him and the Muwaḥḥid Sultan, under whose patronage Ibn Rushd wrote commentaries on Aristotle's corpus. Very little is known about his personal life, and except for some fragments of poetry, *Ḥayy Ibn Yaqẓān (Alive Son of the Awake)* is Ibn Ṭufayl's only extant work. The work has been translated into several languages, including English translations by Simon Ockley (1708) and Lenn Goodman (1972). Goodman's translation is preceded by a significant introduction to the text in which he presents Ibn Ṭufayl's thought as a unique educational philosophy and emphasizes the differences between it and educational philosophies of important Western intellectuals. Sāmī Ḥāwī, whose *Islamic Naturalism and Mysticism* is one of the most significant studies of Ibn Ṭufayl's work in modern scholarship, follows a seemingly different strategy: He attempts to show the strong resemblances between Ibn Ṭufayl's thought and modern Western intellectuality. This is despite the fact that he has interesting things to say, not only in relation to the shortcomings of the Orientalists' treatment of Islamic philosophy but also concerning the limitations of modern philosophical thought in general.[5] In his treatment of Ḥayy, he seems to be struggling between his desire to apply to his study a strict rationalistic approach and the fact that he is dealing with a philosopher-mystic who makes an explicit declaration of the limitation of rationalistic thought.[6]

In arguing for the originality of *Ḥayy*, Ḥāwī insists that Ibn Ṭufayl did not borrow his ideas from Ghazālī or Ibn Sīnā, and that the utmost that one can infer is that they had an influence on his thought.[7] But Ḥāwī infers from *Ḥayy* that Ibn Ṭufayl *intended* not to follow Ibn Sīnā because in his description of the mystical states (*aḥwāl*) in *Ishārāt,* Ibn Sīnā was an imitator.[8] Such inferences, needless to say, go against Ibn Ṭufayl's own statements, and Ḥāwī seems to be one step closer to claiming, as Dimitri Gutas and other scholars did, that in attributing illuminative wisdom to Ibn Sīnā, Ibn Ṭufayl was an inventor of a fiction. Instead, Ḥāwī depicts the difference between Ibn Sīnā and Ibn Ṭufayl in terms of a distinction between a possessor of theoretical knowledge (*naẓar*) and a possessor of immediate knowledge (*dhawq*), which he develops into a distinction between conceptual apprehensions and dynamic existential involvement.[9] He finds the parallel to Ibn Ṭufayl's existential involvement in Kierkegaard's dynamic existential breach, which is contrary to the mediating process of reason. Like Kierkegaard, Ibn Ṭufayl teaches us that immediate experience must not be replaced with an abstraction, that reason has limits, and that propositional knowledge of the truth is impossible: "Rationality is not man's only basic differentia . . . Like most existentialists, he strongly contended that man makes himself, fulfills himself, and becomes himself in the dynamic act of knowing the Truth—Necessary Being. Ḥayy's very nature was a process, a project to surpass the now and reach the everlasting eternal."[10] Thus, Ḥayy, the existentialist, realizes that man's nature is more than his reason and, like the existentialists, he attempts a "hypothetical destruction of, and universal doubt in, the surrounding world of tradition and education."[11]

One might wonder how Ḥāwī's existentialist interpretation can be consistent with his statement that "Ibn Ṭufayl's philosophy becomes almost hollow and indigent if one strips it of its metaphysical locus."[12] Ḥāwī's depiction of Ibn Ṭufayl's existentialistic literary style, which he contrasts with rigorous logic in his description of Ḥāyy's attainment of mystical experience, seems to be in stark opposition to his own rationalistic depiction of his treatise.[13] Ḥāwī's study as a whole seems to be divided into two unrelated parts in which rationalism and mysticism are presented independently of each other. His failure to present a coherent interpretation of Ibn Ṭufayl's thought stems from his insistence on dissociating him from any possible influence by Ibn Sīnā, which prevents him from properly appreciating the significance of the illuminative account that Ibn Sīnā introduces in *Ishārāt* and that Ibn Ṭufayl employs as his basic model of the knowledge of illumination. As we shall see, Ibn Sīnā provides a liminal depiction of the mystical states (*aḥwāl*) and of the possessor of knowledge, who becomes, like them, a limit between presence (existence and manifestation) and absence (nonexistence and nonmanifestation) and a polished mirror facing the Real. In the same vein, Ibn Ṭufayl provides a liminal depiction of the transcendent essences (*dhawāt mufāriqa*), which are *imaginal* reflections of the Real, and Hayy's essence, which becomes, like them, an imaginal representation of the Real.

In his attempt to show that *Ḥayy* is devoid of the symbolic nature of Ibn Sīnā's mystical recitals, Ḥāwī emphasizes that the major part of the treatise consists of a progressive philosophical argument and that even the part that leads to the attainment of mystical enlightenment "is also progressively substantiated by a full-blooded argument."[14] But he falls short of explaining how Ibn Ṭufayl's mystical conclusion is related to the progression of his logical argument. It must be admitted, however, that establishing this sort of relatedness is, in a sense, problematic because it implies that the passage beyond reason is paradoxical in the sense that it is itself the result of a rational necessity. And yet, the recognition of this paradoxicality, and with it the self-transcendent nature of the limits of reason, are fundamental principles of illuminative philosophy. The possessor of reason recognizes this paradoxicality following a mystical exercise depicted by Ibn al-ʿArabī as an exercise of fasting, at the consummation of which it is said of the person who fasts: "The sun has gone down from the world of the witnessed and risen up in the world of the intellect (*ʿaql*)."[15] As William Chittick points out, Ibn al-ʿArabī usually renders the word *ʿaql* as "reason" but employs "intellect" to designate the illuminated reason of the Gnostic. Ibn al-ʿArabī says: "When the affair reaches this limit, he gains the divine uplifting beyond the property of his own nature, and self-disclosure lifts him up beyond the property of his reflection, since reflection derives from the property of elemental nature … *The intellect, in respect of itself, possesses self-disclosure*, so it is lifted up beyond the low reaches of the natural reflection that accompanies imagination and takes from sensation and the sensory thing."[16] Perhaps the best demonstration of the notion that reason in respect of itself possesses self-disclosure can be found in the logic that leads Ibn al-ʿArabī to his paradoxical concept of the essential limit, or *barzakh*.

According to Aristotle, the limit is the ultimate part and essence of each thing because things are known by their limits.[17] This is also what Ibn al-ʿArabī thinks: "For distinction occurs through limits, and knowledge comes to be through distinction."[18] He notices, however, that the limit not only divides two things but also unifies them. Consequently, the (essential) limit must possess *two* faces (to differentiate the two things) that are *one* (to provide for their unity): if the two faces, with which it meets the two things, were not one, a new limit would be required to differentiate between them, and knowledge would be impossible.[19]

Ibn al-ʿArabī says that the possessors of unveiling know the essential limits and stop at them. This knowledge is difficult to attain because, unlike the formal limits (*al-ḥudūd al-rasmiyya*), the essential limits are difficult to *find*.[20] As for those who stop at the formal limits, they are the possessors of belief.[21] Ibn al-ʿArabī associates the formal limits here with the ordinances of religious law, but he also identifies them with the limits that rational thinkers employ.[22] Those who possess the essential limits in addition to the formal limits are perfect. Those who possess only the formal limits are complete but not perfect: "What is sought is perfection (*kamāl*), not completion (*tamām*), for completion lies in creation, but perfection lies in the benefits that the complete acquires and bestows. Someone may not gain this degree despite his completion—for God *has given each thing its creation*, and thereby it has been completed, *then guided* (Q 20:50) to the acquisition of perfection. He who is guided reaches perfection, but he who stops with his completion has been deprived."[23]

He who is guided is guided to bewilderment (*ḥayra*), considered by Ibn al-ʿArabī as one of the highest stages of knowledge.[24] Bewilderment is not negative. On the contrary, bewilderment is essential for realizing the truth of perfect knowledge. Thus, when the knower is bewildered, bewilderment is removed from him *in bewilderment*.[25] Bewilderment is movement, and movement is life.[26] Those who stop in their knowledge at the formal limits, the limits of manifestation or creation, are complete. In the closure or completion of their knowledge, however, lies their imperfection because creation is renewed constantly following the constant self-disclosure of the Real. Those who are bewildered transcend the formal limits and connect with the essential limits, the limits of self-disclosure. They are the possessors of perfect knowledge, and they become such by turning themselves into essential limits—polished mirrors that perfectly reflect the form of the Real. Despite its simplicity, Jābar bin Ḥayyān's story may be useful for illustrating this point: "They say that in a certain valley there are snakes that can kill animals instantly by looking into their eyes. They also say that in this valley there is a great beast whose eyes are like gulfs. As the snake seeks to kill it, the beast lifts up its eyes toward the head so that its sight would not fall on the snake and its eyes become like pure, polished mirrors. The snake sees itself in the mirror and dies."[27]

The knower attains live knowledge by turning himself into a liminal entity that resembles a perfectly polished mirror. By turning himself into such an entity, it becomes possible for the knower to see that which cannot be seen. This is because he sees "with God's eye," not "through his own eye from behind the veil of his essence."[28] In his interpretation of the Prophet's saying, "God has seventy veils of light and darkness, were He to lift them, the glories of His face would burn away everything that the eyesight of His creatures perceives," Ibn al-ʿArabī says that the dark and the luminous veils are the veils of nature and the reflective knowledges. Through the burning of these veils, the essences of the Gnostics become one essence that is identical with God. As for the common people, the veils are not lifted from them, so that they do not witness the truth of this unity. The Gnostics must not divulge this knowledge of unveiling and must take heed of the Prophet's saying: "Do not bestow wisdom on other than its folk, lest you wrong it, and do not hold it back from its folk, lest you wrong them."[29] As I will show in what follows, what Ibn al-ʿArabī says here is, in a sense, a summary of Ḥayy's and Ibn Ṭufayl's stories combined.

In introducing the naturalistic account of Ḥayy's birth, Ibn Ṭufayl presents a tripartite classification of bodies: transparent bodies that do not reflect light at all, such as air; dense bodies that reflect light partially; and bodies that reflect light perfectly, such as polished mirrors. In correspondence to this classification, he divides existents into inanimate objects, in whose form the Spirit, which resembles the light of the sun, does not leave any traces; plants in whose form the Spirit leaves some traces; and animals in whose form, and the form of the human being in particular, the Spirit leaves a full impression. As the presence of the form of the Spirit is reinforced in the form of the human being, its reality eclipses all other forms and whatever stands in its way. It then resembles a mirror that reflects on itself and burns everything else with the glories of its light. Then the form of the Spirit and the human form are united in a bond that is "indissoluble not only according to the senses but also according to reason."[30] The story of Ḥayy Ibn Yaqẓān is the story of the reestablishment of this bond by removing the physical and rational veils that stand between man and his real nature. The story can be divided into three stages. In the practical stage, Ḥayy learns how to remove natural or physical veils. In the theoretical stage, he learns how to remove rational veils. In the mystical stage, he learns how to transform the ultimate veil, his own self, into an essential or liminal entity that turns on itself and burns everything else. Then Ḥayy encounters common religious people and seeks to "bestow wisdom on other than its folk." Prior to the description of this encounter, Ibn Ṭufayl registers his severe criticism of rationalists who are confined within the formal limits of their reason, as religious people are confined within the formal limits of their religious beliefs. He also learns Ḥayy's lesson, as he explains that even as he determined to write his book, he covered it with "a thin veil and a light covering, easily pierced by those who are worthy and too thick for those who are unworthy to penetrate it."[31]

Ḥayy may be regarded as the story of the development of human knowledge. This is different, however, from the story related in Fārābī's *Book of Letters* in the major sense that its author refuses to halt at the formal limits of (Aristotle's) logic. *Ḥayy* may also be regarded as the story of the relation between religion and philosophy. The problem of this relation, however, must not be depicted as external to philosophy and as pertaining merely to the relation between philosophers and religious people, but rather as falling within the limits of philosophy itself and as constituting a major incentive for refining or redefining these limits. This is why this problem cannot find its rather simple Fārābian solution by investing philosophical effort in convincing religious people that their religious beliefs are imperfect imitations of philosophical truths. Such a solution would only bring closure, whereas the story of philosophy is a story about disclosure.

OUTLINE OF THE CHAPTERS

Chapter 1. I argue against the views of three scholars, Dimitri Gutas, George Ṭarābīshī, and Lawrence Conrad, on Ibn Ṭufayl's mystical epistemology and the purpose of writing *Ḥayy*. Gutas claims that Ibn Ṭufayl misinterprets a certain passage in the prologue to *al-Shifā'*, in which Ibn Sīnā mentions his book on Eastern philosophy and falsely ascribes to him illuminative ideas to draw the attention of his readers to his own work. I do not see an act of misinterpretation here. Even if we concede that Ibn Sīnā was no illuminationist, the most that we can charge Ibn Ṭufayl with is naively repeating his words. Ibn Ṭufayl makes it perfectly clear that the *essence* of the knowledge of illumination is not to be found in Ibn Sīnā's *Shifā'*, which agrees almost completely with Peripateticism; or in his own work, in which he revealed whatever he could reveal of its secrets; or in any book, for that matter. He repeats his statement several times and in different places in his work, such that one begins to wonder what makes scholars freeze on one statement, in which he invites the reader to seek Ibn Sīnā's work on Eastern philosophy, and ignore all the rest.

Ibn Ṭufayl's special appreciation of Ibn Sīnā stems from the fact that after making such a remarkable advance in Peripateticism, he was still able to make a declaration to the effect that rationalistic thought is limited. Gutas's reluctance to give serious consideration to this declaration is the outcome of his insistence on making an absolute distinction between philosophy and mysticism. The portion of his writings in which Ibn Sīnā introduces his mystical insights is insignificant in terms of *quantity* and the assumption is that giving serious consideration to his mystical declaration in this meager portion must be inconsistent with the overwhelmingly rationalistic part of his work. Considered from Ibn Ṭufayl's point of view, however, this assumption is not only limited but is actually the root of the extreme rationalistic thought of which he is especially critical. After all, what is *Ḥayy* but such a long (rational) argument culminating in a mystical conclusion?

According to his own testimony, Ṭarābīshī became interested in the study of medieval Islamic philosophy only after reading Muḥammad al-Jābirī's *Critique of Arab Reason*. Because I make a number of references to Jābirī in this book, it will be useful to say a few words about his work. Several scholars consider Jābirī to be the first Modern thinker in the Arab world to provide a serious criticism of Islamic reason. Indeed, Jābirī's insistence on the significance of the rational order and the adherence to *externalist principles* bear a striking resemblance to the ideals of modern philosophies of the Enlightenment.[32] According to Jābirī, medieval Islamic philosophy failed to make any serious change in the epistemological contents that it inherited from the Greeks. However, it succeeded in exploiting those contents for the sake of settling its ideological conflicts, especially the conflict between philosophy and religion. Hence, Jābirī thinks that those who, like the Orientalists, judge Islamic philosophy according to epistemological standards commit a serious mistake because from an epistemological point of view, Islamic philosophy did not possess much of an essence. The problem of the relation between philosophy and religion occupied a central place in Islamic philosophy; and concerning this problem, Muslims were divided into Eastern and Western schools of thought. The Western school included thinkers such as Ibn Rushd, Ibn Ṭufayl, and Ibn Khaldūn, who maintained a view of separation between philosophy and religion. Those thinkers were in opposition to the Eastern school, which included thinkers such as Ibn Sīnā and Ghazālī, who attempted to establish harmony between philosophy and religion. This attempt resulted in alienating the Arabic mind from the path of rationalism. The thinkers of the Western school, the true philosophers, sought to overcome this alienation by building a wall that protects rationalistic philosophy from the esoteric influences of the irrationalists.[33] Muḥammad al-Miṣbāḥī concludes Jābirī's view by saying that he agreed with the Orientalists' claim that Islamic reason produced no new philosophical visions. At the same time, however, he blamed them for ignoring the fact that Islamic philosophers, by whom he meant those who belonged to the Western school, did not occupy themselves with philosophy for its own sake, but only to use it in resolving their ideological conflicts and to build a barrier between rationalism and irrationalism.[34]

In his work, Ṭarābīshī assumes the role of the skeptic, as he confines himself almost exclusively to demonstrating inconsistencies in Jābirī's position. Ṭarābīshī argues that the Western school of philosophy was not as united as Jābirī presents it. He actually considers Ibn Ṭufayl's work, in which he registers his special debt to Ibn Sīnā, as an attack against none other than the figure of Ibn Rushd and the rationalism that he represents. A careful examination of Ibn Ṭufayl's view on the relation between philosophy and religion, however, reveals how close it is to Ibn Rushd's. Rather than lending support for Jābirī's view, this fact should provide grounds for a more consistent reading of the principle of Islamic philosophy, and this is what the present book attempts to do.

Two main views on the purpose of writing *Ḥayy* have been advanced in scholarship. Léon Gauthier argued that the book is primarily about the realtion between philosophy and religion, and George Hourani argued that its principal subject is the possibility of the soul's unaided ascent to philosophical knowledge. Conrad criticizes both views. His criticism amounts to claiming that Ibn Ṭufayl was led to writing *Ḥayy* by societal rather than philosophical considerations. To establish his view, Conrad sought to reveal what he considered to be flaws in the logical structure of Ibn Ṭufayl's work. By doing so, he sought to throw doubt not only on Hourani's view, but equally on Gauthier's, because this is based on the assumption that Ibn Ṭufayl arrived at the concluding part of his work by following a perfectly planned and meticulously executed logical procedure. I attempt to show that what Conrad considers as flaws in the logic of Ibn Ṭufayl's narrative make perfect sense when examined from a liminal point of view and when proper consideration is given to the symbolic import of the treatise.

Chapter 2. Ibn Ṭufayl's employment of central Ṣūfī concepts in the introduction to his book aims to emphasize the element of self-reflexivity intrinsic to his model of illumination and to reveal an important fact about the limitation of the use of language in relation to an experience that defies closure. Ibn Ṭufayl describes the seeker of knowledge as a person who devotes himself (*ḥamīm*) to obtaining knowledge by constantly purifying (*ṣafyy*) the mirror of his heart. The Ṣūfī then becomes one with the state (*ḥāl*), which resembles the essence of time. This act of identification gives rise to utterances that "flow from" the Ṣūfīs (*shaṭaḥāt*) and that involve a claim for unity with Truth. This claim is paradoxical. It is a true claim, because Truth encompasses everything. Once stated, however, the claim becomes false because no matter how carefully unity is expressed, negation always creeps into it with the expression and splits it against itself. The recognition of this paradoxicality distinguishes the Ṣūfī not only from those who do not possess awareness of the limitations of all claims for Truth, but also from extreme skeptics, who by holding unlimitation as their *final* position only impose on themselves another form of limitation.[35]

Ibn Ṭufayl states that it was by the study of Ghazālī and Ibn Sīnā that he could see truth for himself. He describes Ghazālī as a person who was well-versed in *ma'rifa* (knowledge1) and *'ilm* (knowledge2). Knowledge2 is related to the world (*'ālam*), whereas knowledge1 is related to the transcendent essences that are beyond the sensible world. To say that Ghazālī was well versed in both knowledges is to say that he possessed both knowledge of manifestation and knowledge of nonmanifestation. It is to say that he belonged to the category of knowers who are in the image of the light of God, to whom belong both East and West (Q 2:142) and whose resemblance is an olive tree that is neither of the East nor of the West (Q 24:35). Ghazālī wrote *Niche of Lights* as an interpretation of the Verse of Light (Q 24:35). The presence of *Niche* in Ibn Ṭufayl's work is so strong that, together with his depiction of Ghazālī as a possessor of perfect knowledge, one is tempted to explain away his stated criticism of him as irrelevant. The most striking resemblances between Ghazālī's *Niche* and Ibn Ṭufayl's *Ḥayy* lie in their depiction of the cosmos as consisting of a hierarchy of light-reflecting mirrors. This depiction may be traced back to Neoplatonic influence, but I think that originally the influence goes back to Plato's Parable of the Cave.

An important feature of the mystical experience as it is depicted in this parable is the gradual unfolding of the light of illumination. Despite this graduality, the experience proves to be painful to the person who is involved in it. As for the feelings of joy and exultation to which Ibn Ṭufayl gives special attention in his description of the experience, they belong to the person in the state of intoxication (*sukr*). In this state, the person experiences absence. When he is again present, the person struggles to regain his former state. Ibn Sīnā amply accounts for this gradual struggle to attain illumination in *Ishārāt,* and I attempt to show that a similar account is present in his mystical recitals of *Ḥayy Ibn Yaqẓān* and *Salāmān and Absāl,* as well as the Hermetistic version of *Salāmān and Absāl*.

Chapter 3. Ibn Ṭufayl introduces two accounts of Ḥayy's birth: naturalistic and traditionalistic. He opens with a depiction of the naturalistic account, which describes Ḥayy's emergence from earth but interrupts it to add a succinct description of the traditionalistic account, according to which Ḥayy is born to human parents. Then he resumes his discussion of the naturalistic account with rich scientific details. Ḥāwī interprets this interruption as Ibn Ṭufayl's attempt to conceal his philosophical stand, which he identifies with naturalism. I argue against his interpretation.

According to the naturalistic account, Ḥayy was generated on an equatorial island, which enjoyed the most temperate climate, from a portion of earth that was perfectly balanced to receive the human form. Ibn Ṭufayl says also that people on this island were generated from trees. This is to emphasize the continuity between natural existents: minerals, plants, and animals. Ibn Ṭufayl's depiction of the chain of existents is compared to Ibn al-ʿArabī's and a certain resemblance between the two thinkers is detected. The major part of the discussion is devoted to Ibn al-ʿArabī's account of his mystical visions in the Earth of *Barzakh*, the conditions of which are similar to the conditions that existed on the equatorial island in which Ḥayy was born.

On Earth, natural existents live and speak and, unlike objects on our earth, they are not subject to generation and corruption. On it become manifest things that are judged by the rational proofs to be impossible, such as the bringing together of the opposites, the existence of a body in two places, and the subsistence of an accident in itself. The manifestation of these things on Earth enables Ibn al-ʿArabī to provide an interpretation for verses in the Qur'ān that the rational faculties shift from their manifest meanings. These things become manifest, however, only to the person who combines knowledge of manifestation (*ʿālim*) and knowledge of nonmanifestation (*ʿārif*); that is, the person who possesses the science of interpretation (*taʿbīr*) that enables him to cross over (*ʿubūr*) from the world of sensation to the intelligible world. I use Ibn al-ʿArabī's theory to provide an interpretation of Plato's myth of spontaneous generation in *Republic*.

Chapter 4. Upon the culmination of his intellectual growth, Ḥayy encounters human society and with this encounter he connects with the traditionalistic account of his birth. The exoteric and esoteric aspects of the human condition are represented here by Salāmān and Absāl, respectively. Although their relationship is depicted in terms of opposition, I attempt to show that their positions enjoy intermediary characteristics. Salāmān's involvement in theological debates with

Absāl signifies his tendency toward rational deliberation. Although fear for his religion leads him eventually to disconnect himself from Absāl and adhere to the dogmatic beliefs of his community, the very existence of fear indicates an important difference between him and other members of his community. Absāl tended toward esoteric interpretation. When he encountered Ḥayy, however, he also feared that interaction with him would endanger his religious beliefs. His fear was alleviated as he recognized that Ḥayy did not know language. His decision to teach him language was based on the hope that his lord would reward him. Thus, despite his inclination toward esoteric interpretation, Absāl was still subject to the principles of mass religion, especially fear (of God's punishment) and hope (for his recompense).

Using Plato's division of the degrees of reality in the parable of the Divided Line, I present Hayy as occupying the highest segment in the line. Next to him comes Absāl, followed by Salāmān. The (dogmatic) people of the religious community occupy the lowest segment of the line and the most distanced from Ḥayy's, which explains the intensity of their opposition to his attempt to convey his illuminative knowledge to them.

Chapter 5. Ḥayy's reflections on the problem of the eternity of the world signified a turning point in his intellectual development. Ḥayy examined limits between chains of existence in the world, but now he came to examine the limits of the world itself. This led him to thinking about the concept of the infinite and its role in establishing the arguments for and against the eternity of the world. I present Aristotle's analysis of this concept and show its relevance to these arguments. Ibn Ṭufayl presented the positions of the philosophers and the theologians in relation to the problem of the eternity of the world as balanced. Ḥāwī claims that by doing so, he attempted to conceal his eternalist position. I argue against this claim.

Chapter 6. In *The Book of Letters,* Fārābī provides an account of the development of human thought from the commencement of the use of language to the time of the invention of logic by Aristotle. He includes in his account a discussion of the relation between philosophy and religion and the role that the philosopher must assume in establishing harmony between them. There are important differences between his account and the one provided by Ibn Ṭufayl. Ibn Ṭufayl's hero became acquainted with the use of language only after he had exhausted all the stages of the development that Fārābī assigns to his rationalistic philosophers and that culminate in Aristotle's logic. This is important because according to Fārābī, the universal language of logic comes afterward and must therefore be considered prior in significance to ordinary languages. Ibn Ṭufayl, however, makes his "silent speaker" employ logic and then transcend its principles. Thus, he applies to formal logic the same argument that Fārābī applies to ordinary languages and, by doing so, he endows it, and the philosopher who adheres to its categories, with a lesser status.

Another important difference between the two philosophers lies in their treatment of the relation between philosophy and religion. Fārābī seems to be positive about the chances of the philosopher to convince believers that what they have in their religion is only the imitation of higher philosophical truths. Ibn Ṭufayl does not share this optimism with Fārābī, not only because of his especially negative view of the intellectual capacities of dogmatic believers, but also because of his recognition of the limitations of the very rationalistic capacity that Fārābī considers as absolute.

Chapter 7. Despite his critical view of Ibn Bājja,[36] Ibn Ṭufayl had a special appreciation for his intellectual capacities. This appreciation stems from his recognition of the significant contribution that Ibn Bājja made to the principle of illuminative philosophy, especially in relation to his liminal depiction of the levels of comprehension. I emphasize the liminal component in Ibn Bājja's thought and the clear impact that Plato's "mystical" parables had on it.

Chapter 8. In describing the traditionalist account, Ibn Ṭufayl makes an allusion to the (Qur'ānic) story of the Sleepers in the Cave. Aristotle mentions the story in *Physics* in the context of discussing the nature of time. I relate his discussion to Ibn Ṭufayl's depiction of the resemblances in which Ḥayy was involved and in which he imitated natural time and motion, the unitary time and the circular motion of the transcendent essences, and the state of absolute fixity characteristic of God. In the context of this discussion, I elaborate on an important incident in Ḥayy's life: the discovery of fire. The traditionalistic account of Ḥayy's birth bears a clear resemblance to Moses's birth story. I elaborate on Ibn al-ʿArabī's depiction of the figure of Moses in *Fuṣūṣ al-Ḥikam*, especially Moses's birth story and his encounter with the Saint (al-Khaḍir).

Chapter 9. Gilgamesh is the builder of Uruk's great walls and the one who plunged into the Absū (sweet waters) to claim the plant of rejuvenation following his encounter with Utnapishtim, The-One-Who-Found-Life. Enkidu is the child of nature, whose creation story bears a striking resemblance to Adam's. Enkidu was seduced toward civilized Uruk by a love-priestess. He and Gilgamesh undertake a series of adventures that enrage the gods, who determine Enkidu's death. His death gives birth to Gilgamesh's quest for eternity. Gilgamesh goes on a long journey, at the end of which he comes together with Utnapishtim and hears from him the story of the Flood, which is, like Ḥayy's, a story about a new beginning. As Moses failed to obtain the object of his quest for perfect knowledge in his encounter with al-Khadir, so Gilgamesh also failed to obtain the object of his quest in his encounter with Utnapishtim. The main lesson that we learn from both encounters is that the object of the mystical quest is one of seeking, not of possessing.

Chapter 10. In the preface to *Myths from Mesopotamia*, Stephanie Dalley writes: "A few original contributions by this translator are included: recognition that the *Tale of Bulūqiya* in the *Arabian Nights* is related to the *Epic of Gilgamesh*."[37] I consider the recognition that Ibn al-ʿArabī's Chapter 8 of the *Futūhāt* is related to *Bulūqiya* as one of the original contributions in the present work. At the same time, I wish to point out that I have detected a strong resemblance between chapter 8 of the *Futūḥāt* and *Uthūlūjiya*, a highly influential work that was mistakenly attributed to Aristotle, and that I will elaborate on this resemblance in my next book.

I want to discuss a few points at the close of this introduction. First, I consider Plato to be one of the main originators of the liminal notion that I presented in my book *Ibn al-ʿArabī's Barzakh* and that I develop further here. The emphasis on the parable of the Cave (and the parables that lead to it) must be appreciated not only in terms of the obvious resemblance between the story of Plato's enlightened philosopher and Ḥayy's, but also in terms of the obvious impact that it had on the illuminative ideas of other thinkers with whom I deal in this book. Second, Aristotle's thought is equally important for the purposes of this book, not only because of the obvious consideration that the story of Islamic philosophy cannot be accounted for in isolation from his philosophy, but especially because of the fact that Aristotle was perceived in Islamic intellectual tradition as the thinker who perfected rational thought. This does not mean that Islamic thinkers believed that Aristotle was the end of the story. On the contrary, by pushing rational analysis to its ultimate limit, Aristotle played a central role in opening the door for the development of the notion of liminality in Islamic medieval thought.

Finally, I wish to address a concern that readers of this book must be aware of, and that is related to the absence of an elaborate discussion of Suhrawardī's illuminative thought from this book. My simple response is that the treatment of such an important and difficult thinker is beyond the scope of this work.

CHAPTER 1

The File of Illuminationist Philosophy and the Purpose of Writing *Ḥayy*

THE LEGEND OF EASTERN PHILOSOPHY

Ibn Ṭufayl opens the introduction to his philosophical story by saying that he has been asked by a noble friend to reveal to him what could be revealed of the secrets of Eastern philosophy (*al-ḥikma al-mashriqiyya*)[1] mentioned by the Head of the Wise ʿAbū ʿAlī Ibn Sīnā.[2] Ibn Sīnā enjoyed a bad reputation or was, at best, ignored in the Western part of the Islamic state.[3] Ibn Sabʿīn, for example, considers him an "intentionally misleading sophist,"[4] and, like Suhrawardī in the East, claims that he, not Ibn Sīnā, was the first to unfold the secrets of illuminationist philosophy, which had been employed by the ancients before logic and dialectic were invented.[5] Despite the fact that Suhrawardī shows more respect for Ibn Sīnā than Ibn Sabʿīn, his position toward him in relation to illuminationist philosophy is in essence not different from that of Ibn Sabʿīn. Suhrawardī says: "You should know that the great sages … such as the father of the sages Hermes[6] and, before him, Agathadaemon and also Phythagoras and Empedocles and the majestically great philosopher Plato were greater in measure and nobler in significance than all those who excelled from among the Islamic logicians … For even as they elaborated and elucidated, much of the thought of the Ancients remained hidden from their sight."[7]

Ibn Ṭufayl states that the philosophy that had reached Andalusia in the books of Aristotle and Fārābī, and in Ibn Sīnā's *Shifā'*,[8] which agrees almost completely with the works of Aristotle, is not sufficient for the needs of the seeker of illuminationist philosophy.[9] He also refers to Ibn Sīnā's statement, at the beginning of *Shifā'*, that truth is beyond this work, and urges the seeker to look for it in his book on Eastern philosophy.[10] Indeed, this seems to be confirmed by Ibn Sīnā in a passage from the Prologue to *Shifā'* quoted by Dimitri Gutas: "I also wrote a book other than these two [the *Shifā'* and the *Lawāḥiq (Appendices)*], in which I presented philosophy as it is naturally [perceived] and as required by an unbiased view which neither takes into account in [this book on Eastern philosophy] the views of colleagues in the discipline, nor takes precautions here against creating schisms among them as is done elsewhere; this is my book on Eastern philosophy. But as for the present book [the *Shifā'*], it is more elaborate and more accommodating to my Peripatetic colleagues. Whoever wants the truth [stated] without indirection, he should seek the former book [on Eastern philosophy]; whoever wants the truth [stated] in a way which is somewhat conciliatory to colleagues, elaborates a lot, and alludes [*talwīḥ*] to things which, had they been perceived, there would have been no need for the other book, then he should read the present book [the *Shifā'*]."[11]

Gutas claims that Ibn Ṭufayl misinterprets this passage to create "the fiction of an esoteric and exoteric Avicenna"[12] by identifying the exoteric Ibn Sīnā with *Shifā'* and the esoteric Ibn Sīnā with *Ishārāt* and the allegory of *Ḥayy Ibn Yaqẓān*.[13] He makes reference to the passage in which Ibn Ṭufayl says that "Avicenna stated explicitly that in his opinion the truth is something else [*al-ḥaqq 'indahu ghayru dhālika*], that he wrote the *Shifā'* according to the doctrine of the Peripatetics only, and that 'whoever wants the truth without indirection should seek' his book on Eastern philosophy."[14] He then argues that Ibn Sīnā nowhere stated explicitly that the truth is something else, and that the distinction that he draws between the two works is one of style and is not based on a difference in doctrine.[15]

Like Gutas, George Ṭarābīshī claims that Ibn Ṭufayl invented the legend of Ibn Sīnā's esotericism to draw attention to his own work. Ibn Sīnā sought to advance with rather than beyond Peripatetic philosophy. And even if he wished to go beyond Peripateticism, he would then be attempting the impossible because he would have to transcend the epistemological limits of his time. This was impossible for him, however, due to the entanglement between Peripateticism and Neoplatonism and the presence of *Uthūlūjiya*, a work that belonged to Plotinus and that was mistakenly attributed to Aristotle.[16] "Like Fārābī who was caught in this entanglement in his attempt to establish an agreement between Aristotle and Plato, Ibn Sīnā also and each time he thought he could release himself from Peripatetic gravitation would emerge from Aristotle's circle only to enter Plotinus's."[17] Ibn Ṭufayl, adds Tarabishi, composed his work within this context of the presence of *Uthūlūjiya*, making his own solemn contribution to the evolution of the legend of the philosophy of illumination. In the West, he played the role that Suhrawardī played in the East in cultivating and controlling the fiction of Ibn Sīnā's philosophy of illumination, whose control is still effective in the present days.[18]

Thus, Gutas and Tarabishi share the opinion that Ibn Sīnā was not a mystic and that the philosophy of illumination, which is attributed to him, is a fiction that was invented by Ibn Ṭufayl, followed by a host of mystifiers from medieval to contemporary times, who tend to confuse themselves and their readers by reading texts as they are reflected, in a state of misrepresentation, in the mirrors of other texts.[19] More specifically, they claim that the distinction mentioned by Ibn Sīnā in the Prologue to *Shifā'* does not designate a difference in doctrine but only in style. Thus, when Ibn Ṭufayl says that Ibn Sīnā stated explicitly that the "truth is something else," his intention is to misrepresent and misinterpret the latter's words. Let me quote the passage from Ibn Ṭufayl's introduction in Gutas's translation to see whether it is possible to think that Gutas and Tarabishi could be accused of the very misinterpretation that they charge Ibn Ṭufayl with: "As for the books of Aristotle, Avicenna undertook in the *Shifā'* to interpret their contents, proceeding according to Aristotle's doctrine and following the method of his philosophy. But in the beginning of the book, Avicenna *stated explicitly* that *in his opinion the truth is something else [al-ḥaqq ʿindahu ghayru dhālika*], that he wrote the *Shifā'* according to the doctrine of the Peripatetics only, and that 'whoever wants the truth without indirection should seek' his book on Eastern philosophy."[20]

Gutas renders *ṣarraḥa* as "stated explicitly," which is a valid interpretation except that at least two other scholars do not use it. Lenn Goodman employs "admits" and Simon Ockley has it (simply) as "says."[21] As for *al-ḥaqq ʿindahu ghayru dhālika*, that is rendered by Gutas as "in his opinion the truth is something else," which is again a valid interpretation, except that Goodman uses the words "the truth for him is something quite different," and Ockley uses "the Truth was in his opinion different." From "says" to "admits" to "stated explicitly," and from "different" to "quite different" to "something else," something is lost along the way, and that is Ibn Ṭufayl simple statement. Ibn Ṭufayl is making the straightforward statement that Ibn Sīnā says that the truth in *Shifā'* is different from the truth that is to be found in his book on Eastern philosophy. And this is exactly and simply what Ibn Sīnā says, as we can see from the first part of the passage from the Prologue to *Shifā'*: "I wrote a book different from (*ghayru*) these two [*Shifā'* and *Lawāḥiq*] in which I presented philosophy as it is in itself and as required by an unbiased view which neither considers the side of colleagues in the discipline nor takes precautions against those who create schisms against them. This is my book on Eastern philosophy."[22] In the remainder of the passage, Ibn Sīnā explains in what sense the book on Eastern philosophy is different from, or, as Gutas puts it, "other than" *Shifā'*. It is different because the truth that it contains is presented as it is in itself, whereas the truth in *Shifā'* is Peripatetic. This is what Ibn Sīnā says, and it is also what Ibn Ṭufayl repeats.

To say, with Gutas, that Ibn Sīnā "is not talking about a difference in doctrine but one in style," as well as that Ibn Ṭufayl created this fiction of difference in doctrine to win authority for his own mystical epistemology, is to oversimplify Ibn Sīnā's meaning and misinterpret Ibn Ṭufayl's. Surely, Ibn Sīnā wants something more than just a formal difference or a difference in style, even if this does not amount to a strict difference in doctrine or whatever other difference Gutas has in mind.[23]

EASTERN AND WESTERN SCHOOLS OF PHILOSOPHY

In *Critique of the Critique of Arab Reason*,[24] Tarabishi argues against Jabiri's thesis according to which two main intellectual traditions ruled over the Arabic medieval mind: the Eastern tradition, championed by Ibn Sīnā, and the Western tradition, which included the three Andalusian philosophers: Ibn Bājja, Ibn Ṭufayl, and Ibn Rushd.[25] Jabiri affiliates the views of the Western philosophers with a school of logic that stood in contrast to the views of the members of the Eastern school, who advocated esoteric and illuminationist stands. Tarabishi indicates that to support his view that the three Andalusian thinkers were united in their rationalistic stand, Jabiri states that he searched for but could not find one word by Ibn Rushd against Ibn Bājja or Ibn Ṭufayl.[26] Now Tarabishi hurries to connect what Jabiri disconnected by connecting what he had previously disconnected: "In writing the history of the philosophy of Andalusia Ibn Ṭufayl does not disconnect himself from the philosophy of the East. On the contrary, he establishes his relationship with it in terms of continuity, and invests his efforts in presenting his personal attempt, as this is manifested in *Ḥayy Ibn Yaqẓān*, under the banner of the Eastern philosophy which is attributed to the Head of the Wise, Abū ʿAlī Ibn Sīnā."[27] This is a strange statement from one who says that Ibn Sīnā's presence in *Ḥayy* is significant in name but not in actual fact.[28] As for Jabiri's claim that Ibn Rushd never said a word against Ibn Bājja or Ibn Ṭufayl, Tarabishi finds it easy to bring not one but many words of Ibn Rushd against Ibn Bājja. When it comes to Ibn Ṭufayl, he takes the reader on a long tour, with useful (but still not to the point) analysis of the poverty of philosophy in Andalusia. Only toward the end of his discussion does he attempt to say something that seems to be relevant to the point. There, he cites Ibn Rushd's famous statement in *On the Harmony of Religion and Philosophy* that "truth does not contradict truth,"[29] and says that this statement could be an appropriate title for Ibn Ṭufayl's story. But then he insists that the aim of Ibn Ṭufayl's work is the opposite of Ibn Rushd's. Whereas Ibn Rushd attempts to show that only experts in logical interpretation are capable of harmonizing philosophy and religion, Ibn Ṭufayl attempts to show that only gnostics are capable of accomplishing this mission. Now Tarabishi draws our attention to Ibn Ṭufayl's reservation in the introduction to *Ḥayy* against the experts in logical consideration and his claim that their rational deliberation does not come close to the knowledge that is attained through vision and that cannot be committed to writing. He also sees in the concluding passage of Ibn Ṭufayl's book an allusion to the person of Ibn Rushd:

> This is ... the story of Ḥayy Ibn Yaqẓān, brought in a manner of discourse not contained in books or ordinary speeches. It contains hidden knowledge received only by those who know God especially ... In following this [course of open presentation] we broke the habit of our righteous ancestors in their unwillingness to expose [the mystery]. *What made it easy for us to tear the*

veil and divulge the secret is the emergence of corrupt views that have been concocted by [the minds of] the philodoxers[30] *of this era who spread them in the land and caused a considerable harm to the weak-minded, who have abandoned the tradition of the prophets. We feared for them [and wished to protect them] against imitating the light-headed and the ignorant in considering these views as the secrets hidden from those who are not worthy of them, since this only makes them all the more interested in adhering to them.* Thus we saw it fitting to allow them a fleeting [moment of] allusion to the mystery of mysteries in the hope that this will draw them toward realization (*taḥqīq*) away from the way [of the misleading]. Nevertheless, we have not spared these few leaves, which are invested with secrets, a thin veil and a light covering, easily pierced by those who are worthy and too thick to penetrate it.[31]

Tarabishi detects in the emphasized words in this passage an allusion to Ibn Rushd. He also cites another passage in which Ibn Ṭufayl interrupts the narrative to register his fiercest criticism against extreme rationalists, and experiences a temptation to see Ibn Rushd as the target of this criticism.[32] The passage in question is an especially important one and I will attend to it later in this book. For now, it suffices to say that it consists of what seems to be Ibn Ṭufayl's straight depreciation of the rational faculty and a clear declaration of its limitations in relation to comprehending divine truths by employing categories that pertain to the sensible world.[33] And indeed, it seems tempting to read this passage in the light of Tarabishi's interpretation and as indicating a rebellion against rationalism and Ibn Rushd as its chief representative. However, I will attempt to show that Tarabishi's reading must be limited due to his failure to grasp the true nature of Ibn Ṭufayl's "rebellion" against rationalism and his burning desire to freeze the relationship between him and Ibn Rushd.

The weakness of Tarabishi's view becomes apparent upon examining his (mis)interpretation of the third and last indication that he detects for an irreconcilable tension between the two Andalusian philosophers. This occurs in a statement in which Ibn Ṭufayl answers his reader's wish that he introduces the science of mystical visions in the way of rational consideration, and explains that this "can be set down in books and mastered by means of expressions. However, it is rarer than red sulphur, particularly in the region where we live. For it is so extraordinary that only some individuals grasp a slight portion of it here and there. And whoever has grasped something of it does not talk about it except in symbols (*ramzan*).[34] For the community of pristine religion (*al-ḥanīfiyya*) and the genuine Sacred Law forbid one to delve into it and warn against this."[35] Tarabishi completely ignores Ibn Ṭufayl's affirmation that, although it is very rarely done, introducing the science of mystical visions in the way of rational consideration is still possible, and he freezes on his warning that the Law forbids one to delve into this matter. He then contrasts this with Ibn Rushd's insistence that it is not only allowed but even obligatory for the possessor of knowledge to interpret the Law,[36] and comes out with a judgment that is not only based on absence of evidence but that also frustrates the evidence that there is.

A serious examination of Ibn Rushd's view on the subject of the interpretation of the Law reveals how close it is to Ibn Ṭufayl's. Let me begin with a passage from Ibn Rushd's *Incoherence of the Incoherence*: "And this is the meaning of the ancient philosophers, when they say that God is the totality of the existents and that He is the agent. And therefore the chiefs of the Ṣūfīs say: *Not-He is but-He*. But all this is the knowledge of those who are steadfast in their knowledge, and this must not be written down and must not be an obligation of faith, and therefore it is not taught by the Divine Law. And one who mentions this truth where it should not be mentioned sins, and one who withholds it from those to whom it should be told sins too."[37] Although Ibn Rushd was reluctant to write down philosophical solutions to problems that pertain to religion, especially the problem of the relationship between God and the world, he thought that such solutions could be provided in philosophy books.[38] Those solutions, however, must be examined only by true philosophers, who possess the exclusive right to interpret them. This right depends on the philosophers' competence in demonstrative reasoning, which competence renders them capable of deciphering the inner meanings of Scripture. These meanings should not be revealed to the dialectical (theological) and rhetorical classes of people, whose work generates doubt, dissension, and strife in the community of believers.[39] In the same vein, Ḥayy came to realize that "there were men appointed to every work, and that every one was best capable of doing that unto which he was appointed by nature."[40] Accordingly, Ibn Ṭufayl makes his hero leave in peace Salāmān and his companions, who possessed a natural aversion to contemplation, and live in peace with Absāl, who "used to make a deeper search into the inside of things and was more inclined to study mystical meanings (*bāṭin*) and interpretations."[41]

In the passage quoted above from *Incoherence of Incoherence*, Ibn Rushd makes an implicit reference to the distinction between divine and human knowledge. The words "those who are steadfast in knowledge" occur in Q 3:7: "But no one knows its true interpretation except God and those who are steadfast in knowledge." The ancients, by whom he means Aristotle in particular, are included among those who are steadfast in knowledge and also the chiefs of the Ṣūfīs. Hence, I think that for Ibn Rushd, knowledge is of two sorts: rationalistic knowledge, which is with the ancients, and mystical knowledge, which is with the Ṣūfīs. Moreover, Ibn Rushd says that the ancients' grasp of the notion that God is one with his creatures is identical with what the Ṣūfīs think. He insists, however, that this is something that must not be put in writing, and to mention it to those who are unfit to hear it is unlawful. At the same time, this knowledge should not be kept from those who are worthy of hearing it. And this is exactly the mission that Ibn Ṭufayl sets out to accomplish and which he describes in the passage that I quoted above from the conclusion of his work. It is interesting that the meaning of Ibn Rushd's words, as well as Ibn Ṭufayl's, is to be found in a famous passage attributed to Aristotle: "Aristotle was reproached by Plato for revealing whatever wisdom he committed to his books. He apologized by saying: 'As for the sons of wisdom and its inheritors they will not besmirch it. As for its enemies and those who have no interest in it, they will not obtain it due to their ignorance of what it contains. Although I have disclosed this wisdom, I have strongly fortified its walls so that the light-headed and the ignorant may not climb them and put their hands on it.'"[42]

Ibn Ṭufayl urges his readers who want the truth without obfuscation to seek Eastern philosophy and search for it assiduously. This is despite his saying that readers who seek the truth without obfuscation should turn to Ibn Sīnā's book on Eastern philosophy. This does not prove that Ibn Ṭufayl is the inventor of a legend, nor even that his words betray an unaware confession that the book on Eastern philosophy does not exist. On the contrary, Ibn Ṭufayl's seemingly inconsistent statements are in harmony with his main position, as it is stated by means of another two seemingly inconsistent statements. He affirms in one statement that although this is very rarely done, it is possible to provide an account of the science of mystical visions in books according to the way of the people of consideration,[43] and in the other that "as for your inquiry concerning what the people of vision (*mushāhada*) witness and concerning the tastes (*adhwāq*) and presence (*ḥuḍūr*) [that they experience] in the state of sainthood (*walāya*), this is something the truth of which cannot, in itself, be *stated (ithbātuhu)* in a book. As one goes about stating it, either in speech or in writing, its truth is *altered (istaḥālat)* and it joins the theoretical part, which is other than it."[44]

The emphasis here is on two concepts: "stated" and "altered." Stating (*ithbāt*) in Islamic theological and mystical traditions is associated with unification (*tawḥid*) and being (*wujūd*). One cannot make a true statement about something unless it is one thing; otherwise, it will not be a statement about *it*. And one cannot make a true statement about something that does not exist because a statement about something that does not exist is a statement about nothing.[45] What the people of vision witness can be stated, but the moment that it is stated, its truth is altered. Hence, a statement about what they witness is a statement about a state (*ḥāl*) that is altered the moment that it is stated; is a statement about something that is limitless.[46] Ibn Ṭufayl says that, although this is very rarely done, it is still possible to provide an account of the science of (mystical) visions in writing and according to the way of the people of consideration. Is this not inconsistent with his previous statement? Not if his account is presented as consisting of stating that a true statement of what the people of the science of mystical visions witness cannot be made. We can summarize this point by saying that Ibn Ṭufayl makes a distinction between a statement *of* what the people of vision witness and a statement *about* what they witness. As it turns out, the latter but not the former can be put in writing. Ibn Ṭufayl's book may be considered as an example of a statement *about* what a possessor of vision, Ḥayy Ibn Yaqẓān, witnessed, for Ḥayy witnessed what "no eye has seen or ear heard, nor has it occurred to the heart of man."[47]

PLATO AND ARISTOTLE: THE HEART AND THE VOICE OF ISLAMIC PHILOSOPHY

The term "file," which appears in the title of this chapter, occurs in the opening chapter of Tarabishi's book.[48] As I have pointed out, Tarabishi wrote his book in response to Jabiri, who charged Ibn Sīnā with inventing the illuminationist thought that "killed reason and logic in the Arabic consciousness for many centuries."[49] According to Jabiri, Ibn Sīnā's illuminationism contributed a great deal to drawing Islamic thought away from a state of openness to rationalism, promoted by Kindī and the Muʿtazilite theologians, to a murky and self-destructive irrationalism, promoted by Ghazālī and Suhrawardī.[50] Thus, if Muslims wish to reestablish what Ibn Sīnā disconnected, they must detach themselves from him and adhere to Ibn Rushd's rationalism.[51] This is the background to Tarabishi's reopening of the illuminationist file. Unfortunately, no sooner had he opened the file than he began to close it by attempting to convince us that the only secret about the philosophy of illumination is that it had no secret about it.[52] But he does not forget in the attempt to point at a conspiracy contrived by the person of Ibn Ṭufayl, the inventor of the fiction of illuminationist philosophy, and also to convince us not how bad Ibn Sīnā must have been, but how he, and many an Islamic philosopher, must have been irrelevant. They were just pawns that made moves according to the plan set by their master, Aristotle.[53]

ʿAbd al-Raḥmān Badawī presents a picture of Aristotle that seems to be different: Aristotle was used in the Islamic intellectual tradition, as he was used in other intellectual traditions, to satisfy its cultural needs and the necessities of its historical circumstances.[54] In light of this understanding, Badawi seeks to dispel the ambiguity surrounding the attribution of *Uthūlūjiya* to Aristotle. He says that even if the Arabs had known the true identity of the writer of *Uthūlūjiya* or suspected its attribution to Aristotle, they would still have attributed it to him.[55]

In *al-Aflātūniyya al-Muḥdatha ʿinda al-ʿArab*, Badawi describes the attribution of *Uthūlūjiya* to Aristotle as a "lucky mistake." Had the real author of *Uthūlūjiya* been known, it would not have received the attention that it deserved and would have met the destiny that befell Plato's genuine writings.[56] What he says in this work, as well as in *Aristotle Among the Arabs* (cited hereafter as AA), seems inconsistent with what he says in his introduction to *The Platonic Spiritual Forms* (cited hereafter as PS). There, he elaborates on the doubts that Islamic philosophers, Fārābī and Ibn Sīnā in particular, had about the attribution of *Uthūlūjiya* to Aristotle.[57] Ibn Sīnā confessed his doubts in *Letter to al-Kiyā* by saying that *Uthūlūjiya* is somewhat suspect (*muṭʿan*).[58] In *al-Jamʿ*, Fārābī mentions the contradiction between what is discussed in *Uthūlūjiya* in relation to the spiritual forms (*ṣuwar rūḥāniyya*) and Aristotle's stated position against the possibility of their existence. However, he dismisses the possibility that

Aristotle was involved in self-contradiction and rejects the doubts about his authorship of *Uthūlūjiya*.[59] In his attempt to establish harmony between Aristotle and Plato, he resorts to interpreting those things concerning which the two philosophers seem to be in disagreement but are found to be in total agreement when their views are examined at a deeper level. Badawi thinks that the harmony that Fārābī endeavored to establish rendered Plato's figure overshadowed by Aristotle's light, and the outcome was very unfortunate. Islamic thinkers in the fourth and fifth centuries became convinced that the reconciliation between the two philosophers was unattainable. Their preference for Aristotle over Plato was a result of a natural disposition for accumulation, articulation, and prying for details as well as spiritual barrenness and the lack of originality and creativity of the thinkers of those times.[60]

It is interesting how the opposing trends of Hegelianism and Existentialism are at work in Badawi's interpretation of the reception of Aristotle in the Islamic intellectual tradition. In PS, he speaks about a factual or natural necessity that committed Muslims, as a class of human intellectuals driven by the force of historical circumstances, to a certain conduct—namely, preferring Aristotle over Plato. In AA, however, he speaks about exactly the opposite case. As a matter of fact, he mentions something about the necessities of historical circumstances. However, these necessities are presented as coinciding with, rather than driving, the game that Islamic *individuals* played in their overlooking of a historical fact—namely, that *Uthūlūjiya* belonged ultimately to Plotinus's *Enneads*. Looking deeper, however, we might detect in what Badawi says in PS a sort of methodological confirmation of what he says in AA. In my opinion, PS is a very important work, especially in relation to the affinity between Suhrawardī's school of illumination and Ibn al-ʿArabī's thought, and deserves a thorough examination. Here, it suffices to point out that this work had been written sometime in the thirteenth century by an anonymous author in whose writing style Badawi finds clear Hegelianistic as well as Existentialistic elements,[61] but who represents an independent Platonism, different from the Platonism of Suhrawardī's school of illumination or that of the Neoplatonists. Despite the fact that Badawi emphasizes the strong resemblance between our anonymous author and Ibn al-ʿArabī, he sees him as an original Platonic thinker who should not be considered as strictly belonging to this (Suhrawardian) or that (Akhbarian) school of thought.[62] From what Badawi says, it becomes clear that he considers PS as the evidence for Plato's emergence in the Islamic intellectual tradition and, with him, the Islamic thinker as the *individual* that he mentions in AA.

It is interesting that in an intellectual tradition in which naming was almost equal to existence, the ultimate author of *Uthūlūjiya*, Plotinus, was not known by his real name, only as al-Shaykh al-Yūnānī.[63] I find myself in agreement with the general thrust of Badawi's view in AA that the mystery of mystifying Plotinus's name lies in a certain interest that Islamic philosophers had in keeping the name of *Uthūlūjiya* separated from the name of its author, and that this interest is related to reconciling religion and philosophy. It was important for Islamic philosophers to attribute the work to Aristotle because Aristotle was the voice that spoke for philosophy. Aristotle was the voice that spoke for Islamic philosophy, but he was not its heart. As it stands, this statement seems to be inconsistent with a host of scholarly conventions that emphasize the many titles of honor that Aristotle had received in the Islamic philosophical tradition, the massive amount of praise that Islamic philosophers had allocated to him, and the great number of statements expressing admiration of the man's special capacities.[64] Add to this the fact that a considerable part of the work by those philosophers consists of commentaries on Aristotle's writings. It is hard to see, therefore, how Aristotle can be considered anything less than the heart of Islamic philosophy or its uncontested master, as Tarabishi surmises.

Islamic philosophers made, in my opinion, an important distinction between human wisdom (*ḥikma*), Aristotle being its chief representative, and another sort of wisdom, which may be called "divine wisdom." Even Ibn Rushd, who no doubt was the staunchest admirer of Aristotle, saw in his philosophy the culmination of human wisdom. The following passage, which seems to provide evidence to the contrary, only supports this view: "Praised He Who has allocated human perfection to him. People toil and after a prolonged time and much hardship are able to conceive what is easily conceived by him. What is conceived easily in others differs from what is conceived as such in him. This is why doubts occur to interpreters concerning his statements, only to find out after a long time that what he had said was sound and that the rational consideration of others was lacking in comparison with his. Due to this divine capacity that was found in him, he became the founder of wisdom (*ḥikma*) and the one who completed it. This is something that is rarely found in any art so that [it is even more out of the ordinary to find it happening in] this great art [of philosophy]."[65]

Ibn Rushd says that Aristotle was the person who founded and completed wisdom. Surely, Aristotle was not the founder of (divine) wisdom if Plato, Aristotle's teacher, is to be reckoned a revered, wise person and to receive in the Islamic tradition the special title of honor: "Divine Plato." Ibn Rushd, the interpreter of Plato's *Republic*, must be acting, therefore, according to the distinction between two sorts of philosophy: philosophy as a (superior) human profession and philosophy as a divine one. Similar to the passage quoted above, the following passage also creates the impression that Aristotle is being divinized, when he is actually being humanized to the utmost degree of (human) perfection: "How wonderful this man must be and how distinguished is his mental capacity (*fiṭratihi*) from the mental capacities of the rest of humans. It is as if divine providence has fashioned him for their sake, so that they may witness the highest perfection in the human species."[66] Tarabishi states that Ibn Rushd's attempt to purify the Peripatetic doctrine from the faults of Greek and Arabic interpreters and restore orthodox Aristotelianism failed due to the confusion caused by the introduction of Neoplatonism and the lack of more effective critical and methodological scientific tools. He adds that Ibn Rushd succeeded only in establishing Aristotelianism as the subject matter of a sort of religious worship because "Aristotle was for him not only the divine Aristotle as the ancients called him, but the human creature that divine providence had chosen as the materialization of the symbol of perfection as well."[67] The truth is that Aristotle was for Ibn Rushd, as well as for the rest of Islamic philosophers, the symbol of the perfection of the wisdom that I sorted as human and that Ibn Rushd, like other philosophers, was fully aware of the existence of another sort of wisdom that had a different nature, as the passage I quoted above from the Thirteenth Discussion of the *Incoherence of Incoherence* shows clearly.[68] In this passage, Ibn Rushd says that Aristotle and the chiefs of the Ṣūfīs possessed sound understanding of the sense in which God should be depicted as identical with his created existence. Aristotle and the Ṣūfīs are described by him as steadfast in knowledge, a description that Q 3:7 provides for those who have the capacity to interpret correctly God's verses, especially verses that are not of well-established meaning (*mutashābihat*). Similarly, Ibn Rushd says in *al-Athār al-'Ulwiyya* that interpreters of Aristotle raise doubts concerning the meanings of his words, only to come to realize after the passage of time that his opinion was the correct one all along. The analogy that has been drawn here might seem as if lending support to the view that Ibn Rushd sought to establish Aristotelianism as an object of religious worship. However, the account of what Ibn Rushd is trying to do goes far beyond and much deeper than the oversimplified account that Tarabishi provides. Ibn Rushd is sowing the seeds of his complementarity thesis, which establishes a synthesis between religion and philosophy. To do this, he first will have to make al-Shaykh al-Yūnānī (Plotinus) leave his body (Aristotle)[69] one last time and not return therein. This act of restoration or abstracting the original from the mixed is what constitutes the heart and the very definition of philosophical interpretation for Ibn Rushd. Something very similar to that must be accomplished to restore the divine religious from the mixed Qur'ānic verses, as I will explain after citing the following passage from Ibn Rushd's *Kashf*:

> The party from the public that considers the Law to be in opposition to philosophy should know that it is not in opposition to it. Also those who associate themselves with philosophy and consider it in opposition to the Law should know that it is not in opposition to it. Each party must know that it has not discerned the true essence of religion and philosophy. An opinion concerning the Law that is in opposition to philosophy is either an innovation that is not in accord with the principles of the Law or a faulty opinion in philosophy based on a false interpretation of it. This is why we found it incumbent upon us to define in this book the principles of the Law. For when its principles are traced back to their origins, they will be found in full agreement with philosophy, not with what is [falsely] interpreted in it. So also concerning the opinion that considers philosophy in opposition to the Law; it should be known that the reason for it is that comprehensive knowledge of both philosophy and the Law is lacking.[70]

Ibn Rushd employs the term "interpretation" (*ta'wīl*) in its Qur'ānic sense. Q 3:7 distinguishes between true and false interpretations. Misinterpretation arises because of verses that are not of well-established meaning (*mutashābihāt*), in contrast to verses that are of well-established meaning (*muḥkamāt*) usually understood by the commentators as related to the categorical orders of the Law.[71] Those whose hearts are twisted interpret falsely those verses to disseminate dissension (*fitna*) in the community.[72] Likewise, some philodoxers interpret Aristotle falsely to prove that his philosophy is in contradiction with the Law. To establish harmony between religion and philosophy, the foundation of both must be revealed, and this is the task that Ibn Rushd assigns for those who are firmly established in knowledge (*rāsikhūn fi al-ʿilm*). It is here that a possible connection can be found between Ibn Rushd and mystical thought, as I find it difficult to believe that his mention of the ancients and the Ṣūfīs in the same breath and in the context of discussing a major problem—namely, the problem of the unity of being—is accidental. Ibn Rushd saw the task of the philosophers mainly as performing an act of interpretation (*ta'wīl*), which in Arabic means bringing back a thing or a meaning to its original or first (*awwal*) state. This is also the task that the Ṣūfīs, and especially Ibn al-ʿArabī, thought lies at the heart of mystical occupation.

Ibn Ṭufayl's *Ḥayy* can be presented alongside this line of interpretation. This becomes clear toward the concluding part of the book. Not far from the island where Ḥayy Ibn Yaqẓān was born, there was another island inhabited by a religious community (*milla*). Salāmān and Absāl were born and raised in this community. They were faithful in the service of their community and observed the ordinances of its Law. The main distinguishing factor between them was that Absāl inclined toward mystical interpretation whereas Salāmān adhered to the outward meanings of the Law.[73] By means of his natural capacity for interpretation, and thanks to his encounter and spiritual association with Ḥayy, Absāl was able to realize that "all those things which are contained in the Law of God ... were resemblances of what Hai Ebn Yokdhan had seen; and the eyes of his understanding were opened, and he found that the original and the copy did exactly agree together. And the ways of mystical interpretation were easy to him."[74] A perfect harmony was established between the man of (mystical) visions (Ḥayy) and the man of esoteric interpretation (Absāl). Failing to appreciate the real condition of the members of Absāl's community, and mistakenly thinking that they all possessed his mental capacities (*fiṭar*),[75] Ḥayy felt encouraged to reveal the secrets of his visionary wisdom, only to be gravely disappointed and run the risk of losing his life. Once he realized that "there were men appointed to every work, and that every one was best capable of doing that unto which he was appointed by nature,"[76] he turned to Salāmān's companions, apologized to them, and acquitted himself of what he had previously said. He also informed them that his eyes were opened and he was able to see what they had been able to see right from the start. Moreover, he urged them to adhere to the ordinances of the Law and to believe in those verses whose meanings are not well established and accept them without argument.[77]

Ḥayy urged Salāmān's companions to stay within the limits of the well-established ordinances of the Law because he realized that going beyond these limits will expose them to the dangers of false interpretations, which are introduced by those whose hearts are twisted and who seek to disseminate dissention in the community. It is here that Ibn Ṭufayl sees the danger of the false philosophers, the false interpreters, who produce what they introduce as the secrets that are to be withheld from those who are not worthy of them and, by means of that, increase people's desire to obtain them. According to Lawrence Conrad, Ibn Ṭufayl's attempt to counter this danger was one of the main reasons for writing *Ḥayy*. I will discuss his as well as the views of others on the purpose of writing *Ḥayy* next.

THE PURPOSE OF WRITING *ḤAYY*

Léon Gauthier argues that Ibn Ṭufayl's primary goal is to demonstrate the harmony between religion and philosophy: Ibn Ṭufayl composed his work following an impeccable, logical plan,[78] which advanced carefully and step by step toward a concluding section that deals with the problem of the harmony between religion and philosophy. This section must therefore be essential to the work, and the problem of the harmony between religion and philosophy must be its main subject.[79]

George Hourani argues that the most important parts of Ibn Ṭufayl's work are those that deal with the reasoning that led Ḥayy to achieve the highest stage of mystical unity with God. His argument against Gauthier rests first on denying the assumption that the concluding part of a work must be its most important part and that it necessarily defines its subject. Second, he argues that the question of the agreement between religion and philosophy does not receive serious attention in the work, and that Ibn Ṭufayl fails to do what Ibn Rushd, for example, succeeded in doing in *On the Harmony of Religion and Philosophy*—namely, present a well-fashioned argument that compares religious and philosophical thought. As a matter of fact, the sections that deal with the relation between religion and philosophy could be pruned out without seriously damaging the work.[80]

In criticizing the view that *Ḥayy* consists of a flawless and carefully carried out logical plan, Conrad registers the following inconsistencies in the work: (1) At the beginning of his work, Ibn Ṭufayl says that no beasts of prey were to be found on the island. Later, however, he says that Ḥayy came to the help of animals that had been brought down by a beast of prey. (2) The reference to how the mother-gazelle laid Ḥayy in the feathered ark supports the account of the child's human origin against the account of his spontaneous generation, although this incident occurs after the merging of the two accounts. (3) Although Ḥayy is totally isolated from humans, Ibn Ṭufayl endows him with the awareness of the demands that his body makes on him, which distract him from contemplating God, the Necessary-of-Existence. His commitment to the requirements of Absāl's religion raises some awkward problems. For how shall he pay almsgiving *(zakāt)* or perform fasting *(ṣiyām)* when he owns no possessions and is already fasting in the most rigorous way? And how can he perform the pilgrimage to Mecca *(ḥajj)* from his isolated island where ships never visit? (4) Ibn Ṭufayl says in the introduction of his book that he wrote it in response to a request made by a friend who wished to learn some of the secrets of Eastern philosophy, whereas in the conclusion, he says that he wrote the book to rebut the views of the pseudo-philosophers.[81]

An answer to (1) can be provided by referring to what Goodman says in relation to a certain intellectual experiment that Ibn Ṭufayl conducts in his book. The experiment teaches us that if an individual is raised away from society, which is full of harmful imbalances, into a well-established natural environment, in which equilibrium and stability prevail, this individual will grow up free of deficiencies. The experiment must be conducted in a fit and balanced environment. This is why it is important, for example, to provide food in abundance so that the mother-gazelle may find pastures in bounty for her milk to be in abundance and feed Ḥayy.[82] A crucial item in the list that Goodman provides for the experiment to work is the absence of beasts of prey. Now Goodman says that Ibn Ṭufayl recognizes the danger of giving Ḥayy everything. For example, despite the existence of food, Ḥayy must endeavor to find it; and although there are no beasts of prey, there are still some animals that compete with Ḥayy on having it.[83] Presence and absence, therefore, work together in establishing a balanced environment that not only provides for the development of the subject of the experiment but also induces him to improve his potentials. This is why the existence of beasts of prey becomes important as a challenge for Ḥayy to overcome. Another balance that Ibn Ṭufayl attempts to maintain throughout the whole work is between the implications of the traditionalistic and the naturalistic views of man's origin. The existence of beasts of prey is important because it confirms the traditionalistic account. This account is based upon religious principles, since the story of man's control over beasts of prey is a story that religion teaches. It is also a story that natural evolution confirms. What Conrad considers as a contradiction only confirms the fact that Ibn Ṭufayl is working according to a careful, logical plan and is not proceeding randomly.

In response to (2), Conrad must be reminded that although Ibn Ṭufayl says right before the mention of the feathers in the ark that the two accounts of Ḥayy's birth are united,[84] the unity in question is not one that excludes difference. An exclusive unity would be ineffective in actively combining two accounts that complement rather than exclude each other.

I am afraid that point (3) is based on a misinterpretation. Living in isolation from human contact does not necessarily mean that Ḥayy is safe from the demands of his body. One might wonder why Conrad should consider this point as raising awkward problems given his insistence that *Ḥayy* is a work that should be considered as a social act reflecting a broad continuum of socio-intellectual perspectives, and as he draws our attention to the significance of the social realities and concerns of intellectuals in a land fraught with serious social, political, and religious tensions.[85] Add to this his insistence that Ibn Ṭufayl was working in harmony with fundamental Muwaḥḥid doctrine and saw himself as fulfilling his socio-political responsibility, which goes along with knowledge.[86] Thus, Conrad insists that "neither Ḥayy nor Ibn Ṭufayl can be satisfied to 'know' in glorious isolation from the rest of mankind, much as Plato's prisoner in the Allegory of the Cave, once he beholds the form of the Good, recognizes his responsibility to return to free the others, however unwilling they be to follow him."[87] Conrad does not forget to mention that in his commentary on Plato's *Republic*, Ibn Rushd indicated that the ideal conditions postulated by Plato for the philosopher-king had existed in al-Andalus under his patron, the Muwaḥḥid caliph Abū Yaʿqūb.[88] One might wonder how being aware of all these things, as well as the fact that Ibn Ṭufayl wrote his philosophical story a few years before his death and that the caliph participated in his funeral, which means that the work had enjoyed his approval, he failed to see that Ibn Ṭufayl's mention of the formal commitment of the *hajj* in such an isolated setting should not be perceived as an anomaly. Indeed, it is intended to reveal two important political and mystical messages that have much in common, because the isolated island can be a symbol for both the isolated mystic and the isolated al-Andalus.

There can be no doubt that the example of the *ḥajj* enjoys a strong presence in Ibn Ṭufayl's work; and in one case, Ḥayy is depicted as performing what can be seen as circumambulating his island, his Kaʿba.[89] His performance was part of the second resemblance in which he imitated the movement of celestial spheres, which can be related to the fact that the seven circumambulations around the Kaʿba presented a resemblance of the spheres of the celestial order. Let us also remember that Ibn Ṭufayl divides Ḥayy's intellectual development into seven stages, which can be seen as activating Plato's educational plan (in *Republic*) on the philosophical level and the religious plan, as seen through the mystic eye, on a spiritual level. It is hard to see how Conrad is not aware of all this and the impression is made that he is actually aware of much of it, only that he had made up his mind that reconciling religion and philosophy is not the problem that made Ibn Ṭufayl write *Ḥayy*.

Point (4) is inconsistent with what Conrad says: "It was an exceedingly common rhetorical device in medieval Arabic literature to begin one's book or essay by addressing an unnamed colleague who has reputedly asked a question or raised a point for discussion."[90] This takes us back to the question of the purpose of writing *Ḥayy,* as Conrad balances his criticism of Gauthier's view by criticizing Hourani, who thinks that Ḥayy's care for his soul rather than the relation between philosophy and religion is the central subject of Ibn Ṭufayl's work.[91] Conrad draws our attention to the significance of the social realities and concerns of intellectuals in a land fraught with social, political, and religious tensions. The societal aspect cannot be ignored, and it is a mistake to assume that Ibn Ṭufayl's main concern was about the ascent of the self-taught philosopher to intellectual perfection.[92] Conrad attempts to reduce the merits of the rationalistic aspect of Ḥayy's quest by emphasizing that the ultimate level of knowledge sought by Ḥayy belonged to a transcendent level of consciousness that cannot be reached "through intellectual speculation based on syllogistic deduction, postulation of premises, and the drawing of inferences."[93] Then he turns to the passage from the conclusion of the story, which mentions the psuedo-philosophers, and finds in this the answer to the question of why Ibn Ṭufayl wrote his story. "There would seem to be no doubt that this is the problem that compelled Ibn Ṭufayl to write," he says.[94] It is the exact formulation of this statement that is the key to understanding the limitation of Conrad's argument. A distinction must be made between "Why did Ibn Ṭufayl *write* Ḥayy?" and "Why did Ibn Ṭufayl write *Ḥayy*?"

The shift of emphasis might seem trivial but it is not, because it reveals the limitation of an analysis that tends to ignore the second and more important formulation of the question and, to the extent that it does provide an answer for it, it does so only accidentally. Rather than presenting *Ḥayy* as an attempt to reconcile philosophy and religion, as Gauthier claimed on the basis of textual analysis, or as an attempt to describe the ascent of the unaided intellect to the highest stages of wisdom, as Hourani claimed on the basis of what he considers as more comprehensive textual analysis, Conrad's view tends to present the text as a mere reflection of the world in which it was created and which could be substituted for any other creation. Although Conrad insists that the appearance of corrupt philosophers compelled Ibn Ṭufayl to write, he would not insist as strongly that this is what compelled him to write *Ḥayy*.

There can be no doubt that socio-political circumstances exerted a serious influence on Ibn Ṭufayl's work and the very setting that he selects for it—namely, an isolated island is a striking statement to this effect that is more telling than any other fact. Thus, he who argues, as Hourani does, that the account of the encounter with the human society occupied only a negligible part of the story must be wrong because the whole story of isolation is meaningless unless it is mirrored against this part. Hourani's view might still make some sense given that the ascent of the unaided intellect can be a valid description of one of the accounts of the story. However, this understanding must be qualified because Ibn Ṭufayl's attempt at reconciling religion and philosophy extends over the entire text and is not limited to its concluding part. I want to conclude this chapter with one final note concerning the identity of Ibn Ṭufayl's addressee. Conrad includes among these philosophers, simple believers, mystics, and several others. He does not mention one very important person: Ibn Ṭufayl or someone who is like his soul mate, his "noble brother."

CHAPTER 2

The Introduction

In the introduction to his work, Ibn Ṭufayl employs central Ṣūfī concepts to explain the basic themes of his mystical epistemology. I elaborate in this chapter on the use that he makes of these concepts. He also states that he could see the truth for himself only by combining Ghazālī's and Ibn Sīnā's arguments. The major part of the discussion in this chapter is devoted to Ghazālī's and Ibn Sīnā's depictions of the knowledge of illumination and aims to elucidate Ibn Ṭufayl's statement concerning their influence on his work.

MYSTICAL EXPRESSION AND EXPERIENCE: FUNDAMENTAL ṢŪFĪ CONCEPTS

Although it was common in medieval Arabic literature to open a work by addressing a "noble brother," in the case of works such as those of the Brethren of Purity or Ibn Ṭufayl, this sort of opening possesses deeper mystical implications.[1] I will explain my meaning by explicating two terms that Ibn Ṭufayl employs in the opening passage of his introduction: "sincere" and "affectionate": "Noble brother, my sincere (*al-ṣafyy*) and affectionate (*ḥamīm*) friend, may God preserve you and grant you everlasting happiness. You have asked me to reveal to you what can be revealed of the secrets of illuminationist wisdom mentioned by the Head of the Wise Abū ʿAlī Ibn Sīnā. You should know that he who wants the truth that is clear and distinct must seek it assiduously and devote himself to obtaining it."[2]

Edward Lane introduces the following interpretation of the term *ḥamīm*: "A man's brother; his friend, or true friend; because anxious, or solicitous, for him."[3] He renders *walā yudriku al-ashyā'a illā ḥamīmuha* as: "And none will attain the objects of want but he who devotes himself to obtain them; who is solicitous for them."[4] Thus, *ḥamīm* can be related in meaning to Ibn Ṭufayl's reminder to his friend to devote himself to obtaining a clear and distinct truth. This is the description of the friend, and this is what he is expected to do to be worthy of it.[5] The word *ṣafyy* means "A friend who regards one, or behaves towards one, with reciprocal purity or sincerity of love or affection, or of brotherly affection."[6] The element of reciprocity is especially important in this interpretation, as well as in the interpretation of terms that are derived from *ṣ-f-w*,[7] which designates relationships of purity between lovers and dear friends. Such relationships resemble a conception of unity in which the self (the same) communicates with itself in or through the other. By writing *Ḥayy*, Ibn Ṭufayl attempted to communicate first and foremost with his own self, even as he might have been communicating with a real person. This sort of communication can be exemplified by referring to Ibn Ṭufayl's example of the mirror that reflects on itself and burns everything else,[8] and it is what is mainly responsible for the sense of strangeness described by him as follows: "Your request has stirred in me a noble idea which brought me to witness (*mushāhada*) a state (*ḥāl*) that I had never witnessed before and made me obtain a degree so strange that no tongue can describe and no eloquence can make its meaning comprehensible, since it belongs to a different order and a different realm of existence."[9] It is hard to believe that the mere occasion of a simple request could produce this newly arrived vision, as if it had never occurred to Ibn Ṭufayl before. This is why I think that something like the reflection in the same, similar to what is depicted in the example of the burning mirror, is what is transpiring here. This reflection leaves the possessor of witnessing in a state of perplexity that cannot be communicated in words because the communicator has become identical with the state (*ḥāl*) that he is attempting to communicate. It often happens that we find ourselves incapable of communicating to others all sorts of ideas, and this does not leave this strong impression of perplexity in us. Rather, the sense of strangeness and perplexity is the outcome of the recognition that such a communication cannot be made in an articulate form even to oneself. And it is also responsible for the feeling of joy that overcomes the possessor of witnessing: "Due to the splendour, delight, pleasure, and enjoyment that accompany the state, he who comes to it or stops at one of its limits will not be able to hide it or conceal its secret. He will be overcome by joy, liveliness, and exultation that make him give some general expression to it, since he cannot be particular."[10] The individual experiences being a unique and solitary person and catches a glimpse of a unity that cannot be expressed specifically. This experience can be so overwhelming that it gives way to the ecstatic utterances known in the Ṣūfī literature as *shaṭaḥāt*.

According to Jurjānī, *shaṭḥ* is "an expression that carries a smell of unsteadiness of the intellect and a claim (*daʿwā*) made as one of the slips committed by the realizers. It is a true claim by means of which the knower speaks correctly but without a divine sanction in a manner that betrays cleverness."[11] Jabiri, who cites a slightly different version of this definition, indicates that we always find *shaṭḥ* in Ṣūfī literature combined with "claim," and that the claim in question is for unity with God, which is caused by a special state (*ḥāl*) of intoxication (*sukr*) that removes the Ṣūfī from his external existence and compels him to speak uncensored.[12] The examples that Ibn Ṭufayl gives for *shaṭaḥāt* show that the claim made by the Ṣūfīs is indeed for unity with God, such as Ḥallāj's: "I am Truth." *Daʿwā* means any claim, whether true or false.[13] Jurjānī says that the claims made by the Ṣūfīs are true but insists that the *shaṭaḥāt*, which give expression to those claims, are slips committed by persons whose intellects are unsteady. This is like saying that the claim is both true and false. The claim is true because it signifies a fact—namely, that everything is in unity with God. It is false, however, because no matter how carefully unity is expressed, negation always creeps into it with the expression, and alienates it from or splits it against itself. I believe that this is the meaning of Junaid's saying: "Knowledge of unification is separate from its existence and its existence is separate from knowledge of it."[14] I will come back to Junaid's saying shortly.

Qushayrī defines state (*ḥāl*) by distinguishing it from station (*maqām*): "The state according to the Ṣūfīs is a meaning that descends on the heart without intention or endeavor or earning in their part [investing it with] joy or grief or expansion or contraction or yearning or disquiet or fear or want. States come as gifts, whereas stations are earned. States come from beyond existence, whereas stations are acquired by investing effort. The possessor of the station is placed in his station whereas the possessor of the state is above his state."[15] In this, there is an explanation for Ibn Ṭufayl's statement that the state he has witnessed belongs to a realm of existence that cannot be represented by means of language and rational consideration. Rather, the state is a meaning that descends on the heart, which fluctuates constantly, thus causing the owner of the state to be always above or beyond the given state. Ibn Ṭufayl says that he has witnessed such a state, but that he finds it extremely difficult to describe in words what he has witnessed. Only toward the end of his book does he say more about what he had witnessed, using his favorite example of light-reflecting mirrors. There, he emphasizes once more the limitation of the use of language and repeats his warning to his reader not to take his words for their ordinary meanings. Then he proceeds in describing the essences of the spheres that Ḥayy had witnessed, beginning with the essence (*dhāt*) of the highest sphere: "He saw a being corresponding to the highest sphere, beyond which there is no body, a subject free of matter, and neither identical with the Truth and the One nor with the sphere itself, nor distinct from either—as the form of the sun appearing in a polished mirror is neither sun nor mirror, and yet distinct from neither."[16]

The essence of the highest sphere that encompasses the world is given the characteristic of a state, which cannot be captured by means of the categorical limits of either/or, only by means of a liminal or imaginal correspondence. As the heart of the Ṣūfī receives the state and acquires its identity as (a fluctuating) heart, so does the world receive the image of the One/Truth as in a mirror and maintains its true unity only as it remains in its image or insofar as the image of the One/Truth remains in it, which is to say the same because the image of the One/Truth is defined here by Ibn Ṭufayl as the essence of the world. Likewise, the heart fluctuates essentially meaning that it is in its essence to fluctuate, so that it and its state (or states) are one and the same. This situation of complete identification with the state is what stands behind the incapacity of the Ṣūfī to draw as if inside his self and include the state as a moment, because he has become one with the moment.[17] Ibn Ṭufayl gives to the states the same characteristics as the *shaṭaḥāt*,[18] the expressions uttered in a state of intoxication. And indeed, Qushayrī says that "the servant witnesses (*yushāhid*) the state in his intoxication and in his soberness he witnesses [the form of] knowledge (*al-ʿilm*)."[19] This brings us back to Junaid's saying: "Knowledge of unification is separate from its existence and its existence is separate from knowledge of it." He who witnesses knowledge (*ʿilm*) of unification witnesses the Truth through the world (*ʿālam*); that is, the Truth as manifest existence. In the state of intoxication, the servant withdraws from the manifest world and witnesses the Truth as essence. The servant can give but a general expression to the state that he arrives at or at one of its limits, which are likewise states the likenesses of which are images of the essence of Truth reflected in the mirrors of the world. In the following discussion, I will elaborate on the distinction between knowledge of the states (knowledge1) and knowledge of the manifested forms in the world (knowledge2).

KNOWLEDGE1, KNOWLEDGE2, AND GHAZĀLĪ'S *NICHE OF LIGHTS*

The closest state of perfection that the servant witnesses is the state that corresponds to the reflection of the essence of Truth in the mirror of the highest sphere, which encompasses the world. This reflection or image, which constitutes the essence of the highest sphere, is reflected in the mirrors of the other spheres to invest them with their imaginal essences. Those essences possess a liminal nature. They are neither Truth nor the spheres and yet they are distinct from neither.[20] The knowledge of these liminal essences and their reflections in the mirrors of the world that the servant possesses is called *maʿrifa* (hence, knowledge1). It is to be distinguished from the knowledge that is called *ʿilm* (hence, knowledge2) and that is related to the world (*ʿālam*). Lane points at the following distinctions between knowledge1 and knowledge2:

a. Knowledge1 concerns the thing itself, which is its object, whereas knowledge2 concerns the qualities, conditions, or states of its object. The latter is more general in signification than the former.
b. Knowledge1 concerns knowing a thing itself, as distinguished from knowing other things, whereas knowledge2 concerns knowing a thing collectively with other things.
c. Knowledge1 denotes the perceiving of something as a thing that has been absent from the mind, thus differing from the latter.
d. Knowledge1 is the perceiving of a thing by reflection, and by consideration of the effect thereof (upon the mind or sense), so it has a more special meaning than knowledge2. Its contrary is failure to acknowledge (*al-inkār*).[21]

In (a) and (b), knowledge2 is said to be more general in signification than knowledge1 because it concerns itself not with the thing itself or in itself, but with the states that it shares with other things. Knowledge1, however, concerns itself with the thing itself, as distinguished from other things. In other words, knowledge1 concerns itself with the essence of the thing, which must be particular to qualify as essence, while knowledge2 concerns itself with its attributes, which must be general to qualify as such. This is why Ibn Ṭufayl says that one who is overcome by the states (essences) can give only a general expression to them because he cannot be particular. In (c), we find an implicit allusion to the identification between knowledge1 and the state of intoxication in which the states come to the servant from beyond existence. In (d), it is stated that knowledge1 concerns the perceiving of a thing by reflection and the consideration of the effect that is made on the mind. In what follows, I will elaborate on these statements by referring to Ghazālī's *Niche of Lights*. Ibn Ṭufayl says: "As for the Shaykh Abū Ḥāmid al-Ghazālī ... when he arrived at this state he expressed himself with this verse.

> It was what it was and it is now beyond my recollection.
> Think the best and inquire no further concerning the [truth of the] report (*khabar*).[22]

But he was a man who was taught the discipline of the mind and the good qualities of the soul by knowledge1 and who was also well-versed in knowledge2."[23]

Ghazālī possessed knowledge of philosophy and logic, which distinguishes him from Ḥallāj and other Ṣūfīs. It is true that he was seriously critical of the philosophers. However, as Chittick points out, Ghazālī's objection was not to the sort of the training of mind that philosophers advocated, but rather to certain conclusions that they admitted.[24] It is this sort of training that Ibn Ṭufayl means by saying that Ghazālī was well versed in knowledge2. He was also taught discipline of the mind and the soul by knowledge1. As (d) indicates, the contrary of knowledge1 is denial or failure to acknowledge. To be in a state of denial is to fail to distinguish true from false, which pertains to the discipline of the mind, and good from bad, which pertains to the discipline of the soul; it is to fail to observe the limits (*ḥudūd*) in both respects. Thus, in spite of the fact that Ghazālī arrived at the knowledge of the states (that is, knowledge of unity), he was still prevented, as a result of possessing both knowledge1 and knowledge2, from attempting to state this in an articulate form.

Knowledge1 is described in (d) as the perceiving of a thing by reflection and the consideration of the effect of the reflection upon the perceiving mind. Within the Ṣūfī tradition, the organ that functions as a reflecting mirror is the heart (*qalb, lubb*).

This is in harmony with Ibn Ṭufayl's characterization of the state as an image that is reflected in the heart of the servant in correspondence to the reflection of Truth in the mirror of the highest sphere. In the resemblance between Ibn Ṭufayl's and Ghazālī's illuminationist views, this characterization plays an especially important role. The examination of this resemblance is crucial for understanding the general plan of Ibn Ṭufayl's project, which he conducted, according to his own admission, by means of synthesizing Ghazālī's and Ibn Sīnā's teachings.[25] Ibn Ṭufayl mentions Ghazālī's *Niche of Lights* as one of the works that were known in Andalusia by his time.[26] The influence of this work on *Ḥayy* becomes apparent upon comparing the manner in which Ibn Ṭufayl opens his book with what Ghazālī says at the beginning of *Niche*: "You asked me, O noble brother … that I unfold for you the mysteries of the divine lights … With your question you have climbed a difficult slope, one before whose upper regions the eyes of the observers fall back. You have knocked at a locked door that is not to be opened except for the firmly rooted possessors of knowledge. What is more, not every mystery is to be unveiled and divulged, and not every reality is to be presented and disclosed."[27] Another passage that provides a clear example of the influence of Ghazālī's *Niche* is the following: "The gnostics, after having ascended to the heaven of reality, agree that they see nothing in existence save the One, the Real. Some of them possess this state as a cognitive gnosis. Others, however, attain this through a state of tasting … their rational faculties become so satiated that in this state they are, as it were, stunned. No room remains in them for the remembrance of any other than God, nor the remembrance of themselves … Nothing is with them but God. They become intoxicated with such an intoxication that the ruling authority of their rational faculty is overthrown. Hence, one of them says, 'I am the Real!' another, 'Glory be to me, how great is my station!' and still another, 'There is nothing in my robe but God!'"[28] Ghazālī draws a distinction between knowledge of unity that is the outcome of rational deliberation (and that can be considered as the culmination of knowledge2) and knowledge of unity that is the outcome of mystical witnessing (knowledge 1). In this passage, there is a reminder that the claim (*daʿwā*), which is expressed in the sayings of intoxicated Ṣūfīs, is one for unification with God. In it, we find also a reminder of Ibn Ṭufayl's example of the mirror that reflects on itself and burns everything else, and that resembles the very state of the servant who has witnessed the state. As he becomes a polished mirror perfectly reflecting the unitary essences, he is no longer distinguished from these. Ghazālī describes this unique situation in the following words: "It is not unlikely that a person could look into a mirror in an unexpected place and not see the mirror at all. He supposes that the form he sees is the mirror's form and that it is united with the mirror. Likewise, he could see wine in a glass and suppose that the wine is the glass's color. When the situation becomes familiar to him and his foot becomes firmly established within it, he asks for forgiveness from God."[29]

When the servant becomes firmly established in the state of unification (that is, when seeing the state (*ḥāl*) becomes a station (*maqām*) for him), he is no longer intoxicated. He becomes courteous and asks God for forgiveness for failing to observe his limits. It is clear that Ghazālī identifies his own position with that of the people of soberness (*ahl al-saḥw*).[30] Nevertheless, he provides an excuse for the conduct of intoxicated Ṣūfīs, the likes of Ḥallāj; and while doing so, he elucidates an important point in relation to the claim for unification. Despite the Ṣūfī's laborious effort to bring his soul to an absolute match with the signification of his name and establish a perfect state of purification,[31] a claim will always cling to it and set it apart from Truth.

It was actually one of the Ṣūfīs who belonged to the camp of intoxication, Shiblī, who expressed this meaning when he was asked, "Why were they [the Ṣūfīs] given this name?" and responded by saying, "It is because of a certain remainder that lingered in their souls. Were it not for that remainder, they would not have been given this name."[32] It is here that knowledge1, which is defined in (d) as the opposite of failing to acknowledge, is especially important because it protects the servant from failing to acknowledge the fact that a limit will always be set between him and Truth. Hence, it was important for Ibn Ṭufayl to say that Ghazālī was taught courtesy by knowledge1, meaning that knowledge1 made him acknowledge the limits that must be observed between the Ṣūfī and Truth and not fall into a state of denial.

The strongest resemblance between Ghazālī and Ibn Ṭufayl can be detected in their characterization of the cosmos as consisting of a hierarchy of light-reflecting mirrors. We find a neat illustration of this hierarchy in an important passage in *Niche*, in which Ghazālī presents a similitude of the hierarchy of the cosmic lights by imagining the light that the moon receives from the sun, entering through a window of a house, and falling upon a mirror and then is reflected to an opposite wall, to finally turn from the wall to the Earth as to illuminate it.[33] The moon, the mirror, and the wall function in this similitude as intermediaries between the sun, the source of light, and Earth, its final recipient, thus characterizing the hierarchy of cosmic lights in terms of liminality. Ibn Ṭufayl describes Ḥayy's witnessing of the liminal reflections of the essences of the heavenly bodies, drawn from the essence of Truth and reflected through the highest sphere to the sphere of the fixed stars, through the following spheres, until they finally reach the sphere of the moon and the form of the world of generation and corruption.[34] Like the other heavenly forms, which are described as neither Truth nor the spheres and yet are distinct from neither, the form of the world of generation and corruption receives the same liminal characterization. This form is depicted as "possessing seventy thousand faces in each of which there are seventy thousand mouths in each of which there are seventy thousand tongues that praise the essence of the One/Truth."[35] In the introduction to *Niche*, Ghazālī says that he wrote his book in response to a request made to him by a noble brother to unfold the mysteries of the divine lights "along with an interpretation of . . . His words, 'God is the light of the heavens and the earth'[36] . . . and also the saying of the Prophet: 'God has seventy veils of light and darkness; were He to lift them, the august glories of His face would burn up everyone whose eyesight perceived Him.'"[37] Instead of seventy veils, Ibn Ṭufayl mentions seventy thousand faces,[38] which he depicts as the essences or the souls of human beings. Some of these are, like Ḥayy's essence, polished mirrors that reflect the form of the sun and some are rusty mirrors that are turned away from it.[39] Ibn Ṭufayl's characterization of these essences is similar to Ghazālī's, although the latter provides a neat threefold classification of the veiled to those who are veiled by sheer light, those who are veiled by sheer darkness, and those who are veiled by light mixed with darkness.[40]

From all this, it becomes clear that Ghazālī's influence on Ibn Ṭufayl's illuminationist thought is essential. I should emphasize, however, that I have not been unaware of the serious criticism of Ghazālī that Ibn Ṭufayl brings up in the introduction to his work. To complicate his position, Ibn Ṭufayl follows his critical statements against Ghazālī by saying that he was one of those who achieved the supreme divinely goals and attained felicity.[41] A partial explanation for this apparent self-contradiction seems to have been alluded to by Ibn Ṭufayl himself in his mention of Ghazālī's tripartite division of views to those that are held in common with the general public, those that accord with the special quest made for them, those that are held by the mystic, and those who share with him his state of knowledge.[42] The irreproachable Ghazālī can then be identified with those views that he shares with his esoteric compatriots. This explanation, however, seems inconsistent with Ibn Ṭufayl's characterization of Ghazālī as a man whose works "bind in one place and loose in another."[43] I think that considerations that have to do with consistency stand behind the tendency of certain scholars to consider *Niche* a forgery, as the contents of this work seem to be in contradiction with Ghazālī's anti-philosophical stand in his *Incoherence*. I also think that similar considerations stand behind certain scholars' reluctance to acknowledge the significance of the mystical component of Ibn Sīnā's thought. My own opinion regarding this problem rests on a conviction that Islamic thinkers, such as Ghazālī and Ibn Sīnā, share a unifying concept of liminality that enables them to be involved in positions that seem self-contradictory but that are in harmony with the paradoxical requirements of liminal thought.

IBN SĪNĀ'S LIMINAL DEPICTION OF THE MYSTICAL EXPERIENCE

In the introduction to his work, Ibn Ṭufayl refers to the following passage from the Ninth Sort of Ibn Sīnā's *Ishārāt*. The words in italics appear in both works:

Then when his exercise and willpower reach a certain limit, there appear to him glimmerings of Truth, sweet like flashes of lightning that shine upon him and then go out. This is what they [Ṣūfīs] call "the instant" (*waqt*), as each instant is surrounded by two griefs, one because of waiting for it and another because of mourning over it [s passing away]. *The more he exercises himself the oftener the coverings [of light] come upon him, till when he is sufficiently diligent in the exercise, the coverings of light start coming upon him without practice. As soon as he perceives a thing, he will turn his face to the side of*

Truth and something will occur to him from it; a covering of light comes upon him and he sees Truth in everything. At a certain limit, the coverings depart from him and his tranquility (*sakīna*) is disturbed, as a person sitting in his company may notice this. When he perseveres in the exercise, his tranquility stabilizes and he is disturbed no more. *Then he reaches a certain level in the exercise when his moment (waqt) becomes fully tranquil. What came to him suddenly becomes steady and the glimmerings of light become permanent. His comprehension becomes stable and keeps him permanent company*. He will then rejoice in the company [of Truth] and when he departs from it he will be so sorrowful for the loss. *It is within this limit that his state might still be noticeable*. Penetrating into this sort of comprehension the [outward] manifestations [of his state] become less apparent, and he becomes present even as he is absent and stays even as he departs. It is possible that within this limit this sort of comprehension occurs to him only sometimes, but then he gradually takes hold of it as he wishes. Then he advances beyond this degree … and declining the world of untruth he ascends to the world of Truth and resides therein lastingly, as he will have the heedless surrounding and circulating him. Once he has gone beyond the exercise to the [actual] attainment, *he becomes a polished mirror facing toward the Truth. Sublime delights pour over him and he rejoices for the share that his soul gained from [the trace] of Truth. As long as he partakes in two considerations, one that faces toward Truth and another that faces toward his own self, he will be hesitant. Then he becomes oblivious to himself and faces toward the side of Truth alone. Even as he beholds his own self, he will behold it only as a beholder of Truth and will not admire it for something that it gained. There he will have arrived in Truth*.[44]

Ibn Sīnā says that when the seeker reaches a certain limit in the exercise, there appear to him glimmerings of Truth like flashes of lightning that shine upon him and then go out.[45] Qushayrī associates the flashes of lightning with the states (*aḥwāl*) enjoyed by the possessor of knowledge1: "The possessor of the station (*maqām*) is placed in his station whereas the possessor of the state is above his state. When asked about the possessor of knowledge1, Dhū al-Nūn al-Miṣrī said, 'He was here and he went.' Some of the Mashāykh said that the states are like flashes of lightning … and that, following the designation of their name, they vanish from the heart at the very moment (*waqt*) in which they descend upon it."[46] The time of the possessor of knowledge1, like the time of the state, ends as it begins, like a flash of lightning that shines and then immediately goes out. This is why it is situated between two griefs: "This is what they [Ṣūfīs] call 'the instant' (*waqt*), as each instant is surrounded by two griefs, one because of waiting for it and another because of mourning over it [s passing away]."[47] Qushayrī says: "They say that the instant (*waqt*) is something between the two times (*zamanayn*) of the past and the future and also that the Ṣūfī is the son of his time (*waqt*), meaning that he is fully occupied with the state in which he is."[48] The occurrence of the flash of lightning is preceded and followed by darkness. As the time of the past is gone and the time of the future is unknown, what can be a better depiction of the experience of enlightenment than an experience of two griefs surrounding a fleeting instant of delight? And yet Ibn Sīnā presents this instant as mounting to measures that encompass the whole of the soul of the possessor of knowledge1. The possessor of knowledge1 becomes the very liminal instant that he contemplates. This is how "he becomes present even as he is absent and stays even as he departs." In the beginning, this unification with the instant occurs only sometimes. Then it expands to occupy the whole time. The exercise is turned into attainment and the Ṣūfī becomes a polished mirror, facing toward Truth, the ultimate source of light. Even as he observes his own self, this observation becomes in the final consideration a pure and self-reflective observation, a reflection that turns on itself and burns everything else.

Ibn Sīnā provides an interesting account of this experience of liminal self-transformation in his visionary recitals. In what follows, I will elaborate on one important passage from Ibn Sīnā's *Ḥayy Ibn Yaqẓān*, which commences with a conversation between a seeker who joins his companions in visiting a sage whose name is Ḥayy Ibn Yaqẓān. The seeker asks the sage to guide him in the journey toward Truth, but the sage warns him: "For the present, then thou must rest content with a journey interrupted by halts and inactivity[49]; now thou wilt be on the road, now thou wilt frequent these companions. Each time that thou goest alone, pursuing thy journey with perfect ardor, I walk with thee, and thou are separated from them. Each time that thou sighest after them, thou turnest back toward them, and thou are separated from me; so shall it be until the moment comes when thou shalt break with them wholly."[50]

The seeker is invited to partake in a journey and in a spiritual exercise that might qualify him for the attainment of the vision of Truth. But this attainment will not be possible if the seeker does not break wholly with his companions. Meanwhile, the break itself will be broken and he will be vacillating between separation from and arrival at Truth. Although this vacillation seems negative because it indicates distance and alienation, it still carries with it a positive indication of an important difference between the person who undergoes it and others who are deprived of the very possibility of engaging in the attempt. The more intimately the seeker immerses himself in this *difference* from his companions, the closer he becomes to unity with Truth. Like the flash of lightning that breaks the identity of the night by separating darkness from the same, the seeker separates himself from everything that turns his attention away from contemplating the essence of Truth and prepares his soul for unification with it. With the advent of the sun, darkness withdraws, and with it, the flashes of lightning. Likewise, when the seeker has attained unification, he will have abandoned not only things that turn his soul away from contemplating Truth, but also his fragmented soul, which he had identified previously with the momentary flashes of lightning.[51] As we shall see, this gradual unfolding of mystic lights, as well as the accompanying vacillation between difference and unity, constitute the essence of the mystical experience as Ibn Ṭufayl accounts for it in his work. This is an important feature in Ibn Sīnā's *Salāmān and Absāl* as well.

SALĀMĀN AND ABSĀL: THE HERMETISTIC VERSION

Relying on the testimony of Naṣīr al-Dīn al-Ṭūsī, the interpreter of Ibn Sīnā's *Ishārāt*, Henry Corbin points out that there are two different versions of a recital bearing the title *Salāmān and Absāl*. There is the recital that was translated by Ḥunayn bin Isḥāq from the Greek and was drawn from Hermetistic sources, with which Ṭūsī became acquainted upon the completion of his interpretation of *Ishārāt*.[52] There is another version of the recital with which Ṭūsī became acquainted only twenty years after he had completed his interpretation of Ibn Sīnā's work. Following Ṭūsī, Corbin states his confidence that the latter version of the recital is Ibn Sīnā's genuine work, and rightly registers his regret that Ṭūsī brings it in such a meager summary within the context of his interpretation of *Ishārāt*.

The Hermetistic text tells the story of a very special love between Salāmān, the son of a Byzantine king, and Absāl. Salāmān's love for Absāl claimed him entirely and precluded him from assuming his father's throne. The king wished to kill Absāl, but his vizier protested: "Let none make bold to destroy what he cannot himself raise up. If the king put this project into effect, it was to be feared that the very foundations of his dwelling would be overthrown and that the elements brought together to constitute his nature would dissolve. The 'child' must little by little discover for himself what it was incumbent upon him to do."[53] The following developments result in the death of Absāl, but not of Salāmān's love for her. The king consulted a certain sage, who concocted a plan that eventually made Salāmān forget Absāl completely. He promised Salāmān that Absāl would be restored to him under a certain condition: In a cave, he must meditate with the sage. However, while the sage will be meditating continuously for forty days, Salāmān must break his meditations every seven days. The meditations and invocations of the sage made Absāl appear to Salāmān, who rejoiced in the vision of his beloved. At the end of forty days, Salāmān was able to see the sublime figure of the heavenly Venus and soon shunned the vision of Absāl.[54]

Corbin doubts the possibility that Ibn Sīnā knew this Hermetistic version of the recital because his own version is profoundly different from it.[55] Moreover, he shows clear dissatisfaction with Ṭūsī's interpretation of the Hermetistic version. In his view, Ṭūsī's interpretation is based on the attempt to bring the imaginal modes of being, which are transmuted into symbols, to a perceptual level that preceded their transmutation instead of situating the interpretation in a plane of a phenomenology of symbols that is not limited to the consciousness of a rationally closed mode of reflection.[56] Corbin, however, provides an interpretation that possesses, according to his own admission, only the value of hermeneutic implications. Nevertheless, he thinks that his interpretation, rather than Ṭūsī's, is the one that provides for some sort of unconscious harmony between the

Hermetistic version of *Salāmān and Absāl* and Ibn Sīnā's reference to the figures of the recital in his saying that "Absāl signifies your level in gnosis (*ʿirfān*)." Corbin agrees with Ṭūsī's interpretation of the figure of Salāmān as "signifying yourself," but disagrees with him about his conviction that the description of Absāl in the recital is not in harmony with Ibn Sīnā's saying that "Absāl signifies your degree in gnosis."[57]

I wish to complement Corbin's interpretation with Ṭūsī's to get the best understanding of what constitutes an *ideal* connection between Ibn Sīnā's *Ḥayy Ibn Yaqẓān* and the Hermetistic version of *Salāmān and Absāl*. The focal point of connection will be Ṭūsī's view, described as follows. According to Ṭūsī, Absāl in the Hermetistic version cannot signify the realizer's degree of knowledge because she signifies the loss and the absence rather than the attainment and the endurance of knowledge. The knower will be prevented from obtaining knowledge so long as he remains attached to Absāl. It is not Absāl, but her disappearance, that signifies the attainment of a degree of knowledge. This is how the king in the story understands the matter; accordingly, he orders the killing of Absāl, who is inhibiting Salāmān from assuming the throne of reason. His vizier, however, had to warn him that Salāmān must *gradually* discover for himself what was incumbent upon him to do; and getting rid of Absāl in that abrupt manner would have the effect of overthrowing the very foundations of the king's dwelling. This seems to be in harmony with Ṭūsī's interpretation: "And I say that the words of the shaykh make one feel that there is a story in which these two names are mentioned, and which contains reference to a seeker and an object that he seeks and attains *gradually* and, through that attainment, comes to achieve one perfection after another, so that Salāmān might be identified with the seeker and Absāl with the object he seeks."[58] What is this insistence on the gradual growth of Salāmān, and, given the fact that Absāl must go eventually, why not make her go now, following the wish of the owner of the throne?[59]

Two answers may be suggested for these questions. The first has to do with the special nature of the mystical practice of acquiring knowledge, in which the personal effort of the seeker is crucial. The adept must take a personal and active part in the attainment of mystical truths, and these must not be imposed upon him as if he were a passive agent and the external and ready products were to be swallowed in one setting rather than digested gradually. The second answer has to do with the careful correspondence that Hermetism observes between the ontological order of what there is and the epistemological order of the manner in which it is known. As the ascending ladder of knowledge attainment is constituted of degrees or levels, so it is fathomed in correspondence to the descending ladder of truth emanation, also proceeding according to grades or levels. If order and harmony are not observed, the ladders of being and knowledge (that is, the foundations) will be stirred. The truth is that Salāmān needs the ladder (the levels of knowledge) to ascend to the throne. To take away the ladder—the only means by which the son can become the father and inherit his throne—is to overthrow the very foundations of the kingdom of reason. In the operation of mystical attainment, Absāl's disappearance must be depicted as functional rather than consequential. It is not the result of the operation of knowledge, confined to this or that degree, but rather what renders the operation possible. That is why it was imperative to make this disappearance a gradual and continuous process rather than the ready product of a sudden act of transformation. This explains why there was need for two sorts of meditations operating at the same time. The continuous meditation was destined to manifest the true Absāl or her true form, whereas the intermittent meditation was destined to manifest some sort of intermediate entity that functions as a veil that conceals and, at the right time, shall reveal Absāl's true image.

IBN SĪNĀ'S VERSION

Although I can understand the reasons that make John Walbridge and other scholars to claim that Ibn Sina's philosophy is overwhelmingly Aristotelian,[60] I cannot ignore the especially deep messages that he placed in the mystical part of his work. I do believe that the mystical message that this part conveys, as well as the striking hints and allusions that it furnished thinkers with, are of enormous importance. I believe this is the case despite the depiction of Ibn Sīnā as a person who "repeatedly sought court patronage and political advancement. His death, supposedly due to complications caused by sexual excess, scarcely exemplified the ideal of the Illuminationist philosopher."[61] Let us keep in mind that Ibn Ṭufayl, who defined himself as an illuminationist, also sought political power, although we cannot say that he was "excessively concerned with worldly matters and thus neglected the more important spiritual matters," as Shaharzūrī describes Ibn Sīnā and other philosophers.[62] And even more importantly, Plato, Suhrawardī's greatest illuminationist model, also sought political power, although he was probably an ascetic. Indeed, one must feel sympathy with Walbridge's statement after reading the testimony of many Islamic historians and medieval intellectuals who used to contrast Plato's asceticism to Ibn Sīnā's worldliness.[63] Keeping this in mind, we must remember that it was almost impossible for Islamic thinkers to distance themselves from political courts; and sometimes this compelled them to be involved in activities that abstinents would shun. We know also that Ibn Sīnā wrote his mystical recitals following or during a political imprisonment,[64] as those might represent his symbolic way of saying genuine things that he was previously unable to say. Hence, his mystical recitals might be depicted as manuals to guide the adept in his struggle with the other, as well as with his own soul, as the two struggles are necessarily related. It is here that I find the most important mystical message in all of Ibn Sīnā's recitals, which has to do with the crucial significance of the gradual attainment to mystical perfection and which should be translated, given what I have been saying, to the language of mystical individuation. This message presents itself clearly in the Hermetistic version of *Salāmān and Absāl* and the text from the Ninth Sort of *Ishārāt*.

Ibn Sīnā's story presents Salāmān and Absāl as half-brothers. Absāl is younger but disciplined and rooted in intelligence and knowledge2. Absāl's brother's wife attempts to seduce him, but he is able to resist the temptation. She manages to get him wedded to her sister and on the wedding night, she takes her sister's place in the marriage bed. The story reaches a crucial point here: "At that moment the heavens became covered with dense clouds. A flash of lightning shot through them, its brilliant light disclosing the woman's face. Then Absāl pushed her violently away, left the room, and resolved to flee."[65] The occurrence of the flash of lightning shows Absāl the cunning face of worldly reality. Now the flash of lightning carries with it a gift of revelation; but it should be remembered (and can be easily forgotten) that the message of revelation becomes effective only because of the intensification of darkness. Absāl, however, is not aware of this. He realizes how dangerously cunning his brother's wife is and decides that he must avoid the immediate danger. He wages war on his brother's enemies and conquers lands for his sake. However, it was not worldly matter, but rather his soul, that he needed to conquer. As he became a great conqueror, the first Dḥū al-Qarnayn to take East and West,[66] he falsely thought that he could now face his brother's wife. As he returns, she returns to her old ways; and this time she makes the generals of his army wage war against him and leave him wounded on the battlefield. A wild beast nurses him until he regains his full strength.[67]

As we can see, the story goes in what looks like cycles of attempts of the seeker to break loose from the bonds that tie him to his earthly reality. The food that Absāl receives from the wild beast represents the stage of animality, which signifies the near completion of the cycle of liberation from the bonds of this world, including the bond of rationality. This food makes Absāl especially strong, as he gathers together great numbers of well-equipped forces and returns to rescue his brother Salāmān, whom he finds in grave danger. It is here, at the peak of his advancement, that Absāl, who "signifies your degree in knowledge," must die and for Salāmān, who "signifies thy own self," to subsist.

CHAPTER 3

The Naturalistic Account of Ḥayy's Birth

Only part of the naturalistic account is presented in this chapter following Ibn Ṭufayl's own presentation, as he commences it with describing the naturalistic account but interrupts the description to provide the traditionalistic account in what Sami Hawi views as his attempt to conceal his naturalistic position. A significant part of the discussion is devoted to Ibn Ṭufayl's liminal depiction of natural existence, which is compared to Ibn al-ʿArabī's. The discussion of Ibn al-ʿArabī's account of his visions in the Earth of *Barzakh* aims to throw light on the liminal characteristics that Ibn Ṭufayl emphasizes in his description of Ḥayy's naturalistic birthplace.

IBN ṬUFAYL'S METHOD OF CONCEALMENT

Ibn Ṭufayl introduces two accounts of Ḥayy's birth: naturalistic and traditionalistic. The question that presents itself immediately is: why two accounts? According to Hawi, Ibn Ṭufayl applies a method of concealment that involves an exoteric aspect, intended for the public, and an esoteric aspect, intended for the enlightened few. The traditionalistic account comes under the exoteric aspect, which includes the belief of the general public in God through revelation and the creation of the world, whereas the naturalistic account comes under the esoteric aspect, which includes the rational depiction of God's existence, the eternity of the world, the unity of all existence, and pantheism.[1] Since the two accounts are contradictory, Ibn Ṭufayl must be employing a method of concealment to hide his naturalistic views from the general public.[2] To hide his real view, Ibn Ṭufayl opens with the description of the naturalistic account of Ḥayy's birth, interrupts it to provide a succinct description of the traditionalistic account, and then resumes his presentation of the naturalistic account to describe Ḥayy's emergence from nature in rich scientific detail.[3]

It is not clear, however, how starting with a naturalistic rather than a traditionalistic account and elaborating on the former can be an effective method of concealing Ibn Ṭufayl's intentions if those are inconsistent with the beliefs of the exoteric public. I think it can be misleading to state, as Hawi does, that the traditionalistic account accords with the outward meaning of the treatise.[4] As I will attempt to show, Ibn Ṭufayl's presentation of the traditionalistic account carries with it deep mystical allusions meant to be understood as such—that is, allusions to be interpreted rather than outwardly comprehended.[5] Moreover, it seems that Hawi's stated conviction that *Ḥayy* is a purely philosophical treatise precludes him from properly addressing the mystical component of the work. This, however, is strange to come from a scholar who complains, with so many affectionate words, against the manner in which analytic philosophy has detached itself from the broad intellectual involvedness and limited itself to concept analysis.[6] To show some fairness toward Hawi, I must emphasize that the task of relating philosophy to mysticism is especially complex. In a sense, the Ṣūfīs had their share in augmenting this complexity, especially those Ṣūfīs who showed serious antagonism to the philosophical enterprise. Indeed, the very warning of Ibn al-ʿArabī against rejecting certain views only because a certain philosopher expressed them indicates the relentless hostility that some Ṣūfīs displayed toward philosophers.[7] I think that the caution that Ibn Rushd exerted toward the Ṣūfīs, despite his recognition of the possibility of the materialization of the Ṣūfī ideal at the level of the individual,[8] is an indication of the philosophers' general reaction to mystics who were either extremely against the rationalists or so much drawn into their own world and encapsulated in their individualistic shells that he would expect little help from them to make reason a universal judge and ruler and to counter the theologians' attempt at confining it within dogmatic limits. As Ibn Ṭufayl was struggling with these concerns, he followed a method of striking balance and establishing harmony between the conflicting parties, even as this method was tinged with the shade of concealment.

SPONTANEOUS GENERATION

According to the naturalistic account, Ḥayy's birth occurred on an equatorial island in the Indian Ocean in which human beings are born without mother or father, and in which there are trees that yield women. According to Masʿūdī, this is the island of *Wāqwāq*. Fārūk Saʿd points out that Masʿūdī was not the only person to mention the island; he provides a list of names of others who mentioned it. Al-Maqdisī and al-Bayrūnī say that in India, there is a tree that is called *Wāqwāq* that bears women as fruit. Also, Zakariyya al-Qazwīnī mentions an island in the Sea of China in which there are trees that bear fruit in the form of women hanging by the hair and screaming "*wāq wāq*."[9] Qazwīnī describes another island as well, and his description of it can be related to what Maqdisī and Bayrūnī say: "In the Island of Women in the Sea of China there are women and no men are with them originally. They conceive by the wind and give birth to women like themselves. It is said that they conceive by means of a fruit of some tree, which they eat and become pregnant … A merchant relates that the wind cast him onto this island: 'I saw women and no men with them. I also saw gold in this island like soil and I saw gold growing like branches of cane. The women were about to kill me when one of them laid me on a board and threw me to the sea. The wind cast me to China land. I reported to the ruler what I had seen concerning the island and the gold that it contained. He sent people to ascertain the report. They went for three years but could not find the island.'"[10]

Remke Kruk indicates that medieval Islamic science was aware of the fact that date palms bear fruit only if the dust of the male flower is sprinkled over the female, and the additional fact that an individual parent of a certain species could generate a new individual without cohabitation with the sexually different individual from the same species.[11] This seems to be in accord with Qazwīnī's saying that women in the Island of Women conceive either by the wind, which, we might add, carries the fecundating dust, or, by means of some fecundated fruit that they eat and give birth to women like themselves. As Kruk indicates, the date palm (*khūṣṣ*) and the beech (*zān*) are the only trees that Ibn Ṭufayl mentions by name in his work.[12] What is noticeable in Qazwīnī's description of the Island of Women and Ibn Ṭufayl's description of Ḥayy's island is the sense of unreachability posited in both accounts for keeping an island in which the best of minerals and the goal of all alchemical transformations, gold, is abundant and another, in which wisdom that is as rare as Red Sulphur[13] grows and flourishes in the finest souls, out of the reach of humans.[14]

Ibn Ṭufayl proceeds to describe the first account of Ḥayy's birth. The island in which people are generated spontaneously is most temperate and perfectly balanced due to its moderate air and the shining of the supernal light, rendering it the fittest place to receive the noblest form of life of the human being. Ibn Ṭufayl rejects the view of scientists from among philosophers and physicians that the region of the equator is one of a very intense heat, which, they say, explains why the fourth zone is actually the world's most temperate region.[15] Relying on assumptions admitted by those scientists, Ibn Ṭufayl proceeds to show that the sun does not heat the Earth in the same manner as hot bodies heat bodies that are near them; and then he develops the argument to show that the region of the equator is not extremely hot or extremely cold.

There are, he says, three causes of the generation of heat: motion, contact with hot bodies, and light. Now the sun itself is not hot, and the air that surrounds the Earth belongs to the group of transparent bodies that are the weakest in receiving heat. This, says Ibn Ṭufayl, had been demonstrated by Ibn Sīnā: "Likewise they teach that it is the highly reflective bodies, not the transparent ones, that take up light best; next are opaque, non-reflecting bodies; but transparent bodies with no trace of opacity do not take on light at all.

The foregoing point was proved by Avicenna, using an argument which was his original work."[16] The sun itself is not hot, and it does not heat air first and then the Earth by convection because we find that higher layers of air are cooler than those closer to the Earth. Also, the Earth is not heated by motion because it is stationary. From all this, it follows that heat follows light, which can be exemplified by referring to the fact that when light is collected in a burning-glass, it sets things on fire.[17] Now the sun, which is spherical, is much greater than the Earth, and at all times more than half of the Earth is illuminated by it. This constitutes a circle of light where the light is most intense in the center and diminishes toward the circumference of the circle, which is totally covered by darkness. In the location at the center, where the sun stands vertical over the heads of its inhabitants, heat is most intense and it becomes least when the sun stays farthest from the zenith. As astronomy affirms, in equatorial regions, the sun is vertical to the inhabitants of these regions only twice a year. The rest of the year, the sun declines to their north six months and to their south six months. Consequently, their states are uniform and they know neither excessive heat nor excessive cold. Ibn Ṭufayl closes this part of the naturalistic account with the following words: "This account is in need of further clarification, which we will not be able to provide here since it will not be fitting for our purpose. We only have drawn your attention to this matter since it confirms the genuineness of the report concerning the possibility of the generation of man in that region without mother or father. Some people conclude by making a final judgment that Ḥayy Ibn Yaqẓān was one of those who were engendered in that region without mother or father and some disagree and provide a different report that we will communicate to you."[18]

Ibn Ṭufayl disrupts his naturalistic account of Ḥayy's birth to bring up the traditionalistic account. He then reverts to the naturalistic account and ends up merging the two accounts with the first cry of the newborn. Hawi interprets Ibn Ṭufayl's disruption of the narrative as part of a method of concealment. In my view, introducing the traditionalistic account right in the middle of the naturalistic account supports the fact that the latter account completes or complements the former, and it does that at the crucial point of discussing a notion that is central to both. This is the notion of liminality, which had been at work throughout the history of Islamic thought and which took an especially significant turn with the illuminationists to reach full growth in Ibn al-ʿArabī. Having said this, I think it will be useful to consider what Bernd Radtke says about a possible influence exerted by Ibn Ṭufayl on Ibn al-ʿArabī. Radtke follows Hawi in describing Ibn Ṭufayl's views as emanationist, saying that this distinguishes him from the Ṣūfī masters, whose terminology he adopts but not their system of thought. "Nothing is more misleading," he says, "than to see the Ṣūfī masters of the third/ninth century as 'pantheistic' predecessors of Ibn Ṭufayl. On the contrary, his ideas may well have cast down [the seed] for the monism of his compatriot, Ibn al-ʿArabī."[19] Conrad agrees with Radtke,[20] and Vincent J. Cornell seems to agree with both, although his statement that Ṣūfīsm is a unique methodology that encompasses different attitudes and types of mystical doctrines opens the door for a kind of relaxation of the tendency to label thinkers with a categorical designation, such as monism or pantheism.[21] In the following discussion, I will attempt to show how Ibn al-ʿArabī's theory of the mystical unity of existence, properly understood and freed from the pantheistic preconceptions that have been attached to it, can be related to the liminal interpretation of the naturalistic account.

A LIMINAL DEPICTION OF THE CHAIN OF EXISTENTS

In *ʿUqlat al-Mustawfiz*, Ibn al-ʿArabī presents a naturalistic liminal depiction of the chain of existents: "And generation proceeded in descending till it reached Earth. The first generation to take place on Earth was the generation of minerals, then plants, then animals, then man. The last of each kind of these generated existents was made the first of that which follows it. The last of minerals and the first of plants was the truffle,[22] the last of plants and first of animals was the date palm, and the last of animals and the first of man was the monkey. Let us then discuss the matter of the generation of man since this is the aim of this book."[23]

Ibn al-ʿArabī's depiction of the chain of existents bears a striking similarity to Ibn Ṭufayl's. In both, liminality plays a crucial role, as we can see from Kruk's analysis of Ibn Ṭufayl's depiction of natural existence: "Ḥayy does not fail to notice that the boundaries between the different 'realms' of the scale of beings are by no means sharp.[24] Plants ... know how to move their roots toward food, and some flowers even turn their heads toward the sun.[25] In this respect, plants do already possess some 'animality,' which contributes to the notion of the essential unity of plants and animals. Ibn Ṭufayl ... touches here upon an interesting point: transitional forms between the mineral and the vegetable, the vegetable and the animal world have been pointed out since antiquity. Mushrooms[26] can be considered as stony vegetables, and sponges as vegetable animals; date palms, which have male and female individuals, die when their heads are cut off, and can fall in love, stand at the top of the vegetable kingdom as animal vegetables."[27]

Later in his spiritual development, Ḥayy became so intensely aware of the unifying circulation that runs through all existents and saw in its preservation an important part of maintaining his imitation of the eternal unified motion of the celestial bodies, which motion is their sole function, as well as what is responsible for their eternal subsistence. To imitate their unlimited motion, Ḥayy would remove limitations that were inflicted upon animals and plants to the extent that these could be removed. When he observed a plant that was deprived of the light of the sun or an animal that was entangled in a snare, he would remove the interrupting body and release the animal from its entanglement.[28] Ibn Ṭufayl shows such a distinctive sensitivity and care for nature that Kruk finds it suitable to identify him as "the first ecology-conscious person in the

Islamic world."[29] Kruk seems to have another reason for emphasizing the caring behavior of Ḥayy, and that is to draw our attention to the distinction between modern ecologists, for whom this kind of behavior may be perfectly plausible, and Ibn Ṭufayl and thinkers of medieval Islam, for whom "care for nature was a highly unlikely notion."[30] Ḥayy could not have cared less about the world; rather, he sought to free himself from everything that had to do with it and rise above the level of generation and corruption to be part of the eternal world.[31]

Is it true that modern ecologists possess motives "generally of an immanent nature,"[32] to compare with the likes of Ibn Ṭufayl, who could not have cared less about what happened to the world? In the medieval world, there were no ecological problems of the sort that modern man experiences, and so it is pointless to talk about the lack of awareness of thinkers such as Ibn Ṭufayl in the first place. Moreover, it is not completely clear to me what is meant here by motives that are "of an immanent nature." Modern ecologists endeavor to save the body of the world because they fear for the safety of their bodies, whereas Ḥayy sought to care for the body of the world because of a spiritual quest for holism. In this sense, modern man may as well be blamed, not for being selfish but for not being sufficiently so, since as Plato says: "That as you ought not to attempt to cure the eyes without the head, or the head without the body, so neither ought you to attempt to cure the body without the soul. And this … is the reason why the cure of many diseases is unknown to the physicians of Hellas, because they disregard the whole, which ought to be studied also, for the part can never be well unless the whole is well."[33]

IN THE EARTH OF *BARZAKH*

Chapter 8 of Ibn al-ʿArabī's *Futūḥāt* is entitled: "On knowing the Earth that was created from the leftover fermented mass of the clay of Adam, peace be upon him, which is the Earth of truth, and the mention of some of the wonders and miracles therein."[34] The words of the title bear a clear similarity to the words that Ibn Ṭufayl uses upon resuming his discussion of the naturalistic account of Ḥayy's birth: "As for those who claim that he was generated from earth they say that in a depressed portion of earth in that island a mass of clay was fermented over the years that the elements: hot and cold, moist and dry were equally mixed and their powers balanced."[35] Ibn al-ʿArabī opens Chapter 8 with the following words: "Know that when God the All Mighty created Adam, peace be upon him, as the first human body to be generated, and made him a root for the generation of human bodies, there remained from his fermented mass of clay a portion from which he created the date palm. The date palm is therefore a sister to Adam and a paternal aunt for us. Hence, the Law identified it as aunt and likened it to a believer. Unlike other plants it possesses wonderful mysteries."[36] What mysteries? Ibn al-ʿArabī does not tell us, but Qazwīnī does: "The Prophet said: 'Honor your aunt the date palm.' He called it date palm because it was created from the remainder of Adam's clay. It resembles the human being in respect of the erectness and tallness of its figure, the absence of twists and knots in its stem and branches and the distinction of its male from its female. It dies when its head is cut off. Among all trees it alone has pollen. Its seeds smell like sperm and the covering of its fruits resembles the membrane that encloses the fetus… If one of its branches is cut off it will not be replaced like an organ of the human body, and it is covered with fiber that resembles the hair of humans."[37]

Ibn al-ʿArabī says: "After creating the date palm there remained from the mass of clay a portion the like of a sesame grain, hardly perceived. God then laid out Earth in that remaining portion and Earth became [incomparably] spacious … In Earth [God invested] wonders and mysteries that exceed all rational measurement and that render the rational minds baffled … including many of the impossibilities that sound rational proofs have judged to be absurd."[38] One of the mysteries of the Earth that Ibn al-ʿArabī mentions is that everything in it that the possessor of vision sees, such as metals, plants, and animals, lives and possesses a tongue just as all creatures do that live and speak. Unlike creatures in our world, however, they undergo no alteration because their world is not subject to corruption, nor are they made of the human natural clay.[39] The world that Ibn al-ʿArabī is describing is the World of *Barzakh* and its inhabitants are the immutable or fixed entities (*al-aʿyān al-thābita*).[40] The behavior that these entities display is governed by the liminal ideality or ideal relativity of space and time, characteristic of intermediate states. Intermediate states are ideal in the sense that they are immutable. But their immutability does not prevent them from displaying opposite qualities. This is because entities in the World of *Barzakh* possess a liminal ideality, which enables them to partake in opposite qualities without losing their specific identity. Ibn al-ʿArabī explains this with the following example:

> In this Earth I entered a land of red malleable gold.[41] In it there are trees all gold bearing golden fruits. A person would take an apple or some other fruit and eat it to find that it possesses an indescribably delicious taste and a delicate scent. I saw that the size of these fruits was so tremendous that were a single fruit to be placed between Earth and sky it would hide the sky from people's sight or upon Earth and it would surpass it by manyfold. Still when the person takes hold of it with this familiar hand he would contain it owing to its gracefulness and air-like subtlety. Despite its [enormous] size, he would enclose it in his hand. This is impossible according to rational consideration. Upon seeing this, Dhū al-Nūn said what was related by him concerning the large that enters the small while it does not become small and the small does not become large nor the wide becomes narrow or the narrow wide. The size of the apple remains as it was and seizing it occurs with the small hand as I have said. Encompassing it is a witnessed [fact] but except for God it is unknown how this [becomes possible]. Knowledge of this is the Real's exclusively. One day in our Earth is equivalent to several years in that Earth.[42]

The example of the fruit that is incredibly great and incredibly small demonstrates the feature of the relativity of the space dimension of liminal ideals.

Another example that establishes a connection between the space and time dimensions of liminal ideals is the example of the fruits that are regenerated at the same time they are picked, so that the process of renewal of existence is not noticed except by the witty.[43] The example, it should be noted, is related to the mention of the fruits of the trees in the Garden of Paradise in Q 56:32-33: "And fruit in abundance neither picked nor withheld."[44] Consider ʿAbdullah Yūsuf ʿAlī's interpretation of this verse: "And fruit in abundance whose season is not limited, nor (supply) forbidden."[45] Such an interpretation, Ibn al-ʿArabī would insist, takes away from the depiction of liminal entities the element of paradoxicality intrinsic to it, and renders the meaning of the verse inert. This meaning can be comprehended only by the witty, and in a kind of quick shift that corresponds to the shift in the regeneration of the liminal entities. The witty witnesses the shift that connects instantaneously two states of the same liminal entity, while the possessor of rational consideration fixes his gaze on one state and then on another state, thus losing sight of the essential unity of the witnessed entity. This is because for the witty, the limit between the two states possesses a *barzakhī* characteristic in virtue of which it connects even as it separates between the two states; whereas for the unwitty, the limit between the two states is limited to the function of separation. This kind of (rationally) fixed consideration will not be appropriate for capturing the malleable nature of existents in the World of Barzakh. Such malleability seems at odds with the depiction of the inhabitants of the World of Barzakh as fixed or immutable entities. However, as Ibn al-ʿArabī elaborates, malleability does not mean that these entities possess no differentiated identities. On the contrary, their nature seems especially distinguished: "As for [Earth's] seas, they do not mix together as God the All-Mighty said: 'He has let free the two bodies of flowing water meeting together. Between them is a barrier (*barzakh*) which they do not transgress (Q 55:19–20).'[46] You witness the waves of the sea of gold strike at each other upon approaching its limits. Next to it the sea of iron which comes in contact with it but the waters of the two seas do not mix together. The waters of [Earth] are subtler in their flowing motion than air [on our Earth], so transparent that none of the creatures that inhabit them or the ground on which their waters flow are hidden from sight. Drink their waters and you will find them incomparably tasty. As for Earth's inhabitants they grow like plants without mating and bringing forth young. Rather they are generated from soil like worms are generated in our Earth."[47]

What is impressive is the special and, in a sense, elusive use that Ibn al-ʿArabī makes of Qur'ānic verses to connect with mystical notions. The relation of iron, which is considered a low metal, to gold, which is the aim of alchemical transformation, is like that of salt water, which symbolizes inferior knowledge, to fresh water, which symbolizes superior knowledge. Like the salt waters and the fresh waters, which are united by a *barzakh* that brings them together and keeps them apart at the same time, iron partakes in a *barzakh* that connects and, at the same time, separates it from gold. I will come back to this example in the context of discussing Plato's myth of spontaneous generation.

Water on Earth is subtler than air on our Earth. It is essential water, the fixed entity of fresh and salt waters being its complementary individuations in our Earth. The most distinguishing feature of essential water is its transparency (*ṣafā'*), a feature that Ibn al-ʿArabī assigns in different degrees to all things that exist on Earth. He describes Earth as a whole as "the theatre of the eyes of the possessors of knowledge1."[48] Ibn al-ʿArabī says that one of the worlds that God created in Earth is in our own image, so that, "when the possessor of knowledge1 sees the images in this world he sees himself in them."[49] Images on Earth are mirrors. More precisely, they are self-reflecting mirrors because they are our creation. Thus, when they reflect our image, they reflect but themselves.[50] To say that a thing is a self-reflecting image is like saying that it is contained in itself. Given that by definition, images are accidents, an accident might then subsist in itself, which is contrary to the very signification of the term. Ibn al-ʿArabī, however, is ready to admit this as well as other impossible consequences: "And everything that the rational faculty considers impossible with its proofs we have found it possible of existence and manifested in Earth and *Allah has power over all things* (Q 2:20). Thus we have come to know that the rational faculties are deficient and that Allah is able to bring opposites together, make a body exist in two places, an accident subsist in itself . . . and a meaning subsist in a meaning.[51] Likewise, each saying of the Prophet and each Qurʾānic verse that has reached us, whose manifest (*ẓāhir*) meaning the rational faculty has shifted, we found it fixed in its manifest meaning in Earth."[52] Commenting on one passage from the *Futūḥāt*, William Chittick says: "No doubt this means that one should be careful to observe the limits of God's revealed language, and one should not interpret (*ta'wīl*) God's speech in ways that go against the words."[53] The rational faculty is deficient because it shifts the words of Scripture from their original meaning by means of an interpretation that goes against the manifest implication of the words. This is especially the case in examples that contain what seems to be a straight violation of rational principles, such as the principle that a body cannot exist in two places at the same time. Consider the verse that depicts fruits that are neither picked nor withheld. For Ibn al-ʿArabī, neither picked nor withheld means *both* picked and withheld.[54] According to rational consideration, however, this is impossible because it means that a body might exist in two different places at the same time. And yet, Ibn al-ʿArabī states this as a fact that he personally witnessed on Earth. Having said this, I must warn us against thinking that Ibn al-ʿArabī would be in the least satisfied with an interpretation that neglects the nonmanifest (*bāṭin*) aspect of reality. Such an interpretation will not be true to the essential signification of the term, and the reasons of those who adhere to it are not more than the reasons of little children:

> Since we have come to know that God tied each sensible form to an intelligible spirit by means of a divine inclination according to the property of a lordly name, we interpreted (*iʿtabarnā*) the nonmanifest (*bāṭin*) in the speech of the Lawgiver according to [the proper determination of] the property of

> the manifest (*ẓāhir*).[55] This is because what is manifest from [the Qur'ān] is its sensible form while the intelligible spirit in that form is what we call the crossing over (*iʿtibār*) in the nonmanifest as we say: "you have crossed over the valley' and we mean: 'you have passed [from the one to the other side of] the valley." This is His saying: "In this there is a reminder [*ʿibra*] for those who have eyes to see" (Q 3:13) and "*re*member (*iʿtabirū*) you who have eyes to see!" (Q 59:2) meaning: pass from the forms that you see with your sensible eyes to the meanings and the spirits that these forms invite in your nonmanifest domain (*bawāṭinikum*). Then you will [truly] be able to perceive the forms with your eyes. Hence God commanded and urged us to exercise crossing over (*iʿtibār*). This is a matter that the *ulama* and especially those from among them who adhere dogmatically to the manifest (*ẓāhir*) [interpretation] have neglected, so that all they have from crossing over (*iʿtibār*) is reduced to expressing wonder. Thus you find no difference between their reasons and the reasons of little children, since they have never crossed over from the manifest form as God commanded them.[56]

How strange that after citing Ibn al-ʿArabī's famous love poem, in which he says that his heart takes every form including the form of the holy Qur'ān and that of the temple of the idols, Goldziher still insists on affiliating him with the Zahirites, the followers of the school of Law that adheres to the exoteric interpretation of the Qur'ān.[57] In an attempt to cope with the strong presence of both exoteric and esoteric tendencies in Ibn al-ʿArabī's thought, H. A. R. Gibb and J. H. Kramers state that as to ritual, Ibn al-ʿArabī belonged, like Ibn Ḥazm, to the Zahirite school of Law; but in matters of belief, he adhered to esotericism.[58] Even stranger is the special manner in which certain scholars, such as Jabiri, relate Ibn al-ʿArabī to Ibn Ḥazm. Jabiri depicts this relation as based on a gnostic conspiracy started by Ibn Sīnā and his "alleged" illuminationist philosophy, and brought to maturity by Ibn al-ʿArabī. Such a conspiracy, Jabiri tells us, involves the gnostics' claim that they are sound adherents to the words of the Qur'ān (in the manner of the Zahirites) and that they actually draw all their knowledge from it. Jabiri says that the claim is false and is destined to make a cover for those esotericists who had drawn all their knowledge from the well of the ancient gnostics and clothed it with Qur'ānic garment to carry out their conspiracy without incurring blame upon themselves.[59]

The Qur'ān, however, is not detached from the wisdom of the ancients so as to approve of reflecting on it in absolute isolation from the general history of human intellectuality. Consider, for example, the strong presence of elements from ancient myth in the Qur'ān, which presence is attested by the Qur'ān itself: "We relate to you the most beautiful *stories* by revealing this Qur'ān. Before it you were among those who are heedless." (Q 12:3) In fact, the presence of myth in the Qur'ān is so strong that the Qur'ān itself found it proper to warn against mistaking it for a myth: "When our verses (*āyāt*) are rehearsed to him he says: 'myths of the ancients (*asāṭīr al-awwalīn*).' No but their hearts were stained by what they had obtained." (Q 83:13) The heart in the Qur'ān is the organ of understanding, just as the ear is the organ of hearing and the eye of seeing. It is not the eye that sees not but the hearts are blind (Q 22:46). For a soft heart is light that guides in the way and those whose hearts are hardened their light has become weak and they are lost (Q 39:22). Q 83:13 does not condemn the myths of the ancients, but rather the persons who interpret them falsely.

They have eyes but they do not see, and they have ears but they do not hear. They are the epistemological opposites of the possessors of hearts.[60] I think that Ibn al-ʿArabī would agree with this interpretation, as well as the interpretation along the same line of the condemnation of the Qur'ān of poets in Q 26:224–226 and Q 36:39.[61] Ibn al-ʿArabī says: "When someone's heart is in a shelter, or a lock is upon it, or its insight is blind, or it is tarnished, or rust upon it, then God has come between him and understanding from God, even if he interprets the speech."[62] As we have seen in the passage quoted above, Ibn al-ʿArabī links interpretation to crossing over (*i'tibār*) from the manifest to the nonmanifest domain, according to a property of determination that unites the two domains and, at the same time, keeps them apart. Thus, interpretation (*ta'wīl*) or crossing over (*ta'bīr*) fulfills the creative function of remembering the two complementary aspects of the reality of the manifest and the nonmanifest, as it takes them back to their first (*awwal*) principle in which they originated. God tied each sensible form to an intelligible meaning. By crossing over from the sensible to the intelligible, the realizer gains knowledge of the tie, the limit between the manifest and the nonmanifest faces of reality. At the limit, the nonmanifest is brought to manifestation. This is called "creation." Creation is continuous and permanent. Creation that took place at some point in a distant past and elapsed, not to be repeated again, is a myth. Indeed, it is the greatest of all myths because, properly interpreted, it is the root of the coming into existence of all things. This coming into existence, this passage from essence (the nonmanifest face of reality) into existence (its manifest face), is incessant and endless. That is why the act of creation, which signifies an endless beginning, can be depicted only by means of a tale (*ḥikāya*) or a myth (*usṭ ūra*), and interpretation is called for to cross over from the mythical to the logical, and *re*member what otherwise would be irrecoverably dismembered.

PLATO'S MYTH OF SPONTANEOUS GENERATION

In *Critias*, Plato mentions a certain division of the Earth that had been executed by the gods. Hephaestus and Athena, being brother and sister and sharing the love of wisdom and artistry, obtained one district that contained "an excellent soil, a generous water supply, and an eminently temperate climate,"[63] and in which they produced a race of good men from the soil.[64] Plato also mentions the myth of generating humans from the earth in *Republic,* where he refers to a Phoenician myth that mentions something that happened in many parts of the world in ancient times but that would not be likely to happen in his own days—namely, delivering people from the earth. Plato mentions this myth in the context of discussing the special education that citizens should receive in the ideal city. He suggests that an attempt should be made to persuade citizens, rulers, and soldiers alike that the training and education that they imagined, as if in a dream, that they had received in their own city had actually originated somewhere else. Rather, in reality they had been molded, together with their weapons, within the Earth. When their construction had been completed, the Earth delivered them, being their mother and nurse. For this reason, they ought to take good care of Mother Earth and defend her against any attack. Moreover, they should regard other citizens as their brothers because they are the children of the selfsame Mother Earth.[65] As God fashioned those that are fitted to rule, he mingled gold in their generation, but he mingled silver in the generation of helpers and iron and brass in the farmers.[66] If sons were born with an infusion of iron to golden rulers their fathers should not give pity in their treatment and should "assign to each the status due to his nature and thrust them out among the partisans or the farmers."[67]

This depiction of the social order has caused serious criticism in modern scholarship because it was perceived as highly deterministic and as precluding mobility and social justice.[68] If the educational lot of citizens had been long allocated and their intellectual status, which is an important factor for determining their social rank, had been fixed accordingly, what mission could ideal educators accomplish but open their brothers' eyes to a bad situation that can only get worse given the constantly deteriorating conditions of the human society as it travels farther away from the age of gold?

What transpires in the nonmanifest domain (down within the Earth) should be interpreted as to tie it to things that are in the proper manifest domain. This, however, cannot be the manifest domain that constitutes our own sociopolitical reality but rather the manifest domain in its ideal reality. For example, to compare with rulers in our reality, golden rulers in the ideal state must possess no gold. Hence, their social rank is measured by what they are essentially, not by what they possess—that is, what they are accidentally.[69] The ruler in the ideal state resembles a Ṣūfī who keeps polishing his soul to preserve his golden essence. Helpers and farmers are made of less valuable metals, such as iron. But iron in the ideal state does not resemble iron in our own reality. The iron in the ideal state is incomparably more precious than gold in our reality, like water on Earth is subtler than air on our Earth. In the ideal state, everything is ideal; and in this sense, it can be said that all things are ideal to the same extent, for, as Plato says, all things are ultimately of the same original stock.[70]

This also explains the possibility that sons are born with an infusion of iron to golden rulers, in which case fathers should give no pity in their treatment of them and assign to each the status due to his nature, and that sons with an unexpected gold are born to fathers made of iron, in which case they should be honored and bid them go up higher.[71] In the ideal state, the act of sorting out is executed without complications because proper education allows for that. But in our state, things do not work this way, as Plato makes this clear in the Allegory of the Cave. To interpret our myth properly in relation to our own reality, we must consider, as Plato attempts to persuade us, that the state in which we thought that we had received our education is a dream state.[72] Surely the ideal situation that exists on Earth and in Plato's ideal state is far from any resemblance to the situation that governed the human society at which Ḥayy arrived. The situation in this society is basically the same as the situation that existed in the society in which Ḥayy was generated according to the traditionalistic account. I will discuss this situation in the next chapter.

CHAPTER 4

The Traditionalistic Account from the End

DIVINE ORIGINS AND ILLUMINATIVE GRADATIONS

Ḥayy went through seven stages of intellectual development, each consisting of seven years. This period of seven sevens can be divided into three main stages. In the practical stage, Ḥayy developed useful capacities to cope with his physical needs. In the theoretical stage, he examined the nature of the structure of the world and scrutinized the problem of the existence of God. In the mystical stage, he occupied himself with the problem of the relationship between God and the world and the manner in which the enlightened philosopher must conduct his life to connect with the divine, even as he is situated within the confines of the physical reality and detained in a prison (his body) within a prison (the world). At the age of fifty, he succeeded in attaining stabilization in illumination:

> One time after another he was able of arriving at that noble station, more and more easily, and linger therein longer until he was able to render arriving at it and departing from it subject to his free choice. Then he held fast to that station and did not turn away from it except for the sake of attending to the needs of his body, which he managed to reduce to minimal measures. In all this, he wished that the All-Mighty God would deliver him from [the distractions of] his body, which diverted him from that [noble] station, so that he might achieve unadulterated pleasure and be released from the pain that he found upon departing from it to care for his physical needs. He remained in that state until he had passed the seventh septenary and became fifty years old. Then he chanced to gather together with Absāl and enjoyed his companionship, the tale of which I shall, God willing, relate to you.[1]

The model of mystical illumination, as Ibn Sīnā presents it in *Ishārāt* and Ibn Ṭufayl represents it in the introduction of his book, finds its conclusion here. The visitations of the flashes of lightning had become more frequent and lasted longer. The moment that commenced with a single and short-lived flash of lightning, surrounded by darkness, had expanded to encompass the entirety of the seer and bring him close to contact with Truth. His earthly vehicle, however, claimed what was due to it, thus preventing the communion from becoming an absolute reality. The solitary learns that physical reality imposes limitations that must be acknowledged. Later, he will also understand that the relation between his unitary soul and his complex body has its parallel in the relation between the solitary and the human society.

Near Ḥayy's island (discussed in detail in Chapter 3), there was another island populated by a community of believers who followed the religious teachings of an ancient prophet and imitated spiritual truths by means of the imaginal representations that were communicated to them in their religion. Absāl and Salāmān were raised in this community. They observed its Law and loved and desired that which is good. They were also involved in theological discussions concerning such matters as the nature of the attributes of God. Absāl showed clear inclination toward inward meanings, which he discerned by means of esoteric interpretation (*ta'wīl*), whereas Salāmān inclined toward the outward implications of the Law.[2] To interpret is to draw the original, nonmanifest (*bāṭin*) meanings of the words from their manifest (*ẓāhir*) designations. Hence, interpretation seems to be esoteric by definition, and to say that in his theological discussions with Absāl Salāmān avoided interpretation means that he seriously opposed the latter's ways of inquiry, which is why their separation was inevitable. Salāmān was afraid to think freely and adhered to his community because by doing so, he would be able to drive out evil thoughts and resist opposing opinions.[3] This hardly seems to be an appropriate characterization of a person who desired that which is good, especially considering the rather intimidating description that Ibn Ṭufayl provides for the community to which Salāmān adhered.[4] It turns out, however, that Salāmān's personality is more complex than it seems at first sight, for he occupies a kind of intermediate position between his people and Absāl, who occupies, in his turn, an intermediary position between Salāmān and the ideal spiritual figure represented by Ḥayy. To elaborate, I will use Plato's parable of the Divided Line.[5]

Plato divides reality into the visible and the intelligible, and represents this concept by a line divided into two sections, each of which he divides in the same ratio into two more sections. He represents the visible section as comprising visible objects and their images, and the intelligible section as comprising intelligible objects (forms) and their images (intermediate objects). Plato presents the four sections as corresponding to the four affections occuring in the soul: intellection, which corresponds to the first and highest level; understanding to the second; belief to the third; and picture, or image thinking, to the last.[6]

It is clear from Ibn Ṭufayl's description of the people of Salāmān's community that they occupy the lowest section in this example, for they perceive by fixing images of visible things in their souls and comprehend truths through imitation and by means of the imaginal representations that they store therein.[7]

Although Salāmān partakes in this dogmatic adherence to image reality, he seems to occupy a slightly different position; he shows tolerance, and even some passion, for rational deliberation. It is true that his final position was adherence to whatever dogmatic beliefs he previously held. But it is also true that, "even the most stubborn politician or sophist, who in public will not listen to the philosopher, still is man and can be stirred up in private. The hard shell of his corruption can be pierced and the anxiety of existence can be touched."[8] Dogmatic people can be stirred up in private if, as Plato says, they are "men enough to face a long examination without running away,"[9] meaning if they are sufficiently free of binding dogmatic conventions to allow for the introduction of some flexibility in their rigid stands. Salāmān fell short of being such a person—he chose to run away and seek protection in the dogmatic conventions of his community. He was afraid that his beliefs would be shaken because of Absāl's distracting opinions, and his fear alienated him from his friend. Hence, fear must be considered to play a negative role here, as it tipped the scales in favor of dogmatism. At the same time, the very existence of fear implies that Salāmān ought to be distinguished from the rest of the members of his community because he could and actually was affected and stirred up by the debates that he had conducted with Absāl. Had Salāmān failed to be stirred up by a certain inclination (*hawā*) for Absāl's opinions, he would not have fled and sought refuge with his people.[10]

Absāl, whose state of mind corresponds to the reality of the third and the closest to the highest section in Plato's Divided Line, made up his mind to ascend even higher. He joined Ḥayy on his isolated island, and there he spent his time leading the life of an ascetic. At this time, Ḥayy was deeply immersed in his sublime stations (*maqāmāt*), emerging from his cave only once a week. This should explain why his encounter with Absāl was so delayed. When Absāl saw Ḥayy for the first time, he had no doubt that he had come across a solitary like himself, and he feared that his presence might interrupt Ḥayy's meditations. Thus, he ran, but Ḥayy caught up with him and held fast to him so that he could not escape. Sensing Ḥayy's great strength and the swiftness of his movement and noticing that the greater part of his body was covered with hair and the skins of animals, Absāl was so terrified that he began to beg for mercy. Ḥayy then managed to calm him down by using his body language and employing the sounds that he learned from animals.

IMITATION AND INTERPRETATION

An important moment in this encounter occurs when Absāl, who due to his special interest in interpretation had acquired knowledge of many tongues, attempted to communicate with Ḥayy. His attempt failed, however, except for the wonder that it left in Ḥayy's baffled mind.[11] Ḥayy was fascinated with Absāl's pleasant voice and distinct words, which sounded distinct from the calls of the animals that he was familiar with.[12] However, in spite of the fascination that the music of the words and the ordered logic of the combinations of their letters created in him,

Ḥayy was out of discursive reach. When Absāl saw that Ḥayy did not know how to speak, his fear of any damage that his company might inflict upon his religious belief was eased, and he became determined to teach him language.[13] Despite his natural inclination towards mystical contemplation, Absāl's intellectual conduct at this stage was still affected by considerations of what Goodman defines as mass religion, especially considerations that are based on fear and hope.[14] Absāl feared for his belief and hoped that by imparting knowledge of the principles of religion to Ḥayy, he would be rewarded by God. In teaching Ḥayy language, Absāl applied a method based upon imitation. He would pronounce the names of things over and over while pointing at them, and persuade Ḥayy to imitate him. Absāl was able to teach Ḥayy nouns in a very short time in this fashion.[15]

It may seem odd that Ḥayy could arrive at the highest levels of intellectual cognition without knowing language. The fact that he was able to learn language in a very short time seems equally odd, given what we know of cases of abandoned children who were raised by animals and who failed to develop any substantial language capacities.[16] As Goodman points out, however, Ibn Ṭufayl puts Ḥayy in the place of Adam as the archetype of mankind.[17] Thus, Ḥayy's example must be interpreted at the general level of mankind, rather than the individual level of this or that specific person.

The problem of the origination of language and the related problem of the relationship between expressions and their meanings were subject to serious debate in the Islamic intellectual community in medieval times. These debates were fueled by the controversy among the theologians over questions of whether the Qur'ān was created and the nature of God's attributes,[18] in addition to the controversy between them and the philosophers over the introduction of Greek philosophy into the Arabic world. Two main views were endorsed: the view of conventional agreement (*muwāḍaʿa, iṣṭilāḥ*), which was the view of the Muʿtazilities and the philosophers, and the view of direct inspiration (*tawqīf, ilhām*), which was the orthodox view. The former view held that a certain philosopher assigned specific nouns to things and then spread knowledge of this among the people of his community. The latter view held that knowledge of nouns was conferred by God on a prophet, who transmitted this knowledge to his community. Those who held the view of inspiration sought support for it in Q 2:31: "And He taught Adam the names of all things."[19] Notice how ingeniously Ibn Ṭufayl entwines the naturalistic and traditionalistic views in depicting the birth of language, the same way he did in depicting the birth of man. He describes a process of acquiring language by convention and imitation, but he does not forget to allude to the religious teaching that it was God who taught Adam the names of all things.

Now that Ḥayy was able to use language, he was ready to describe to Absāl how he ascended the ladder of knowledge and came to witness the sublime essences until he made the Station of Arrival his limit:

> When Absāl heard his description of the realities and essences which are beyond the sensible world and which possess knowledge of the essence of the

All-Mighty Truth and his depiction, which he tried to present as adequately as possible, of what he had seen at the Station of Arrival concerning the bliss of those who arrive and the pain of those who are veiled, he had no doubt that all the things that had come in the Law concerning God's Command[20] and angels, His paradise and hell, His books and messengers, and the Day of Judgment were but resemblances (*amthila*) of the things that Ḥayy had seen. The eyes of his heart were opened, the fire of his mind was kindled, and the rational concept (*maʿqūl*) coincided for him with the transmitted word (*manqūl*), as the ways of esoteric interpretation and all things masked were revealed to him. There was left no difficulty in the Law or any obscure matter but clarified and solved. He had become one of the possessors of hearts.[21] Then he looked at Ḥayy Ibn Yaqẓān with the eyes of veneration and admiration and was certain that he was one of the *friends of God* (*awliyā' Allah*) *who know neither fear nor grief*.[22] He put himself in Ḥayy's service and imitated him by following his intimations concerning the truth of the religious practices that he had been taught in his community.[23]

The encounter with Ḥayy provided Absāl with a perfect test of verification. Ḥayy had seen through direct experience what Absāl had learned through the examination of the transmitted texts of religion.[24] He had seen the essential meanings (*ma ʿ qūlāt*) that are transmitted (*manqūl*) by means of the words. Absāl had stood face to face with such a person, who had seen the reflections of essences on the polished mirror of his heart. Placing himself as another polished mirror against Ḥayy's, he could now watch his heart being kindled with light. He had placed himself as a faithful, although lesser, member in the ordered chain of the friends of God, thus rightfully earning the title of a possessor of a heart and a master of esoteric interpretation.[25]

The fact that no human taught Ḥayy knowledge provided an especially strong support for Absāl's belief in the superiority of his wisdom. The fact that his immediate wisdom coincided perfectly with the mediated knowledge that he had acquired in his religious community made him see and understand for the first time the principle of his own relationship with his mysterious, supernal self. The rank that Ḥayy occupies in comparison to Absāl's corresponds to the rank that Ibn al-ʿArabī assigns for the first Intellect, which in the order of lights is considered the first Lamp that is prior to all other intellects. The other intellects resemble lamps, the wicks of which possess less clarity and limpidness of oil. Consequently, they are less receptive of the light. Although they draw their light from the first Intellect, the light of the first Lamp suffers no decrease:

> Each says, "I am like it. How is it more excellent than I? For [light] is taken from me, just as it is taken from it." So it leaps up and speaks, but it does not see the First Lamp's excellence over itself in respect of the fact that it is the root and possesses priority. Moreover, the First Lamp is not found in any sort of matter, and there is no intermediary between it and its Lord. Nothing else has any being [*wujūd* in Chittick] save through it and the sorts of matter that

> receive burning from it, such that the entities of the intellects become manifest. All this is absent from the intellects, or rather, they have no tasting of it. How can that which has no *wujūd* save from a father and a mother perceive the reality of that which has *wujūd* without any intermediary?[26]

As Chittick points out, for Ibn al-ʿArabī, the First Intellect is another name for the Universal Spirit, while the other intellects are angelic and human intelligences.[27] This is the spirit that attached itself to the fermented mass of clay in Ibn Ṭufayl's naturalistic account of Ḥayy's birth: "In the very middle formed a tiny bubble divided in half by a delicate membrane and filled by a fine gaseous body, optimally proportional for what it was to be. With it at that moment joined 'the spirit which is God's,'[28] in a bond virtually indissoluble, not only in the purview of the senses, but also in that of the mind. For it should be clear that this spirit emanates continuously from God. It is analogous to the sunlight that constantly floods the earth."[29] Ibn Ṭufayl is making a reference here to Q 17:85, "And they ask you concerning the Spirit. Say: 'The Spirit is from the Command of my Lord. And you have been given but a little knowledge.'" He likens the spirit to the light of the sun. As the sun's light never ceases to emanate on the world, so also the spirit is indispensably inseparable from the well-proportioned and adequately prepared matter. Notice that Ibn al-ʿArabī says in the passage quoted above that compared with the First Intellect, the other intellects possess no knowledge of tasting. The First Intellect has knowledge of tasting because there is no intermediary between it and its lord. This does not mean that a relationship *does not exist* between the First Intellect and its lord, only that the relationship *is nonexistent*. Ibn al-ʿArabī would say that Absāl has gained a certain capacity for interpretation due to the preparedness and the cleanliness of his heart. The mirror of his heart had been polished to such a degree that it enjoyed a state of nonexistence. Then he could see with the eye of understanding that all the things that he had been taught by the Law were resemblances (*amithila*) of the divine essences that Ḥayy had witnessed in an immediate fashion. Unlike the secondary intellects, however, he was able to distinguish between his own capacity and that of Ḥayy. Absāl regarded Ḥayy as an example to be imitated and a provider of allusions to be followed for the sake of interpreting those things in the Law that seemed to him ambiguous.

IBN ṬUFAYL'S LIMINAL DECLARATION

The encounter with Ḥayy enabled Absāl to achieve the aim that was his purpose for coming to the philosopher's isolated island. He departed from his religious community to care for his own individual spiritual interests, and as far as those were concerned, he was fully rewarded. On the other hand, in his zeal for realizing the potential of his inherent archetypal nature, Ḥayy wished for no less than lifting all individuals to the status of the universal. In the process, he shunned Absāl's solemn implorations to refrain from taking a regretful step—one that will almost cost him his life. One might wonder, therefore, what real benefit came to Ḥayy as a result of his encounter with Absāl, and whether, considering the dangerous consequences of the encounter, we should regard it as a sort of false promise made to the enlightened philosopher, who is bound as if in a tragic scene to replay his own fate and flee from human society twice.

To begin with, there is some sense in Moses Narboni's argument that the very fact that Ḥayy ended in seclusion from human society with Absāl, rather than being utterly alone, means that spiritual isolation need not be total and that, in principle, it could be achieved within society.[30] Abraham Melamed ascribes Narboni's interpretation to a certain influence exerted upon him by Ibn Bājja, the author of *Governance of the Solitary* and *Conjunction Between the Active Intellect and the Human Intellect*.[31] In addition to Ibn Bājja's influence, Ibn Ṭufayl's depiction of the relationship between the solitary and the human society can be best understood in comparison with Fārābī's depiction of the role of the philosopher as a social reformer. Ibn Ṭufayl's view of Fārābī, similar to his view of Ibn Bājja, was rather negative. He applies against him the same method of criticism that he applies against Ghazālī and that consists of revealing the self-contradictory nature of their works. His references to the two thinkers differ, however, because he seems to find excuses for Ghazālī's shortcomings and, to a lesser degree, for Ibn Bājja's, but he does not seem to be concerned with paying the same courtesy to Fārābī. In my opinion, the reason for this has to do with the fact that he detects a strong mystical element that is explicit in Ghazālī and implicit in Ibn Bājja, but he fails to detect such an element in Fārābī. Fārābī resembles for him the state of philosophy in its (almost) accomplished rationalistic turn. It is important to keep in mind, however, that Ibn Ṭufayl was not against rationalism as such, but only against limited rationalists who fail to see that persons are more than their reasons. Otherwise, what would be the difference between persons reduced to mere believers, dogmatic as to be cut off from the light of illumination, and persons reduced to a close system of rationalistic truths that have become dogmatic even as they have become evidently axiomatic? This will be like a prisoner who is confined in a cave, boasting before his fellow prisoners that his fetters are made of gold while theirs are made of bronze, or, like a blind bird that can fly but cannot see the way out of its confinement.

The examples that I have presented are inspired by the words that Ibn Ṭufayl puts in the mouths of extreme rationalists. He likens those to bats whose eyes are dazzled by the sun and who move in the chain (*silsila*) of their madness and utter follies against the illuminated, accusing him of losing his rational instincts and of discarding the axiomatic rules of the intelligible, such as the rule that a thing must be either one or many.[32] In what sounds like total despair, Ibn Ṭufayl suggests that we leave the rationalist in peace with his reason and fellow rationalists because what he is concerned with is the rational faculty that examines the sensible existents and extracts universal meanings from this examination, while the possessors of knowledge that Ibn Ṭufayl wants are situated at a level that is above the level of rational consideration.[33]

This statement is significant, as in it can be found the explanation for my insistence on situating the discussion of Fārābī, as well as Ibn Bājja, in the context of the traditionalistic account. As we shall see, despite the effort that the former invested in achieving harmony between religion and philosophy and the serious and, in a sense, unprecedented attempt of the latter to advance towards liminal philosophy, both thinkers considered rationalism to be the ultimate limit of the philosophical enterprise. However, Ibn Ṭufayl seems to have placed rationalistic philosophy at a level that is transcended by a higher one. He has made a declaration to the effect that rationalistic philosophy plays only a limited role on the stage of the physical world. On this stage, rationalistic philosophers play not the liminal part preserved for illuminationists, but the part of a sect (*milla*), such as the sect that Fārābī invested great effort in contrasting with philosophy in *Book of Letters*. What holds as axioms in this sect of rationalism, even the axiom that the whole is larger than its part, is rather irrelevant in the divine realm, in which "we cannot justly say, *all*, nor *some*, nor express anything belonging to it by such words as our ears are used to, without insinuating some notion which is contrary to the truth of the thing, which no man knows but he that has seen it; nor understands, but he that has attained to it."[34]

From the perspective of illuminationist philosophy, the limits of rationalism are the limits of the spoken or written word. The knower uses words as he uses the steps of a ladder to ascend and arrive at a certain limit. The knower must transcend the ladder to immerse himself in the abyss of illumination or otherwise be stuck forever with it. This was the fate of Ibn Bājja, who promised but failed to provide a satisfactory account of illuminationist vision.[35] One might wonder whether this downgrading of the significance of words is what lies behind the fact that we have so little in writing by Ibn Ṭufayl. As a matter of fact, *Ḥayy* is the only work that we have from him, and it is only through this work that we know his philosophical thoughts.[36] Given this fact, one might feel that the blame that Ibn Ṭufayl incurs upon Ibn Bājja for not elaborating on the state of unity with the divine (*ittiṣāl*) is simply exaggerated. Add to this the fact that many of the things that he says in his work had been previously said by his predecessors, and Ibn Bājja is a prominent example among these. Thus, his attack on Ibn Bājja's rationalism might seem exaggerated, and his promise to establish the principle of a philosophy of illumination that extends beyond rationalism might be exaggerated as well.

I find myself in agreement here with Hawi that although Ibn Ṭufayl's work shows a clear evidence for the influence of his predecessors, it would be wrong to see in it an amplification or merely an elaborate exposition of their philosophy.[37] I also agree with the testimony of the historian ʿAbd al-Wāḥid of Marrakesh that Ibn Ṭufayl's book, although slim, is of tremendous benefit in the study of the condition and meaning of human existence according to philosophical ideas.[38]

Ibn Ṭufayl succeeds in interweaving mystical and rationalistic threads of thought in an especially unique manner. The significance of his book stems not from this or that part that deals with this or that subject, as scholars have attempted to show, but rather from the sort of declaration that it makes. This declaration has the radical reexamination of the limits of human understanding as its subject matter and is fueled by a unique concept of liminality that had emerged from a long history of debates between Islamic theologians and philosophers. In the center of these debates stood the problem of the origination of the world. This will be the subject of the next chapter.

CHAPTER 5

The Origination of the World

BETWEEN PLATO AND ARISTOTLE

The problem of the origination of the world was the first problem that Fārābī mentioned in explaining his motives for writing his treatise on the agreement between Plato and Aristotle: "I have seen that most people in our time have engaged themselves in vain discourse and contended over the subject of the origination/eternity of the world, claiming that there is disagreement between the two ancient philosophers in relation to the affirmation of the existence of a first creator and his being the author of the causes … I wished by making this statement to combine their views and unfold the substantial meaning of their words, so that agreement between their views becomes manifest and doubt is removed from the hearts of those who examine their books."[1] This was also the first problem that Almohad Sultan Abū Ya'qūb Yūsuf raised in his enquiry to Ibn Rushd in the meeting that Ibn Ṭufayl arranged between them: "The first thing the Commander of the faithful asked me was 'What do they (he meant the philosophers) believe about the heavens? Are they eternal or created?' I was seized with consternation and did not know what to say … He turned to Ibn Ṭufayl and began to discuss the question with him, referring to the positions of Aristotle and Plato and all the other philosophers, and citing the arguments of the Muslims against them."[2]

From Fārābī's and Ibn Rushd's words, we learn of the special significance of the problem of the origination of the world and that Plato and Aristotle were the main originators of the polemics concerning it and, consequently, those who held the key for its solution. The problem of the origination of the world was at the heart of medieval Islamic thought, and this explains why it was important for Fārābī to establish harmony between the opinions of the two philosophers in *al-Jam'*, and that is also why Ibn Rushd made a similar, although more successful, attempt in *Faṣl al-Maqāl*.

In his attempt to establish harmony between Plato and Aristotle, Fārābī argues that they made different, even conflicting, statements about the same subject matter in different kinds of scientific treatments. This is how he attempts to explain the difference between Plato's universal (or intelligible) depiction of substance and Aristotle's individual (or sensible) depiction of it.[3] In his attempt, he affirms the existence of the intelligible forms in Aristotle of *Uthūlūjiya*. Notice, however, that his interpretation of the Platonic forms is rather Neoplatonic, as he relies on the notion that the forms exist in the First Intellect. Hence, he denies that forms exist as actual substances transcending the world because this must create an infinite number of worlds, which is absurd according to Aristotle's demonstration in *Physics*.[4] Following Neoplatonic principles, Fārābī thinks that forms must exist as thoughts in the intellect of the supreme divinity rather than actual entities existing independently: "Since God the All-Mighty is live and since it is he who brought the world into existence with all that it contains, it is necessary that he possesses in his self (*fī dhātihi*) forms of the things that he wills to bring into existence. And nothing bears likeness to him (*walā ishtibāh*)."[5] This account of the forms is different from the account that Plato provides in *Timaeus*, which depicts creation as a process in which the maker of the universe employs eternal and unchangeable patterns in fashioning the created things as copies of their originals.[6] To render the forms independent and eternal is to assume the existence of something that shares in the creator's eternal existence. This is why it was important for Fārābī to say that nothing bears a likeness to God.

One might wonder: what difference does this depiction of the ontological status of the forms make to Fārābī's notion of creation since, according to him, the emanation of the world from God does not occur in time (assuming a beginning for the world's origination in time negates logical principles) and never one part after another.[7] We are indeed face to face with what seems like a slim but is actually a significant difference between two theories of the origination of the world. The one belongs to Plato and depicts this as a real occurrence, not in but with time; and the other depicts it as an imaginal occurrence that takes place in the "mind of God" and the minds of those who, like the Aristotle of *Uthūlūjiya* (Plotinus) combined with the Aristotle of Aristology (Aristotle), have returned to themselves to see themselves as the knower, the knowing, and the known. To depict the origination of the world as a *real* occurrence not in but with time is to depicit it as paradoxical. In my opinion, Ibn al-ʿArabī was the first thinker in the Islamic world to give full expression to this sort of paradoxical depiction; he truly deserves to be called Son of Plato.[8]

Ibn Ṭufayl says that the first thing that Ḥayy saw after attaining self-annihilation (*al-fanā' al-tāmm*) and achieving union with the divine was the essence of the highest sphere, which is the limit of all bodies. He saw an essence that is pure of matter and is "neither identical with the essence of the One/Truth or the sphere itself nor other than both, as the image of the sun that appears in a polished mirror is neither identical with the sun or the mirror nor yet other than both."[9] As I indicated above, in describing the essences, Ibn Ṭufayl emphasizes that each essence is neither identical with nor other than the other essences. Rational consideration takes this to mean that essences are identical in some respects and different in other respects. This, however, will completely miss Ibn Ṭufayl's emphasis on the paradoxical nature of the essences, which is responsible for their *flowing* with perfect, unified, motion.[10]

Ibn Ṭufayl's first overt explication of this conception occurs at the culmination of the metaphysical stage in Ḥayy's life, which extended from age twenty-eight to age thirty-five. The problem that occupied Ḥayy's mind throughout this period is none other than the problem of the world's origination. In liminal terms, the problem is related to the question whether or not the world has a limit. One is easily tempted to draw a distinction here between limitation in time and limitation in space. One is further tempted to think of this distinction as a dividing line between philosophers and theologians, as the former perceive of the world as limited in space but not in time, and the latter see it as limited in both space and time. If there is a story of temptation in philosophy, as there is in religion, then this is the story, its hero being Aristotle influenced by Platonic epistemological principles, rational analysis being its general incentive, and scrutinizing the notion of infinity the specific reason for the fall. In what follows, I will turn to Aristotle's analysis of this notion.

ARISTOTLE'S CONCEPT OF THE INFINITE

In *Physics*, Aristotle states that the science of nature is concerned with spatial magnitudes, motion, and time, as each of these is necessarily either finite or infinite. Therefore, he thinks it is necessary to inquire whether there is an infinite and, if there is, what it is.[11] He indicates that Plato and the Pythagoreans made the infinite a principle as a self-subsistent substance rather than a mere attribute of some other thing, while all the physicists considered the infinite as an attribute of a substance.[12] Antonio Capizzi points out that the infinite as a noun does not exist in the Presocratics and as an adjective only in some of them. Aristotle had introduced into earlier scholars a concept not to be found with them and "forced the thought of the most recent ones to extract from the 'infinite being' and 'infinite matter' an 'infinite' which 'all posit as the principle of beings.'" As for the reason that led Aristotle to introduce this concept, Capizzi finds it in a principle that is employed as an essential technique in the Platonic dialogues and that renders it illegitimate to apply a category without having first abstracted and defined it.[13] To abstract and define the infinite, however, proved to be extremely problematic and, at the same time, especially fruitful—it led Aristotle to the distinction between potentiality and actuality.

Aristotle defines the infinite as "what is incapable of being gone through, because it is not its nature to be gone through."[14] The infinite cannot be an actual body or substance: "For any part of it that is taken will be infinite, if it has parts: For 'to be infinite' and 'the infinite' are the same, if it is a substance and not predicated of a subject. Hence, it will be either indivisible or divisible into infinities. But the same thing cannot be many infinities."[15] At the same time, the infinite cannot be indivisible because in its full completion, it must be a definite quantity.[16] Should we say, then, that the infinite does not exist? Aristotle thinks that to suppose that the infinite does not exist leads to impossible consequences because time, which is infinite, will then have a beginning and an end.[17] This cannot be the case, however, because time is defined as a limit that is always perceived in moving from a moment of *before* to a moment of *after*.[18] This leads Aristotle to the distinction between potential infinite, whose parts exist successively, and actual infinite, whose parts exist simultaneously.[19]

In *Metaphysics*, Aristotle defines *complete* as "that outside of which it is not possible to find any, even one, of its parts," and identifies actuality with complete reality.[20] In *Physics,* he states that a "quantity is infinite if it is such that we can always take a part outside what has been already taken. On the other hand, what has nothing outside it is complete and whole."[21] Two important ways in which the infinite is exhibited are in time and in the division of magnitudes, as in both "one thing is always being taken after another, and each thing that is taken is always finite."[22] Aristotle admits that the phrase "potential existence" is ambiguous and comes very close to saying that the infinite does not exist. It turns out that the examination of the nature of (infinite) time makes him distinguish not only between potential existence and actual existence, but also between two sorts of potential existence and eventually between sorts of being.[23] He says that the potential existence of the infinite should not be perceived in the same way as we perceive the potential existence of a statue, for example, which will become an actual statue, although it has not become one yet. "There will not be an actual infinite."[24] This is the reason why Aristotle says that "'being' has more than one sense"[25] and that, "we must not regard the infinite as a 'this', such as a man or a horse," or a substance, but rather as things whose being consists in a process of coming to be or passing away.[26]

Aristotle's analysis of the concept of time seems to have created a split in the unitary conception of being. Time may not exist as an actual infinite because actual infinity means incomplete actuality. Time may not also exist as a potential infinite, if by "potential" we mean something that will but that has not yet existed. It is not merely incomplete but will always be incomplete. It will never *be* something, and yet somehow it *is*.

IBN ṬUFAYL'S LIMINAL STAND

Aristotle's depiction of the nature of the infinity of time, together with his distinction between potentiality and actuality and eventually between two sorts of potentiality, played a significant role in providing Islamic philosophers with a crucial means for debating their position on the problem of the origination of the world. Paradoxically, it also created a fault line in their conception of the unity of being and opened their position to the skepticism of theologians.[27] As I indicated above, Ibn Ṭufayl situates the discussion of the problem of the origination of the world in the twenty-eighth to thirty-fifth years of Ḥayy's life. Right at the commencement of this period, Ḥayy was able to sense with his innate nature (*fiṭratihi*) the notion that the body of the world must be finite. Then Ibn Ṭufayl makes him *speak to himself* one of several arguments that he was, in principle, capable of articulating to convey the simple notion that he received intuitively.[28] As a matter of fact, this was not the first time that he presented Ḥayy as "speaking to himself." He did that when he employed a logical argument for demonstrating that the spirit of life that resided in his mother-doe and left upon her death was located in the heart's left chamber.[29] Ibn Ṭufayl insists on reminding us that the notion of the finitude of the world had been perceived intuitively (*fiṭra*), both before and after introducing the argument in support of it. The impression is made that he is trying to assure the reader that he is not making a slip of the tongue—he is fully aware that his hero cannot speak. I think, however, that Ibn Ṭufayl is trying to do more than just guard himself against the reader's careful discernment. Let me explain my meaning by comparing the use that he makes of the notion of "intuition" or "innate nature" (*fiṭra*) with the use that Ibn Sīnā makes of "insight" (*ḥads*), a capacity that renders the possessor of knowledge capable of swiftly concluding a logical argument without having to go through the regular steps of cogitation.

As Herbert Davidson indicates, there is a certain link between Ibn Sīnā's "insight" and Aristotle's "quick-wit" (*dhakā'*), which appears in the Arabic translation as a certain fineness of insight (*husn ḥads*) for seeking out middle terms in the syllogism in no time.[30] Davidson says that the concept of insight attracted the attention of Ibn Sīnā more than the concept of quick-wit because he regarded insight stronger than cogitation in finding out the middle term, which is an abstract concept emanated from the Active Intellect.[31] Ibn Sīnā discerns an important difference between the function of insight and that of cogitation. He says that cogitation is a movement of the soul among notions (*ma'anī*), especially notions that are within the imaginative faculty. There, the soul seeks an image that prepares it for the emanation of the middle term from the Active Intellect. Insight, however, brings forth the middle term and the conclusion instantaneously—that is, without movement.[32] As we shall see, this statement is important not only in the present context but also in the context of discussing Ibn Bājja's depiction of perfect knowledge, as the knower ceases from moving toward the object of knowledge because he has become identical with it.[33] Rather than downgrading the significance of motion, which plays a cardinal role in Aristotle's *Physics*, this depiction of the fixity of perfect knowledge indicates a necessary passage beyond physical reality.[34] Ibn Bājja establishes the possibility of this passage solely on rational consideration and the work of, what Aristotle calls "quick-wit," whereas Ibn Ṭufayl combines quick-wit with intuition, as we can see from his articulation of the notion of the impossibility of the infinity of the body of the world: "Then he [Ḥayy] with the power of his intuition (*fiṭratihi*) and the quick-wit (*dhakā'*) of his mind (*khāṭirihi*) thought that it is false to think that a body that is infinite can exist, since this is an impossible thing and an inconceivable meaning."[35] We can say with some caution that with quick-wit, Ibn Ṭufayl wished to connect with the abstract reality of Ibn Bājja, the rationalist, and with intuition, he wished to connect with a central principle that defines the starting point as well as the ultimate aim of Ṣūfism.

Like Fārābī, Ibn Ṭufayl assumed that logic is a real language prior in significance to ordinary languages. Specific arguments, such as the argument that Ḥayy spoke to himself, can be translated into many languages; and yet the logical import, which is conveyed through the language of logic alone, remains one. More important, the relationship between ordinary languages and the language of logic is paralleled by the relationship between the many logical arguments that Ḥayy could have articulated in support of his intuition and the one and simple notion that he *witnessed* by means of it.

Ibn Ṭufayl says that thinking about the notion of the eternity of the world made Ḥayy come across several difficulties due to arguments similar to those that led him to the conclusion that the existence of an actual infinite is impossible. Although he does not articulate the detailed argument or arguments he has in mind, it is clear that he aims at two major arguments that Islamic theologians employed in demonstrating that the world had a beginning in time. The arguments are based on two Aristotelian principles: the principle that the infinite cannot be traversed and the principle that one infinite cannot be greater than another.[36] In *Incoherence of Incoherence*, Ibn Rushd identifies a certain argument as the most serious of all the theologians' arguments and says that a proper solution for it should end all the doubts that they raised against the philosophers. The argument is based on Aristotle's first principle: If we assume that the movements in the past are infinite, then it is impossible for a movement in the present to take place unless an actual infinite number of preceding movements is terminated.[37] In his solution to this argument (hence referred to as "argument1"), Ibn Rushd refers to another argument (hence referred to as "argument 2") that is based on Aristotle's second principle and that is introduced in Ghazālī's *Incoherence*: "The eternity of the world is impossible, for it implies an infinite number and an infinity of unities for the spherical revolution, although they can be divided by six, by four, and by two. For the sphere of the sun revolves in one year, the sphere of Saturn in thirty years, and so Saturn's revolution is a thirtieth ... of the sun's revolution ... But the number of revolutions of Saturn has the same infinity as the revolutions of the sun, although they are in a proportion of one to thirty."[38] In his answer to this argument, Ibn Rushd employs Aristotle's distinction between actual and potential infinity. It is impossible to assume that one infinite is greater than another if the two infinites are taken as actual, because then there will be a ratio between them, but it is possible if the two infinites are regarded as potential infinites because no ratio can be found between potential infinites.[39] This, says Ibn Rushd, solves all the doubts that are generated by the theologians, argument1 being their most threatening one.

Ibn Rushd's solution to both argument 1 and argument 2 was brought by Ibn Sīnā in *Ishārāt*, a work that was known to Ibn Ṭufayl.[40] From the facts that

Ibn Rushd considered argument1 a major source of the theologians' doubts and that before him, Ibn Sīnā provided an identical solution to the same argument, it is possible to draw the following conclusion. By presenting the argument in the form of an argument that balances that of the philosophers rather than an argument that had found its ready solution, Ibn Ṭufayl meant what he said when he stated, "Do not think that the philosophy that has reached us in Aristotle's and al-Fārābī's books and in Ibn Sīnā's *Shifā'* are sufficient for our purpose nor has anyone in Andalus provided a sufficient account of it in writing."[41] After stating the difficulties that the philosophers had introduced against the possibility of the temporal origination of the world, Ibn Ṭufayl states that for years, Ḥayy kept vacillating between the conflicting positions as the arguments proved to be equally balanced.[42] Hawi argues that this statement is part of Ibn Ṭufayl's method of concealment. Ibn Ṭufayl is a philosopher-pantheist and, therefore, he must believe in the eternity of the world. In the treatise, "he presents this *belief* with a semblance of uncertainty and contradictions in order to guard himself against possible repercussions by the orthodox public and the ruling class."[43] Hence, Hawi rejects the thesis that by admitting neither the eternity of the world nor its temporal creation, or by presenting the arguments for and against the eternity of the world as balanced, Ibn Ṭufayl was assuming a skeptical position similar to that of Immanuel Kant, who was led by his famous antinomies to the conclusion that reason is limited.[44] Hawi emphasizes that Ibn Ṭufayl differs considerably in this respect from Kant because his reflections on the problem of the eternity of the world led him to affirming the existence of God, whereas Kant's epistemological investigations led him to the rejection of metaphysical thought. To support his view, Hawi argues that only in a small part of his work does Ibn Ṭufayl affirm that knowledge gained through philosophy accords with knowledge gained through revelation; and that in the major part of the work, he makes it clear that demonstrative knowledge possesses the higher standing.

Moreover, Hawi refers to what he considers as Ibn Ṭufayl's hint to his true belief by saying: "The world with its entirety … is *logically posterior to God in nature but not in time*; just similar to holding something in your hand while moving your arm. The object you held would undoubtedly move with your hand, a movement that is logically posterior to your hand, but coexisting with it in time. For in time the two motions are simultaneous. It is in this way, in nature but not in time, that the universe is caused and created by its maker."[45] The fact that Ibn Ṭufayl says those things after he concludes that the arguments for and against the eternity of the world are balanced proves that he "*believed* in the eternity of the world in the vein of most Muslim Neoplatonists."[46]

If Ibn Ṭufayl only *believed* in the eternity of the world, then what is the difference between his position and the position of the believer in its origination? If demonstration leads to the conclusion that the arguments for and against the eternity of the world are balanced, then is not his *belief* in the eternity of the world and his statement that the world is only posterior to God logically, not in time, in contradiction with the demonstrative knowledge that enjoys the higher standing in his work? Most likely, Hawi would use this very consideration to support his view of concealment. And indeed, he is obliged to do so if he wants to avoid the Kantian position, which renders reason limited and which is itself inconsistent with Ibn Ṭufayl's metaphysical thought. Ibn Ṭufayl, however, does not deny that in principle, reason is limited. But he seems to have a different understanding of the nature of this limitation and indeed a different understanding of the very concept of limit around which rational delimmas revolve. On the basis of this understanding, he can maintain that the world is limited but that the limit of the world is different from the limit that both theologians and philosophers conceive of. The limit of the world possesses a paradoxical nature and owing to this paradoxicality, it can be said that God is related to the world without having to be either in contact with it or cut off from it.[47] This paradoxical depiction of the relationship between God and the world is at the heart of Ibn Ṭufayl's metaphysics and constitutes his solution to the problem of the origination of the world.

CHAPTER 6

The Shadow of Fārābī

In *The Book of Letters,* Fārābī provides an account of the evolution of human thought from the commencement of the use of language to the time of the invention of logic by Aristotle, and he declares that by Aristotle's time, philosophy was complete. Ibn Ṭufayl states that even with the commentaries of Fārābī and Ibn Sīnā on Aristotle's works, philosophy was still incomplete and is actually destined to remain so. Both declarations prove to be problematic and, at the same time, especially creative.

PHILOSOPHY'S ULTIMATE MISSION

According to Fārābī, religion comes naturally after the completion of the philosophical sciences. If religion originates in a nation prior to philosophy, then it will be possible to have the philosophy of another nation transferred to this nation. In this case, religion in the new nation might be in conflict with philosophy, and its followers might struggle against the philosophers and cast their philosophy aside.[1] It goes without saying that Fārābī is describing here the case of Islamic religion and the difficulty in which Islamic philosophers were involved in introducing Greek thought to the Islamic intellectual tradition. One immediately thinks about the conflict with the theologians as a major source of the difficulty. This is undoubtedly true. And yet, there was another related difficulty that was not less troubling to the philosophers; and that had to do with defining the very essence and range of the philosophical enterprise, especially in light of the view that philosophy had been perfected by Aristotle.[2] The assumption is that conflict with religion should aggravate this difficulty. Although not entirely incorrect, this assumption is limited and, if not qualified, might even be misleading. It can be argued that conflict with religion was more of a bliss than a curse because it allowed a philosopher like Fārābī not only to compose philosophical "harmonies," but also to play the role of a philosopher-prophet and to establish a whole new order in a whole new situation. He will then be restoring the natural order and adjusting what needs to be adjusted in the noble situation that is created following the introduction of religion. The conflict with religion can give fresh air to the philosophical pursuit of truth, and Fārābī must be most satisfied with a title such as the Second Teacher, to replay the role of the First Teacher (Aristotle, or Muḥammad) on the stage of the new theatre.[3]

In Chapter 1, I mentioned Hourani's view that the main aim of Ibn Ṭufayl's work is to assert the possibility of the unaided assent of human reason to philosophical perfection. How could this be different when Ḥayy not only lived apart from humans but, as Hillel Fradkin points out, he did not have even awareness of their existence, as he was kept from the very possibility of considering political life?[4] This also distances Ibn Ṭufayl from the naturalistic account of acquiring language because conventional agreement is a crucial element in the development of language according to this account. If we add to this that Ibn Ṭufayl showed clear dissatisfaction with rationalistic thought and made it obvious that philosophy had not reached perfection with Aristotle, who stated that man is a political animal,[5] we must begin to wonder what can Ibn Ṭufayl's naturalism have in common with Fārābī's naturalism, if anything. And as if all this is not enough, Goodman wipes out the very possibility that Ḥayy attained perfection in knowledge unaided. After all, was he not motivated by his *fiṭra*, "his congenital endowment of capacities," to achieve the "successive realization of Ḥayy's potentials, the progress of his soul *upward*, toward God"?[6]

Ibn Ṭufayl presents the two accounts of naturalism and traditionalism in such a manner that they ought to be seen not as two separate opposing accounts, but rather as two faces of the same account, mirroring and complementing each other. Ibn Ṭufayl's account can be depicted as an account of mystical naturalism. This account does not exclude the possibility of divine intervention. In this respect, it is akin to traditionalism. But divine intervention exists only potentially here. It is a drive that is found in a state of latency in all humans, constituting their *fiṭra*. It can be revealed as well as concealed. The author of the materialization of revelation or its privation is the human being. If divine intervention is a possibility, then only man can make it an actuality. In this respect, the account is akin to naturalism.

In Ibn Ṭufayl's account, there is to be found that which is missing in models of mysticism that depict the mystical experience as consisting of sudden illuminations and passive receptions of momentary revelations that are, no matter how wonderful, irrelevant to what is needed in the community of mystics: a guiding manual for the solitary. As we shall see, the guiding manual that Ibn Ṭufayl provides for his mystical philosophers incorporates the guiding manual that Fārābī presents to his rationalistic philosophers, but it makes a crucial addition to it. This addition is best seen as a declaration to the effect that essential man, the mystic, is more than his reason, the rational philosopher in him. Rationalistic philosophy constitutes a section of man, exactly as rationalistic philosophers are members of their own sect and as theologians are members of theirs. It is true that mystics also have their own community and, in this sense, they connect with traditionalism. But the difference between the Fārābī of *Book of Letters*, who represents the tradition of rationalistic philosophy, and Ibn Ṭufayl, who represents the tradition of mystical naturalism, is that whereas the former depicts the history of the development of the philosophical sciences as coming to a halt, the latter leaves it open-ended and seeks to transcend it.

According to Fārābī, dialectic and sophistry precede certain philosophy; that is, philosophy established on the basis of rational demonstration, just as the nourishment of the tree or its flowers precede its fruits. In turn, demonstrative philosophy precedes religion just as the user of the tools precedes the tools, and religion precedes theology and jurisprudence just as the user of tools precedes the tools or the master the slave.[7]

Both depictions of the precedence of master to slave and the user of tools to the tools are employed by Ibn Ṭufayl in his description of the relationship between spirit and body. After the death of his mother-doe, Ḥayy sought to find the organ that was responsible for the ceasing of her movement and the cause of the impairment of her bodily functions. He performed several operations on her, only to conclude that the being that he was looking for is not to be found in the body, for the body was but a tool that was being used, as he used sticks to defend himself against animals.[8] Ḥayy realized that this being is a spiritual unity responsible for the many bodily functions. Thus, when the animal spirit uses the eye, the act is called seeing, and when it uses the ear, it is called hearing, etc.[9]

The relation between body and spirit is one of dependence, which is also the sort of relation that holds between religion and philosophy in Fārābī's account; for religion "aims to instruct the multitude in theoretical and practical matters that have been inferred in philosophy, in such a way as to enable the multitude to understand them by persuasion or imaginative representation, or both."[10] A similar relationship of dependence holds between religion from the one side, and theology and jurisprudence from the other. Now, if religion is dependent on a dubious philosophy, theology and jurisprudence will be in accordance with it, especially if religion further distorts the things that it takes from such a philosophy and substitutes similes and images for them, presenting these as certain truths. Theology then seeks to verify them with arguments that only create more doubt and confusion.[11] Because religion teaches theoretical matters by means of persuasion and imaginative representation, theology employs arguments that are of this nature as it is aware (*tash'ur*) only of the ways of persuasion and imagination.[12] Fārābī makes here a clever use of the term *tash'ur* to depict the mode of cognition characteristic of the theologians. *Sha'ara* means "perceived with any of the senses." It also means "had knowledge of, was cognizant of."[13] Thus, it can be said that by employing this term, Fārābī wants to draw our attention to the fact that the theologians' mode of comprehension is situated somewhere between sensation and knowledge.

Upon the death of his mother-doe, Ḥayy was considering which bodily organ was responsible for her death. He had observed that the parts of dead animals are solid except for the head, chest, and abdomen. It occurred to him then that the organ that he was looking for must be in one of these places. His opinion (*ẓanihi*) strongly inclined toward thinking that it must be in the center of the three because the other organs must be dependent on it. "Then, as he came back to himself, he could feel (*shaʿara*) that organ in his breast, since he could see that he could do without all the other organs, even the head, but that he could not do without the heart, not even for an instant. It is for this reason that when he was fighting with beasts of prey he would protect specifically his breast from their horns as he felt that thing in it."[14] At such an early stage of his development, and due to the limitation of his logical capacity, it is only natural that Ḥayy's mode of thought is depicted by employing designations of low cognitions, such as opinion and feeling. Ḥayy's thought resembles at this point an early stage in the development of human knowledge, which is depicted in Fārābī's account as a stage in which feeling prepares the way for rational consideration by making the person incline toward logical thinking.

Fārābī states that in verifying theoretical matters, the theologian employs rhetorical methods and seeks to persuade the multitude by appealing to common preliminary opinions. In this, the theologian is one with the multitude. The highest level of certainty that the theologian can attain is the level that is reached by employing dialectical methods, methods of negating opinions dialectically.[15] As religion is servant to philosophy and the theologian is servant to religion, so theology is also servant to philosophy because it seeks to verify, by means of common preliminary opinions, things that are verified in philosophy by means of demonstrative reasoning. This renders the theologian different from the multitude and, in this sense, he is of the select. The philosopher, however, is the select in relation to all people and all nations—that is, absolutely: "The jurist (*faqīh*) uses as principles acquired premises transferred (*manqūla*) from the founder of the religion in the deduction of particulars, whereas the man of practical wisdom (*mutaʿaqqil*) uses as principles premises commonly accepted among all and premises drawn from his experience. That is why the jurist is one of the select in relation to a certain specific religion and the man of practical wisdom is one of the select in relation to all. Therefore, the select without qualification are those who are philosophers without qualification. All others, who are considered of the select, are only considered as such because they bear resemblance (*shabahan*) to the philosophers."[16]

Ibn Ṭufayl presents Salāmān and Absāl as involved in improving their knowledge through theological study. Surely Salāmān felt that he was of importance as a jurist in his religious community. However, as can be inferred from Fārābī's account, he is of the select only in relation to the multitude. Absāl enjoyed a similar position to that of Salāmān, as he was also engaged in improving his knowledge of the Law. However, he enjoyed a highly developed capacity for interpretation, which set him apart not only from the common people of his religion but also from Salāmān. Absāl, therefore, is to be considered more of the select than Salāmān. Upon his encounter with Ḥayy, and following the latter's description of what he had witnessed upon contact with the divine,[17] Absāl came to realize that things that had been delivered in the Law resembled things that Ḥayy had witnessed. As the jurist in Fārābī's account is in the resemblance of the philosopher, so Absāl in Ibn Ṭufayl's becomes in Ḥayy's image. Only Ḥayy is to be considered absolutely of the select. For Fārābī, this means that he has become a concluding part of a consummated process of rational deliberation, whereas for Ibn Ṭufayl, it means that he has become a liminal entity that transcends this very process and, possessing no point of reference except reference to the same, it reflects upon itself and burns everything else.

Fārābī says that the jurist employs premises transmitted from the founder of religion, whereas the man of practical reason uses premises based on universal validity and his personal experience. Again, we find here a clear resemblance to the divergence between Salāmān, who adhered to the manifest or outward signification of the religious ordinances, and Absāl, who excelled in rational interpretation and sought nonmanifest or inward meanings.[18] As for Ḥayy, because he lived apart from humans, he had to rely completely on his own experience in cultivating his intellect and attaining the best of rational deliberation.[19] The consideration of the fact that Ḥayy not only attained truth through direct experience, but that he also arrived at it unaided, might convince us that Fārābī's depiction of the man of practical reason is an appropriate account of Ḥayy. However, although in its greatest part Ibn Ṭufayl's work consists of a description of a personally driven rationalistic progression, the mystical assumption that motivates and sets in motion the whole process makes a considerable difference as to the essential import of the story. Let us bear in mind that rational argument may be employed in different and even opposite ways, as it can be directed against itself in a sort of dialectical turn that is considered inferior in Fārābī's *Book of Letters* but that is responsible for the passage that Ḥayy was able to make beyond rational consideration. This dialectical turn is motivated by an extremely influential notion in Islamic mysticism; namely the notion of intuition (*fiṭra*). I will elaborate on this notion in the following discussion.

THE ORIGINATION OF LANGUAGE

Shortly after drawing the distinction between the jurist, who relies on transmitted premises (*manqūla*), and the man of practical reason (*muta'aqqil*), who relies on rational argument and his personal experience, Fārābī commences his discussion of the origination of language. The connection between the two subjects can be located in a contrast so significant in Islamic medieval debate between the view of transmission (*naql*) and the view of reason (*'aql*). This debate is related to the two views of the development of language; namely, the views of inspiration and conventional agreement. Fārābī's own account of the development of language is based on conventional agreement, which is conditioned by the possibility of social interaction. In a sense, the example of Ḥayy provides confirmation for this view. Ḥayy, who lived away from human beings, grew speechless and remained so until he met Absāl who taught him language. And yet, this fact does not prevent Ibn

Ṭufayl's hero from attaining the intellectual level of the rationalistic philosopher, the select without qualification in Fārābī's account. It is actually what enables him to transcend this very level and turn into a unique liminal entity and the meeting place of the two accounts of his birth.

In the following passage, Fārābī depicts the process of the development of language as strongly governed by natural predisposition and makes a special connection between the two concepts of innate nature (*fiṭra*) and movement (*ḥaraka*). As we shall see, Fārābī's use of *fiṭra*, which is identical for him with natural disposition, is significantly different from the use that Ibn Ṭufayl makes of it: "A human being who is left alone at the point at which he acquires his first nature (*yufṭar*) will rise and move (*yataḥarrak*) towards that which is easiest to move towards by nature and in the manner that is easiest. His soul undertakes to know, think, conceive, imagine, and intellect whatever he is most intensely disposed towards by nature, for that is what comes most easily to him…The first time he acts in this way, he acts through a capacity that is in him by nature and a natural attribute, not by prior habituation nor by art. If he repeats an action of one kind many times he will acquire a habitual attribute, either moral or artificial."[20]

By *fiṭra,* Fārābī means the person's natural disposition that is determined by his natural composition. This determines the sort of motion or action that a person makes and the regulating rules that he draws from observing the recurrence of a certain act. Given that multitudes originate in different natural abodes, they come to possess specific natural forms that render their souls "disposed towards and prepared for cognitions, conceptions, and images to specific degrees both quantitatively and qualitatively."[21] Thus, *fiṭra* seems to possess no inspirational connotations for Fārābī. This makes it significantly different from the concept of *fiṭra* that designates a primordial state in which the souls existed prior to and independently of the conjunction with bodies and their specific configurations. In his spiritual struggle, Ḥayy came to realize that not motion, but the absence of it, is what will bring him back to that sublime state. This is because motion is a natural (*ṭabīʿī*) phenomenon joined to natural bodies, to be distinguished from the state of fixity characteristic of the unitary state of souls existing by their instinctive nature. This state of fixity directs the realizer toward the state of unity characteristic of the solitary existence of the divinity. It is this unitary state that the souls witnessed and confessed upon being asked: "Am I not your Lord?" on the Day of Covenant.[22] And it is different from the state of universal unity that Fārābī makes the possessor of reason halt at, and that Ibn Ṭufayl makes the possessor of *fiṭra* arrive at and yet surpass it for the sake of a higher state of unity.

Motion is crucial for the commencement of the process of communication. When a person wants to inform another person of his intention, "he will first use a sign to indicate what he wants from whomever he seeks to make understand."[23] Then he uses sound. The first sounds are calls, "for that is how one who is being made to understand realizes that he is intended to the exclusion of others."[24] It is true that communication between human beings was not an option for Ḥayy.

But this does not mean that he did not possess the very concept of communication, since he communicated with gazelles, "imitating their sounds so accurately that his voice and theirs could no longer be distinguished. He also imitated all the sounds of the birds that he heard and the sounds of animals. His imitation was most exact as he was greatly affected by things that he wanted. Most often he would imitate the sounds of gazelles when they called for help and defense or courtship and companionship, as animals make different sounds in different situations. As things were absent from his observation, their resemblances were fixed in his soul and he developed attraction to some things and dislike for some others."[25] Thus, it is safe to say that Ḥayy knew some form of language, even as this form was confined to the level of employing sounds in Fārābī's account. Notice also that the different sounds that animals made were related to the sort of motion that they had to undertake. It turns out that in principle, not only human beings possess the sort of disposition that enables them to set out in the process of communication; in fact, animals possess a similar disposition. This is to emphasize the sort of continuity between existents that is characteristic of the naturalistic account.

Fārābī's account of the development of language enjoys a strong presence in Ibn Ṭufayl's description of Ḥayy's encounter with Absāl. As Absāl reached Ḥayy's island, his sole aim was to lead a solitary life, a life of proximity to the divine and release from the limitations of human affairs. This is how he came to engage himself in performing prayers and reciting holy verses with a voice that sounded very appealing to Ḥayy. Next, a chase develops in which Ḥayy hunts Absāl down as he would prey; the process of communication commences.

As Absāl wished to share his food with Ḥayy, he ate and made a sign (*ashāra*) for Ḥayy to do the same. In what Ibn Ṭufayl says next, there is an allusion to the story of sin that led to the fall of man. Upon eating Absāl's food and realizing how tasty it was, Ḥayy felt that he forfeited his vows (*ʿuhūdihi*) not to rejoice over food.[26] Hence, he decided to leave Absāl and return to his familiar place to resume his state of witnessing. This was impossible for him now that he had broken his sublime state of spiritual contemplation. Like the first man, Adam, who had to descend to Earth to labor in order to find his way back to his lost heaven, Ḥayy sought to return to Absāl to possess the knowledge of what he possessed, thinking that then he would be able to rid himself of the temptation and regain his pure state of witnessing. The actual process of learning human speech commences: "Absāl began teaching him by pointing at (*yushīr*) perceptible existents (*aʿyān al-mawjūdāt*)[27] and pronouncing their names. Then he would repeat this act and urge him to say the words. Ḥayy then would say the name while pointing at the thing. This way *he taught him all the names* and made him advance in stages until Ḥayy was able to speak in the shortest time."[28] As must be clear from the following passage, Ibn Ṭufayl's depiction of the actual process of acquiring language is very similar to Fārābī's: "It so happens that one of them uses a sound or expression to indicate something when addressing someone else and the hearer memorizes it. Then the hearer uses the same expression when addressing the first inventor of that expression. In this case the hearer will have followed the example of the inventor and will have fallen in with it, in such a way that they will have agreed upon that expression and acted in concert (*iṣtalaḥa wa-tawāṭa'a*)."[29]

THE QUEST FOR UNITY

The first things to be given expression are sensible things. People then begin to give expressions to their conceptual or universal knowledge as they take their starting point from the sensibles. They notice that sensibles are different in some respects and alike in other respects. What sensibles have in common is an intelligible, universal meaning (*ma'nā ma' qūl*) predictable of many sensibles. Sensibles are called "particulars" and "individuals" (*ashkhās, a'yān*), while universals are called "genera" and "species" (*anwā'*, aj*nās*). Without employing language, Ḥayy arrived at the same conclusion. "He examined objects in the world of generation and corruption such as animals, plants, minerals, and the elements and what is composed of them and noticed that they were … one in respect of being alike and many in respect of being different."[30] With this recognition, Ḥayy commenced the theoretical stage in his intellectual development. This stage came after a practical stage at the end of which he was able to excel in the art of surgery and to gain mastery over competing animals.[31] At this stage, things appeared to Ḥayy as a manifold that lacks limitation and existence seemed to him dispersed and disorderly.[32] It is only expected from a person who sees reality as such to spend so much time *dissecting* animals and examining the peculiarities of their organs and *controlling* them by means of invention and trickery. Such a person sees disorder (chaos) and seeks to rectify it; he is in the right mode to create only that to create the light of understanding is to be acquired. That light emanates necessarily from the One and pervades all dimensions of existence. Upon examining the individuals of the animal species, he saw that these individuals are alike, as he could discern only slight differences between them. Thus, he judged that the animal spirit is one in all: "The spirit in all the species was one and undifferentiated, only divided among numerous hearts. If what had been dispersed of that spirit in the hearts were to be gathered in one vessel then it would be one thing like the one body of water divided among numerous vessels and then collected to become one again … With this sort of consideration he thought about the [nature of the] species and assumed that the plurality of its individuals is like the plurality of the members of the body of the one person, which is not really a plurality."[33] This is what Ḥayy quickly grasped when he examined first the identity of his own person. At first, differentiation is not an issue here because there was only one Ḥayy in Ḥayy's solitary world. But Ḥayy's body is composed of many parts, so his identity might be manifold as well. Quickly, however, Ḥayy saw the one in the many as he realized that the animal spirit, which is the essence of his identity, is the one, and the rest of the body organs are but many tools that are used by it.[34]

Ḥayy's examination of the members of the animal kingdom yielded the same result, and he obtained the same result upon examining the realm of plants. Here also, Ibn Ṭufayl returns to the example of the single body of water that is divided into many vessels.[35] Next, Ḥayy examined physical objects that do not sense, like animals, or feed and grow, like plants. He found that the differences between these objects are accidental, and that they are essentially one, as it is the case with animals and plants.

In depicting the nature of inanimate things, Ibn Ṭufayl makes an allusion, rather than an explicit mention, to the example of the divided waters. Thus, the example of divided waters is stated explicitly in Ibn Ṭufayl's depiction of the unity of animals, mentioned concisely in his depiction of the unity of plants, and only alluded to in his depiction of the unity of inanimate objects. As I see it, there is an implicit reference here to two Qur'ānic verses. Q 21:30 reads: "Do not the unbelievers see that the heavens and the earth were joined together … before we clove them asunder? We made from water every living thing. Will they not then believe?"[36] Q 24:45 reads: "And Allah has created every animal from water. Of them there are some that creep on their bellies; some that walk on two legs; and some that walk on four."[37] Notice that in the first verse, water is depicted as the source of living things; that is, plants and animals but not inanimate objects. In the second verse, water is depicted as the source of animals but not of plants or inanimate objects. At any rate, I hope that the reader is convinced, as I am, that Ibn Ṭufayl's reference to the example of the divided waters in particular is most likely related to the religious teaching of the Qur'ān.

As we have seen, Ḥayy was able to arrive at the distinction between universals and particulars without using words. It turns out that the fact that he did not possess knowledge of language actually quickened his arrival at and stabilization in unity away from difference and plurality. Words were not there for him to fix and perpetuate differentiation by giving it a definite designation. Ḥayy's observation of differentiation was itself made to flow. In other words, although Ḥayy was able to recognize both unity and difference, he did not perpetuate the *difference* between them by fixing names for specific individuals and, consequently, for the very concept of individuality, as persons in Fārābī's account did. The fact that Fārābī builds his account of the development of the human sciences following the development of language, which makes its starting point in communication between people and designating expressions for sensible things, is mainly what distances his hero from Ibn Ṭufayl's.

THE DEVELOPMENT OF MEANINGS

Although the initial point of reference for Fārābī is the sensible reality, in building his account, he talks about the development of intelligible meanings (*ma'ānī ma'qūla*) transmitted by the vehicle of language. The process of the development of language is a gradual unfolding of the latent meanings of scientific knowledge, which are arranged in specific forms that become more and more orderly as the meanings develop. The first intelligible meanings that appear are entirely rhetorical. The art of rhetoric, which is the first of the syllogistic arts, develops when over the course of time, events and special occasions make the people of a certain nation use speeches. Then they use similes and imaginative representations to convey their meanings. This leads to the invention of poetry as the next syllogistic art. Poetry is a syllogistic art because it "stems from the natural inclination (*fiṭra*) of human beings to seek order and organization in all things. The rhythms of expression are orderly, well composed, and organized relative to the time uttered."[38] In the evolution of meaning, the formal structure of language is improved to harmonize it with the order and composition of meanings in the soul. This task is assigned to those who are eloquent (*fuṣaḥā'*) and those who are experts in composing language suitable to the occasion of speaking or writing with perspicuity (*bulaghā'*).[39] A process of memorizing language commences, which is based on transmitting sayings from one generation to another. At some point, it becomes practically impossible to memorize all the material that has been accumulated and there arises a need to put language in writing.[40]

What Fārābī says next is especially important. One should know from whom to acquire the language to be written and transmitted to future generations, as one should seek it from those whose nature forbids them from imagining other than their own letters and from acquiring foreign words. For this reason, a nation is sought that has not mixed with foreign nations and has not been exposed to hearing foreign tongues. In the case of the Arabs, this nation was found with the inhabitants of the wilderness in the interior regions of the land, who dwelled in houses of hair or wool and who were rough and wild because they had not mingled with the inhabitants of civilized towns and were therefore immune from errors.[41]

Goodman points out that for medieval Arabs, primitive life meant the life of the Bedouins, with the simplicity of their manners and the purest standards of their language as well as the best poetry. He brings Ibn Khaldūn's statement that urban inhabitants are weaker and more prone to luxury, and his comparison between the Bedouins and the urban inhabitants as the former were closer to the early natural state of the soul (*fiṭra*). Then he elaborates on the relevance of this statement to Ibn Ṭufayl's project: "Ibn Ṭufayl ... believed that crime and positive law, mass ritual and the need for ritual, and all the culturally specific traits of man, arise together under the social pressures of built-up centers of population. Thus Ibn Ṭufayl's thought-experiment endeavors to give man a fresh start, to choose ground far from the crowded tenements of the great cities—which have settled owners and restrictive traditions, and are not, like the desert, equally hostile or hospitable to all. The object of the exercise is to see whether a man by himself can build a better home, starting only with a firm, straightforward foundation, and the mind God gave him."[42]

Once the practical arts have been developed, the investigation of natural and mathematical sciences commences. Rhetorical methods are used first. Then dialectic is discovered and is distinguished from and favored over the sophistical methods. The dialectical method is then turned against itself to establish the fact that it is insufficient for attaining certain science. By this time, mathematical sciences will have been perfected and people show interest in political investigations while still employing dialectical methods mixed with certain methods. This was the state of philosophy by the time of Plato. Then philosophy was further improved by Aristotle, and with him, the door of investigation is closed and philosophy becomes an art to teach and be taught only. It is taught publicly by employing rhetorical, poetical, and dialectical methods and privately by employing syllogism. Then the need arises for lawgiving and the methods to teach the public theoretical matters by means of persuasion and imaginative representation; religion is born.[43]

Fārābī no doubt displays great confidence in stating that philosophical investigation had attained a state of perfection with Aristotle. This is in contrast with Ibn Ṭufayl, who considers it inadequate to think that the works of Aristotle, even in combination with the commentaries of Fārābī and Ibn Sīnā, are satisfactory for attaining philosophical illumination. Philosophy is still incomplete and perhaps will remain so, notwithstanding the effort that Ibn Ṭufayl invested in writing his work and revealing whatever he could of the secrets of Eastern philosophy. It seems that Ibn Ṭufayl has taken on a major challenge, for to open the end in this way (that is, to claim that philosophy was not completed by Aristotle) is to unavoidably alter the order of the stages that are presented in Fārābī's account as leading to his thought. Ibn Ṭufayl might be able to deal with this challenge by adding to the process one or more stages that complete a new body of knowledge and present Aristotelian thought as constituting an earlier development in this process. This way is blocked, however, because Ibn Ṭufayl reflects on illuminationist philosophy in terms of transcending rather than supplementing Aristotle's philosophy. It turns out that the account of the new story is in accord with dialectical or transcendental methodology as this is depicted in Plato. Ibn Ṭufayl's move can be portrayed as a *re*turn from Aristotle to Plato to compare with Fārābī's, which consists of advancing from the latter to the former. Therefore, I suggest that one way to look at the difference between Fārābī's and Ibn Ṭufayl's methodologies is to depict it in correspondence to the difference between Plato's and Aristotle's conceptions of dialectic.

TWO CONCEPTIONS OF DIALECTIC

In *Topics,* Aristotle explains the difference between demonstrative and dialectical reasoning: "Now reasoning is an argument in which certain things being laid down, something other than these necessarily comes about through them. It is a 'demonstration,' when the premises from which the reasoning starts are true and primary … Reasoning, on the other hand, is 'dialectical,' if it reasons from opinions that are generally accepted."[44] Aristotle defines "true" and "primary" as things that are believed on the strength of themselves and not of other things, as each of the first principles of science should generate belief in and by itself. He defines "generally accepted" as things that are accepted by all or by the majority or by all or the majority of philosophers.[45] Aristotle defines induction as the passage from individuals to universals and distinguishes it from dialectical reasoning: "Induction is the more convincing and clear: it is more readily learnt by the use of the senses, and is applicable generally to the mass of men, though reasoning is more forcible and effective against contradictious people."[46] Compare this with what Plato says in *Republic*: "This ... is the very law which dialectic recites, the strain which it executes, of which, though it belongs to the intelligible, we may see an imitation in the progress of the faculty of vision, as we described its endeavor to look at living things themselves and the stars themselves and finally at the very sun. In like manner, when anyone by dialectic attempts through discourse of reason and apart from all perceptions of sense to find his way to the very essence of each thing and does not desist till he apprehends by thought itself the nature of the good in itself, he arrives at the limit of the intelligible, as the other in our parable came to the goal of the visible."[47]

By means of the art of dialectic, one captures the essence of things and arrives at the limit of the intelligible to obtain a clear vision of reality as it is in itself. All other arts have for their object the opinions of men or things that are subject to generation and corruption. Only the art of dialectic produces a waking vision of true being, while even arts such as geometry and the studies that accompany it are only dreaming about it. There is no adequate way of inquiry except for the way of the art of dialectic that "attempts systematically and in all cases to determine what each thing really is."[48]

Thus, it becomes clear that for Plato, dialectic plays the role that demonstrative reasoning plays for Aristotle: It provides knowledge of the essence of things and does not depend on the opinions of men. It also removes itself from the study of things subject to generation and corruption unless this assists the ascent of the knower to the intelligible world in a manner similar to what Plato describes in *Symposium*.[49] Aristotle, however, depicts induction, which proceeds from sensible individuals to universals, as surpassing dialectic in being "applicable to the mass of men" and "is more readily learnt by the use of the senses."[50]

To provide an "account of the essence of each thing," and to render this "account to himself and to others,"[51] the seeker of the art of dialectic must embark on a journey in which he ascends above the things for the essence of which he seeks to provide an account and those for whom he seeks to provide the account. Indeed, the dialectician must be involved in an act of self-transcendence because before he became an account provider, he had been one of the public. Self-transcendence is a major feature in Plato's depiction of the state of the dialectician. It is also a major feature in Ibn Ṭufayl's illuminationist philosophy, as his hero goes through similar spiritual developments and meets the same fate as that of Plato's enlightened philosopher. No such feature is to be found in Fārābī's *Book of Letters*. The process of the development of philosophy seems to have a linear design, as it is based on transcending the other. Dialectical transcendence, however, resembles a dialogue of the self with itself, as Ibn Ṭufayl's hero, much like Plato's enlightened philosopher, was a silent speaker.[52]

CHAPTER 7

The Shadow of Ibn Bājja

Two of Ibn Bājja's works had a special impact on Ibn Ṭufayl's thought: *Conjunction Between the Active Intellect and the Human Intellect* and *Governance of the Solitary*. The former is badly organized and suffers from apparent confusion. Ibn Ṭufayl has an explanation for this confusion and the fact that most of Ibn Bājja's works are unfinished. An attempt is made here to show that Ibn Bājja's confusion was in part the result of his struggle with the liminal consequences of his rationalistic deliberations.

IBN BĀJJA ON THE CHAIN OF EXISTENTS AND SELF-INTELLECTION

Ibn Bājja opens his *Conjunction* by mentioning the senses in which the term "one" is employed and refers the reader to Fārābī's discussion of this subject. Then he says that man is said to be one as a principle of motion.[1] Man as a mover employs two sorts of tools: material and spiritual. Material tools are of two sorts: artificial tools, such as the musical pipe, and natural tools, such as the hand that moves it. Natural tools are prior in significance to artificial tools. This is why it is said that the hand is the tool of tools.[2] Ibn Bājja states, however, that the real tool of tools is the instinctive heat which exists in animals that have blood. Plants also possess a principle of motion, but this hardly resembles the principle of motion in animals.[3] There is a state in which the human being resembles plants. In the womb, the human being feeds and grows, which is what plants do. In this state, the human being is an animal potentially. When the human being is a child that is suckled, he resembles an animal in action and a human being potentially.[4] When he leaves the womb and begins to use his senses, he resembles animals in possessing sensation and locomotion.[5] In the actual human being, the first mover is the imagined form, in addition to the two moving powers that he shares with plants in charge of nutrition and growth.[6]

As we can see, motion occupies an important role in Ibn Bājja's depiction of the chain of existents. This is also the case in Ibn Ṭufayl; he says that nutrition is "an interchange by which the being nourished replaces matter that breaks down by ingesting material similar to itself and assimilating this to its own substance."[7] He says, "Growth is movement in all three dimensions at once, according to a set proportion," and he adds that "these two functions are universal among plants and animals and must therefore issue from a form shared by both plants and animals. This form is what is called the vegetative soul."[8] Thus, the form is posited as a differentiating factor that determines the specific nature of each existent. At the same time, it is by virtue of this factor that existents are situated in one continuous unity as their forms connect with and continue each other. Thus, the form or the soul divides and, at the same time, connects. This is, in my understanding, the meaning of its being a principle of motion. It is a principle of motion not merely because it is located at the limit between one existent and another, but because it *is* the limit that fixes the very identity of existents.[9] This seems like reading Aristotle through Platonic eyes. And indeed the examination of Ibn Bājja's *Conjunction* reveals that he also attempts to combine Aristotle's and Plato's teachings to present a unified conception of the development of the intellect. His presentation, however, suffers from apparent confusion, as becomes evident from what he says at the conclusion of his work:

> As I finished reading it, I found that it fell short of rendering my meaning comprehensible. For this consists of a proof (*dalīl*) that is not to be found in what is stated here, except with the greatest difficulty and the most strenuous effort. Still my statement contains an indication (*dalāla*) of my meaning. Once the terms are refined, and the meaning is comprehended, it becomes clear that none of the acquired knowledges2 can reach its level. Once its corresponding concept is realized, the meaning, which is comprehended,[10] sees itself in a level as distinct from all previous levels and as related to notions pure of matter and too noble to be attributed to natural existence. Rather, they are states that belong to the blessed (*su'adā'*), who are worthy of the title "divine," granted by the All-Mighty God to his servants as he wills. I also found that in some places the expressions are not put in the best arrangement but I did not have the time to replace what needed to be replaced. Hence, I depend on you to do this since I know that you are capable of it.[11]

This apology, which concludes a work that is poorly organized, suffers from confusion. Ibn Bājja does not make it clear whether he is referring to a person to whom his meaning is revealed or whether he is implying that the meaning is revealed or reflected upon itself. I will attempt to show that both readings of the text are reasonable.

Ibn Bājja says that the highest domain of existence within which the possibility of conjunction may be actualized is the domain of the human being. As a child, the human being resembles an animal in action and a human being potentially. The passage from infancy toward rational maturation occurs when the human being acquires rational concepts (*ma'qūlāt*), concepts that create in him the desire to move toward rational consideration. Ibn Bājja explains that the rational concept is not a material or imaginal bodily form. Rather, it is a form whose matter is the intermediary, imaginal form.[12] Here, he refers the reader to two of his works in which he discusses intermediary forms, and then states, rather hastily, that "the first mover in the human being is the intellect (*ʿaql*) in act and the intellected (*maʿqūl*) in act, since the intellect in act is one with the intellected in act, as others have explained and I summarized their account in *On the Soul*."[13] Majid Fakhry indicates that the reference to this work is void.[14] Herbert Davidson's summary of Alexander of Aphrodisias's account of the subject of conjunction will be useful in explicating Ibn Bājja's statement.

Alexander refers to Aristotle's statement that actual intellect is identical with what is actually thought.[15] He explains that if a form is not attached to matter, then it is actually intelligible—that is, intelligible by its own nature, the thinking subject being identical with it. "A pure form would, in other words, be both an actual object of thought and also the subject having it as the object of thought. It would be an incorporeal being having itself as a permanent actual object of thought, an intellect thinking itself."[16] Compare this with what Ibn Bājja says: "As for the intellect whose thought is identical to itself…it is one and does not become many in the manner that form becomes many in relation to material things…Since seeing the thing and conceiving it occur when the seer obtains the meaning of the thing and abstracts it from its material substance and since the meaning that we want to conceive is a meaning that possesses no additional meaning, the act of this intellect becomes its essence…and the mover, who performs it, becomes identical with the moved. It is, as Alexander says in *On the Spiritual Forms*, an intellect turning back to itself."[17]

As the intellect becomes identical with the comprehended meaning, and the mover and the moved become one, it makes no difference whether we interpret the word "comprehend" in the passage quoted above from the conclusion to Ibn Bājja's *Conjunction* as referring to a comprehending person or a meaning that comprehends or sees itself. Ibn Bājja presents thinking and seeing as identical. By doing so, he seeks to differentiate between propositional and direct or immediate thinking. The intellect that is identical with its thought does not think by means of propositions, nor does it mean to. Standing as a mirror facing its object of comprehension, the object is already there.[18] In this sense, even saying that the intellect "turns back" to itself can be misleading because its movement, unlike the movement of lesser intellects, is identical to itself.

Ibn Bājja introduces a tripartite classification of the human intellect following the passage of the human soul from potentiality to actuality through the embryonic, infantile, and mature stages of its development. The first level in this classification corresponds to the level of the common public. Those who belong to this level conceive of concepts always in connection with material or natural forms. In this category is included knowledge of the practical skills. The second level pertains to theoretical knowledge. The possessor of practical knowledge considers first the objects and then the concepts. The possessor of theoretical knowledge considers first the concepts and then the objects. Nevertheless, the latter's knowledge is still related to the material forms, and when he sees the concept, he sees it mediated "as in the case of the reflection of the sun in the water. What is seen in the water is not the sun itself but its image. As for the common people, they see the image of the image as in the case of the image of the sun that is reflected in the water and from the water in a mirror. The third is the level of those who are blessed and who see the thing in itself."[19]

THE PRESENCE OF THE PARABLE OF THE CAVE

Ibn Bājja says that the state of the common public resembles the state of those who dwell in a cave and who, whether in the heart of the cave or at its entrance, see colors only in the shadow and in a state that resembles darkness. There are those who have managed to leave the cave, and on the outside, they are able to see light free of colors, in which case they have become able to discern the true nature of colors. Their situation resembles that of the possessors of theoretical knowledge. "As for the blessed they are free from any resemblance to any sort of vision, since they have become the thing. Were vision to turn into light this would be their rank."[20] As must be clear, Ibn Bājja is referring here to the Parable of the Cave. Notice, however, that even when he makes a direct reference to Plato, Ibn Bājja seems to be thinking of other thinkers. His choice to speak about colors as the objects of seeing, for example, is such a case, and reference to statements such as Alexander's "light is the cause of making colors that are potentially visible, actually so," and Themistius's statement that when "light becomes present in the potential faculty of vision and in potential colors, it turns the former into actual vision and the latter into actual colors," are clear indications of this. Since I cannot elaborate on this point in the context of the present discussion, I refer the reader to Davidson's discussion of the subject of the relationship between the active intellect and the human thought, in which the two statements quoted above can be found.[21]

What Ibn Bājja says next is extremely obscure, and I think that a summary account of the Parable of the Cave can be helpful in making his words more comprehensible. Plato describes prisoners dwelling in a cave with a long entrance open to the light. They have their hands and necks fettered from childhood, so they cannot move or turn their heads, and all they can do is look forward. Behind them, there is a fire burning, and above and between them and the fire is a road. Along the road, there is a wall past which men carry all kinds of implements and images of animals and humans and material objects that rise above the wall. The prisoners cannot see each other or themselves because they cannot move their heads, and all they can see are the shadows cast from the fire on the wall in front of them. As for the voices, they deem that they are coming from the shadows in front of them. The prisoners, therefore, must think that reality is identical to the shadows of the artificial objects shown on the wall.[22]

As Socrates was describing the situation of the prisoners in the cave, Glaucon, his interlocutor, commented that he was speaking about a strange image and strange prisoners. Socrates had to remind him: "Like to us, I said, for to begin with, tell me do you think that these men would have seen anything of themselves or of one another except the shadows cast from the fire on the wall of the cave that fronted them?"[23] This is an important reminder to readers who read the Parable in the manner that Glaucon was receiving it. Even after Socrates's reminder to him that the prisoners are like us, he does not seem to realize that the Parable was actually about none other than himself and that Socrates was only playing the role of the very wall that he was speaking of, mirroring and reflecting the image of his interlocutor so that he can see himself and, when he has done that, see others.[24]

Self-reflexivity is a crucial element in Plato's dialectical epistemology. In his way to release, the prisoner must acquire the capacity to reflect on himself, even as this calls for a considerable amount of suffering. There are physical difficulties to overcome. To leave his spot, the prisoner must stand up and *walk*, while lifting his eyes to the light, and, for the first time, *see* real objects.[25] Walking, as Ibn Bājja tells us, resembles making judgments. The prisoner who can walk for the first time also can make judgments for the first time.[26] He is able, when he is no longer motionless, to lift his eyes to the direction of the light and see the objects that he mistook for their images. Still, the prisoner cannot see the light itself. If he is compelled to look at it, that would hurt his eyes and he would flee to the shadows, which he will see more clearly, since he is accustomed to seeing in the dark.[27] This is to confirm Ibn Bājja's view that whether in the heart of the cave or at its entrance, the state of the dwellers in the cave is a state of seers in darkness.

By saying that the prisoner is *dragged* by force up the ascent and *drawn* into the light of the sun, Plato wants to emphasize that the motion that the prisoner exercises in his way to enlightenment is not purely self-activated. It is important to remember that even after leaving the cave and completing the journey, all the way to looking upon the sun, the prisoner's motion will still not be purely self-activated. Even then, he will be forced to walk back to his dark cave to teach others what he had been taught. Should he try to stir or move them by force, as he was also stirred and moved by force, he will then and only then come to close the circle of his journey of illumination. By doing so (that is, by seeing himself in the mirror of the other), he will achieve the state of unity with the same.

The prisoner is drawn out into the light of the sun. The dazzling beams fill his eyes, and instead of seeing real objects clearly, the prisoner goes blind. That is why habituation is needed. First, he sees the images of things reflected in water, and later the things themselves. Then he sees the appearances in the heavens, first in the night by looking at the stars and then by day by looking at the sun's light. Finally, he will be able to look at the sun itself,[28] which represents the idea of the Good and which will be "the last thing to be seen and hardly seen" in the region of the known and "this is indeed the cause for all things of all that is right and beautiful, giving birth in the visible world to light, and the author of light and itself in the intelligible world being the authentic source of truth and reason, and that anyone who is to act wisely in private or public must have caught sight of this."[29]

Ibn Bājja situates those who belong to the common public in the dark cave, whereas he situates the possessors of theoretical knowledge outside the darkness, in the light of the sun. They differ from the common public in that, while they are able to see the image of the sun as in the water, the common public can see only the image of the image as if the sun's image in the water is reflected in a mirror. As for the blessed, they are neither in the darkness nor in the light because they have become the light. In terms of the objects of knowledge, the first group sees sensible forms, the second intermediate spiritual forms, and the third concepts or universals. As for the sensible forms, they designate immediate and least durable existence. Their existence is so fleeting, indeed, that even as we point at them, they perish.[30] The spiritual forms live longer because they consist of the two extremes: the intelligible, from which they receive durability in existence and permanent subsistence; and the sensible, from which they receive impermanence. Because their existence is limited in relation to the everlasting existence of concepts, it makes no difference whether their lives are long or short,[31] for they are forms that are related to material bodies and all such forms must ultimately perish. A concept is a universal form to be distinguished from all other forms because it "possesses no material form nor is it a spiritual form of a body that exists in the form like an imagined entity. Rather it is a form whose matter consists of spiritual intermediate (imaginal) forms."[32] To distinguish concepts from intermediate forms, Ibn Bājja calls the former "universal spiritual forms" and the latter "particular spiritual forms." Universal spiritual forms possess a single, specific relationship, which is their relation to the person who cognizes them, whereas particular spiritual forms have two relations: one is specific and that is their relation to the sensible object and another that is universal and that is their relation to the person who comprehends them.[33]

Let us see how what has been said connects to the possibility of achieving conjunction or unity because this is what Ibn Bājja aims to do. As it turns out, unity is related to the sort of relationship that each form possesses toward the knowing subject and the manner in which this affects the state of his motion. Let us consider first the sensible form. As Ibn Bājja says, the sensible form is the form that enjoys the shortest duration of subsistence.[34] The simple act of pointing at the thing suffices to give us all the knowledge that can be had about it because that is all that sense perceptual knowledge consists of. It is not clear, therefore, whether a relationship can be established between the knowing subject and such an object in the first place. In a sense, it makes no difference whether we say that the sensible form possesses no *fixed* relationship, or that it possesses no relationship at all with the perceiving subject. In the Parable of the Cave, this is the state of the prisoners, who dwell in a complete state of motionlessness, and the shadows on the wall, which are mere images and which only seem to be moving.[35] The ascent of the prisoner toward the light and his encounter with the intermediate forms, which are represented by the reflections of higher entities in water, signify an important stage in the development of the prisoner's judgmental or rational capacity. In Ibn Bājja's theory of knowledge, the intermediate forms occupy a central place. I will elaborate after quoting the following passage from his *Governance*:

> It is clear that no idea can be formed or a logical conclusion drawn out in a rational or any form of spiritual contemplation from sensible forms. For when we have sensed a body and acquired its spiritual particular form and wished to reproduce it we do so by abstracting it from its particular relationship to its substance. The substance itself cannot be brought into existence since it exists already. Rather it is by means of the spiritual intermediate form that we bring what is nonexistent into existence. This does not include all that is nonexistent but only what exists potentially...He, whose spirituality is imparted to him through sensation, reflection, and imagination that are limited to this sensible form, is found to be incapable of performing many acts...He who delimits his sensible form's spirituality to what he draws from sensation becomes careless. For the imaginal capacity of the particular spiritual form, which is caused by sensation, is reduced to a mere motion in place. As for the other motions they belong to the form that is specific to the nature of the human being, that is, the intermediate form. When the human being possesses a nature that is limited to the measure of spirituality that is allocated to sensation, he becomes dull and is found not to be effective in performing many acts...You find the eyes of the dull and the careless as if frozen and their moves few, while you find the eyes of the noble swift in their moves and the black of their eyes humid as if in a melted state.[36]

It is interesting how Ibn Bājja seeks to establish a synthesis between the physical movement of man's eye and his spiritual capacity, and how he seeks to locate this synthesis in that part of the human being that Aristotle regards the noblest, and that contains the human of the eye,[37] the resemblance of which is an image-reflecting mirror. Indeed, it is in the context of discussing imaginal or intermediate forms that a proper synthesis can be sought between the physical and the spiritual because the intermediate form is "a middle between material and conceptual existents."[38] Being in the middle, the intermediate form possesses two relationships: a particular relationship to the sensible and a universal relationship to the person who apprehends it. This is to compare with the universal form, which possesses only one particular relationship to the person who apprehends it.[39] This means that when the person turns to the apprehension of the universal form, the form actually returns to itself. Returning in the part of universals, however, does not mean that the concept makes a move. The concept is permanent and fixed compared to the sensible form, which is the agent of change and ceasing.[40] Ibn Bājja says that in none of its states, the concept resembles things that are in motion. For example, when Zayd's form changes from a state of nobility to a state of wickedness, this change is something that is like moving, but it is not motion. ʿAmr is the one who moves from imagining one spiritual intermediate form that belongs to Zayd to another form that is also acquired by ʿAmr. Zayd's concept remains fixed. The bodily imaginal or intermediate existence seems to have moved from one state to another because of its proximity to the sensible. Concepts, however, have no relationship whatsoever to bodily existence. Otherwise, if Zayd is noble and ʿAmr is wicked, then the unifying concept will be both noble and wicked, which is absurd.[41] This explains the significance of the intermediate forms in the process of acquiring knowledge and Ibn Bājja's rather enigmatic statement that there is nothing in the human being's walking that is for the sake of his universal form and that his actions belong to his intermediate form.[42]

Ibn Bājja arrives here at what he describes as an extremely serious difficulty. Although he says that the concept of a human being is the purest of all concepts,[43] he is undoubtedly hesitant about the nature of the human being in general. This is because human nature seems to be an intermediary between the nature of the everlasting and the nature of the generated or the nature of that which continues incessantly in time (having neither beginning nor end) and that which is generated and corrupted. The human being in this sense follows the way of nature. "For nature does not move from one genus to another except by intermediation, as this is witnessed in all genera of existing substances. For there is an intermediate existent between inanimate things and plants such that man cannot judge whether this is a plant or an inanimate thing. Likewise there is an intermediate existent between the genus of animals and the genus of plants, which partakes in both."[44] Ibn Bājja concludes, therefore, that the human being must consist of a duality of meanings, such that in virtue of the one meaning, which conforms to everlasting nature, he is everlasting; and in virtue of the other meaning, which conforms to the nature of generation and corruption, he is subject to generation and corruption. No sooner had he stated his conclusion than he proceeded to invalidate it. For one thing, speaking about two meanings that oppose one another and that enter into the definition of the same human being is absurd. Ibn Bājja ends this confusing account of the essence of the human being, and with it his *Governance,* with a rather strange statement that the human being is a natural wonder.[45]

Ibn Ṭufayl says that Ibn Bājja was occupied with the affairs of this world and passed away before the storehouses of his knowledge were opened. He made a promise to elaborate on the state of the blessed, but due to lack of time or his fear that this would be seen in contradiction with the way he conducted his life, he failed to keep his promise.[46] The truth is that what rendered Ibn Bājja's project incomplete was mainly his hesitation to acknowledge the very liminal conclusions to which his rational analysis led him. Ibn Bājja was able to recognize that the notion of liminality played a major role in the depiction of the unity of natural existents. His naturalistic reflections led him to extend this depiction to establish a state of conjunction between natural and spiritual existence. Once the paradoxical implications of conjunction started to impose themselves as a logical necessity, however, he found himself backing away.

In my view, Ibn Ṭufayl admired Ibn Sīnā for being able to make an early and important declaration of the limitation of rationalistic thought, but he refrained from expressing whatever admiration he had for Ibn Bājja because he fell short of making the same sort of declaration. Apart from the manner in which thinkers conduct their social life, the declaration that they make in relation to the limits of intellectual inquiry is crucial not merely for *being* a mystic, but rather in relation to the very understanding of the same theoretical or philosophical knowledge at their disposal. Ibn Bājja is a unique case because, as I have attempted to show in this chapter, his works seem to be full of bits and pieces of liminal declarations; but somehow he seems to have failed to pull them together and produce a major liminal declaration to the effect that rationalistic thought is limited.

CHAPTER 8

The Traditionalistic Account from the Beginning

THE EMPHASIS ON BALANCE AND EQUILIBRIUM

Those who deny the account of Ḥayy's spontaneous generation say that opposite the island on which the naturalistic birth took place, there was another populated island ruled by a proud and jealous king. His sister secretly married a relative, whose name was Yaqẓān, and gave birth to a child. Fearing for his life, she put the child in an ark, sealed the ark tightly, and cast it into the sea. The ark was brought to the coast of an island. The tide was high, and the waters cast the ark into an elevated thicket protected from the rain, wind, and sun that *turned away from it when it rose and when it set.*[1] The wind heaped sand that blocked the entrance to the thicket, and the ark remained dry. The violent waves plucked the nails of the ark and shattered its boards. The baby cried of hunger and his cries reached the ears of a doe that had lost her fawn. The doe followed the voice of the crying child, while imagining her lost fawn, until she reached the ark and removed its cover. She showed great affection for the child and tenderly provided him with all that he needed.[2]

The first thing that attracts our attention in relation to this account is the special sense of protection that Ibn Ṭufayl surrounds Ḥayy with in this, as well as the following stages of his early development. This point has been noticed and amply analyzed by Goodman in his depiction of Ibn Ṭufayl's project as a thought experiment intended to demonstrate that in separation from society, man will be able to attain the highest values of spiritual maturity.[3] The sense of providing to which Ibn Ṭufayl gives special emphasis seems sometimes to be exaggerated to include details that seem insignificant, such as the fact that the thicket to which the ark had been brought was of pleasant soil. It turns out, however, that this detail is far from being insignificant—it establishes a linkage with the fuller description of the excellent quality of the spot of earth in which Ḥayy was born, according to the naturalistic account. The rich soil was responsible not only for the generation of Ḥayy, but also for the fact that the island was abundant with vegetation, so that the doe would be rich with milk and the newborn would receive proper nutrition.

Together with the sense of providing comes the need for balance. As Goodman points out, there are fruits in abundance in the island, but Ḥayy must find them; there are no beasts of prey, but there are animals that compete with Ḥayy over his supper; the doe must weaken and eventually die so that Ḥayy may develop responsibility and gain independence.[4] Balance and equilibrium are shown to be crucial for man's birth, according to the naturalistic account. Life originates when the opposite components of matter are balanced and equilibrium between their conflicting powers is attained. When balance is shaken, as is the case when human societies evolve, there is need for a new beginning to regain balance and reestablish the broken harmony. Such was the ultimate purpose of Ḥayy's birth as it is depicted in the traditionalistic account. This account bears clear resemblance to Moses's birth story as it is related in the Bible and the Qur'ān. Later in this chapter, I will dwell on Ibn al-ʿArabī's depiction of the figure of Moses and explicate its relevance to Ibn Ṭufayl's traditionalistic account. I will also provide a discussion of the encounter that took place, according to the Qur'ān, between Moses and al-Khaḍir because I believe this will be useful in elucidating important aspects of this account. The story of this encounter is one of four stories that constitute the Qur'ānic Chapter of the Cave. The relevance of the first story, the story of the People of the Cave, to the traditionalistic account is straightforward. Ibn Ṭufayl says that when the ark reached the seashore, the waters cast it into an elevated thicket protected from the rain, wind, and sun that *turned away from it when it rose and when it set*. Reference is made here to Q 18:17, "Thou wouldst have seen the sun, when it rose, declining to the right from their cave, and when it set, turning away from them to the left, while they lay in the open space in the midst of the cave."[5] The mention of the cave occurs for the first time in the context of describing the incident of the discovery of fire. The incident is significant for the purposes of our discussion and it will be useful to elaborate on it.

THE DISCOVERY OF FIRE

> As chance would have it, a fire was kindled by friction in a thicket of reeds. When Ḥayy caught sight of it, he was terrified because he saw a being (*khalqan*) that he had never seen before. For a good while, he stood wondering at it. As he drew closer, he could see what a piercing light it possessed and how, with its overwhelming capacity, it consumed and turned into its own nature everything it touched. Wonder, courage, and the potency that God the All-Mighty implanted in his nature made him stretch out his hand to take a portion of it. When he touched it, it burned his hand and he was unable to take hold of it. Then he thought that he could seize a piece of firewood not wholly

consumed by fire. He held it from the side that fire had not burned … and carried it to his dwelling, a cave that he found suitable for living. He kept the fire up … and tended it day and night, full of amazement and admiration for it. He was pleased with its company, especially at night because it took the place of the sun in providing light and warmth. His love for it increased, and he deemed it the best of all the things that he possessed. He observed it moving always upwards, seeking elevation, and was convinced that it was one of the celestial jewels [adorning] the sky.[6]

First notice the careful manner in which Ibn Ṭufayl combines two explanations of the "birth" of fire. According to the first, it was by chance (*ittafaqa*) that fire was kindled. Although the second explanation, which has it that fire was made by friction, seems closer to being an explanation in the scientific sense, the use that Ibn Ṭufayl makes of *chance* has, in my opinion, philosophical implications that are rooted in Aristotle and Ibn Sīnā.[7]

The Arabic translation of Aristotle's *Physics* renders *chance* as *tilqā' al-nafs*, meaning in Aristotle that a thing acts for a cause or a reason that is spontaneous or that comes from within itself, and therefore generates an act that is contrary to nature. The naturalistic explanation has it that fire was kindled not spontaneously or simply by chance, but because of a definite natural cause—namely, friction. How then can we still speak about chance as an *explanation* for the burning of fire? One possible explanation is that, for Aristotle, chance is a cause of effects caused by nature; it is only that this cause is accidental and, in this sense, it is indefinite and thus posterior to nature.[8] Another related explanation has to do with the possibility that Ibn Ṭufayl's employment of *ittafaqa* is linked to Ibn Sīnā's use of *ittifāq* (coincidence) for *chance* instead of *tilqā' al-nafs*. Catarina Belo thinks that the use that Ibn Sīnā makes of the term is significant because *ittifāq*, which does not exclude the deterministic view that every event has a necessary cause, is distinguished from *min tilqā' nafsihi*, which has an indeterministic tone, suggesting that something is coming without a cause and by itself.[9] As she points out, for Aristotle, chance is found in events that do not always occur, for the most part, but rather in rare events, which is also what Ibn Sīnā believes. She emphasizes, however, that for Ibn Sīnā, events that come by chance are linked to necessary causes. They are considered the outcome of chance only because they are unexpected, not because they are not related to necessary causes. Rather, when its conditions are met, the rare event that comes by chance is to be considered necessary.[10] Ibn Ṭufayl, the reader of Ibn Sīnā's *Shifā'*, might therefore be using *ittafaqa* to tell us that the burning of fire by friction, although rare in nature, is still an event that is linked to necessary causes. This is important because, as Ibn Sīnā says, chance is a cause especially because it provides an account of the thing's occurring neither always nor for the most part.[11] The starting point is, therefore, the introduction of chance as an account for the occurrence of an unusual event. The making of science proceeds by filling this rather empty account with scientific content. Hence, recognition of chance is an important step in scientific discovery, and it is not by chance that Aristotle dedicates so much attention to it in *Physics*, nor I believe it was by chance that Ibn Ṭufayl opens with it the account of such an especially important discovery.

A careful examination of the description of the birth of fire reveals three phases or stages of evolution. Seeing the fire for the first time and observing its powerful action, Ḥayy is filled with fear. His relationship with fire at this stage is characterized by alienation and distance. This characterization is appropriate for the state of the possessor of (public) religious belief, which is based on fear of God's chastisement and hope for his mercy and forgiveness. Distance implies unfamiliarity, which is caused by lack of knowledge. Due to this lack of knowledge, the servant is always in a state of fear of his lord, even as he observes his religious duties fully and most faithfully. This is also why he needs hope to balance his fear so that he may maintain a stable relationship with his lord. Fear, however, remains the dominant incentive, and it plays an important role in urging the believer to shorten the distance between himself and his lord by acquiring knowledge of him. In this sense, the process of acquiring knowledge commences in accord with the biblical words: "The fear of the lord is the foundation of knowledge."[12]

The second reaction is depicted in terms of wonder, characteristic of the philosophical mode of thought. "For it is owing to their wonder that men both now begin and at first began to philosophize."[13] Ḥayy's wonder, which was caused by the observation of the fire's penetrating light, made him draw closer and act to bring light into his dark cave; this symbolizes bringing knowledge into his ignorant soul. The third reaction is that of love. Ḥayy falls in love with fire, as he finds in it the provider of heat and light that are most needed at night. This reaction to fire, which is based on love and adoration, is characteristic of the mystical mode of thought, which seeks unification with and illumination from the side of the lord.

The discovery of fire falls in the practical stage of Ḥayy's development, which precedes the theoretical and mystical stages. The discovery of fire might therefore be presented as one moment that potentially includes the main tripartite division of the story, and the mirroring in one incident of the whole process of its development.

Another important observation is related to the presence of Plato's Parable of the Cave in Ibn Ṭufayl's description of the incident. Both cave and fire play an important role in Plato's parable, as well as in Ibn Ṭufayl's account of the discovery of fire, as fire is placed in a dark cave to assist the enlightened person in ascending to the highest levels of illumination. In both cases, it is presented as representative of the sun, the source of truth and the entity responsible for the very existence and essence of beings, as their existence is sustained by its heat and their essence is illuminated by its light.[14]

The resemblance between the two thinkers does not end here. Consider Plato's words in describing the method of acquiring knowledge of justice: "But if something different manifests itself in the individual, we will return again to the state and test it there and it may be that, by examining them side by side and rubbing them against one another, as it were from the fire sticks we may cause the spark of justice to flash forth, and when it is thus revealed confirm it in our own minds."[15] Plato speaks about a method of acquiring knowledge of justice by comparing the justice that the individual has in his mind with the form of justice in the ideal state by way of rubbing them against one another. If fire is kindled, then there is confirmation. Otherwise, we must say that the knowledge of justice that is achieved in the mind is knowledge of injustice. In his encounter with Ḥayy, Absāl heard his description of the essences that are beyond the sensible world and the knowledge that they possess: "He had no doubt that all the things that had come in the Law … were but resemblances (*amthila*) of the things that Ḥayy had seen. The eyes of his heart were opened, the fire of his mind was kindled (*inqadaḥat*), and the rational thought (*ma*ʿ*qūl*) coincided for him with the transmitted word (*manqūl*), as the ways of esoteric interpretation and all things masked were revealed to him."[16] Ḥayy's intuitive account of the essences and the knowledge that they possess functions as the ideal against which Absāl rubs the truths of his religious community and, by means of that, attains realization. Discerning the coincidences between the resemblances and their originals, in whose image they are fashioned, kindles his mind with fire and opens his eyes. He becomes a possessor of the knowledge of the Law, which accounts for what is just and what is unjust.

THE SLEEPERS IN THE CAVE

In *Physics*, Aristotle places the story of the Sleepers in Sardinia in the context of discussing the nature of time and the view that time exists only with motion or change: "On the other hand, time cannot exist without change; for when there is no change at all in our thought or when we do not notice any change, we do not think that time has elapsed, just like the legendary sleeping characters in Sardinia who, on awakening from a long sleep in the presence of heroes, connect the earlier with the later moment into one moment, thus leaving out the time between the two moments because of their unconsciousness … So thinking that no time has elapsed happens to us when we specify no limits of a change at all but the soul appears to *rest* in something which is one and indivisible, but we think that time has elapsed when sensation has occurred and limits of a change have been specified, evidently time does not exist without a motion or change."[17]

When the Sleepers connected the earlier to the later moment, the two moments became one and, in the absence of motion, time froze. This is because time is known "when we limit a motion by specifying in it a prior and a posterior as its limits; and it is then that we say that time has elapsed."[18] Thus, knowing time is related necessarily to the perception of motion, as "time is the number of a motion with respect to the prior and the posterior."[19] The Arabic translation of Aristotle's text renders Sardinia as *sard*.[20] It is interesting that the meaning of *sarada* is: "He carried on a thing, or put it forward from one stage to another, in regular order, consecutively, or one part immediately after another, uninterruptedly."[21] As examples of this sort of action, Lane mentions the act of reciting the Qur'ān (*sard al-Qur'ān*) by carrying on the reading rapidly and uninterruptedly and the example of the tears that follow one another (*tasarrada*), like as do pearls.[22] Words and tears in these examples compare to the (many) times or moments that are connected by the one time or one moment. The "moment," is the designation for both "moment" and "now," is not part of time because it does not admit of division, being one and indivisible. Yet time (*zamān*) does not exist without the moment that provides for its very unity. "For the moment is the cause of the actual continuity or unity of time. We only imagine that the moment is the cause of the division of time. The time which is the number of the First Motion, however, is incapable of halting although we imagine the moment dividing the year to months and the month to weeks."[23] The first motion is the motion of the circle that encompasses the whole and consists of the *returning* of the whole to the point of origin in one indivisible moment. This moment is not divided into parts so that it is not identical to the time that is divided into parts that are also times.[24] This analysis of the nature of time finds its correspondence in the three resemblances that Ḥayy performed for the sake of attaining mystical witnessing (*mushāhada*).

The first resemblance is related to sensible existents that are made up of differentiated parts and powers and that act according to different drives. As Ibn Ṭufayl says, this resemblance hinders the attainment of mystical witnessing because sensible things are but veils that cover up the inner vision. And yet Ḥayy imitated the motions of sensible existents as a means to preserve the spirit that dwells in his heart.[25] In virtue of possessing this spirit, he was able to engage himself in the second resemblance in imitation of the circular motions of the celestial spheres. This imitation enhanced his spiritual witnessing a great deal. However, he still possessed self-awareness, which obstructed the stability and continuity of his vision. Through the third resemblance, Ḥayy attempted to imitate the Necessary-of-Existence. His state was so intense that he felt that his self was totally annihilated.[26] The interpreter of Aristotle's *Physics*, Abū ʿAlī bin al-Samḥ, writes: "Nature is necessarily related to time. This is because nature is a principle of motion … and motion exists only in time since it is from something and to something and what is from something and to something is incapable of being in one moment so that it must be in time."[27] The interpreter Yaḥyā bin ʿAdī adds that natural existents dwell in an actual and divisible time; it is divisible because the mover halts and thus renders the motion, which is originally continuous, actually divisible.[28] Ḥayy had to acknowledge the limitations of natural existence and natural time because his unitary or essential nature is related in this world to this divisible nature and divisible time. However, he endeavored to minimize his dependence on physical existence and to attain more continuity and perpetuity. For example, he would eat only the minimum amount that kept him going and, even then, he would refrain, when gathering his food, from rooting out plants or destroying their seeds.[29] Ḥayy then was ready for the engagement in the second resemblance, through which he attempted to imitate the circular motion of the celestial bodies. The major characteristic of the motion of the celestial bodies is that it never halts, the divisions that are witnessed in their motions being the work of our imagination. Yaḥyā bin ʿAdī compares this to the moment that is responsible for the essential continuity of time, although in our imagination we deem it divisible.[30] In the third and last resemblance, Ḥayy attempted to situate himself not at the limit of the moment, as this finds its resemblance in uniting with the motion of the highest sphere, but rather in the moment itself, as this finds its resemblance in uniting with the very being of the Necessary-of-Existence. By doing so, Ḥayy was able to achieve the ṣūfī ideal of becoming *son of his time*.[31] He resorts to his cave, shunning all that is sensible and abstaining from motion. His awareness of the sensible world vanishes, and eventually he is able to annihilate that which generates this awareness.[32] Ḥayy attains the state of sainthood. It was this state that al-Khaḍir enjoyed and Moses eagerly sought, according to the story of their encounter in the Chapter of the Cave.

THE ENCOUNTER BETWEEN MOSES AND AL-KHAḌIR

The story begins with Moses telling his servant, Yūshaʿ bin Nūn, that he will not give up until he reaches the Meeting-Place-of-the-Two-Seas (*majmaʿ al-baḥrayn*) or he will spend years journeying.[33] When they reach the designated place at the rock, the fish that Moses was ordered to carry with him makes its way as in a tunnel in the sea. The allusions are to the incident during Passover of Moses's people passing through the Red Sea and the rock that Moses split asunder with his rod and waters gushed forth from it.[34] As water is the source of life and the symbol of knowledge, the association of the rock with the figure of al-Khaḍir, who drank from the waters of life, becomes plain and is confirmed by the interpreters of the Qur'ān.[35]

They went back to the place in which the fish was restored to life. There they found "one of our servants, on whom We had bestowed mercy from Ourselves and whom We had taught knowledge from Our own Presence."[36] From this point on, Yushaʿ bin Nūn disappears from the story, which is, in my view, an indication of the imaginal or *barzakhī* nature of the encounter with sainthood in which Moses was about to be involved and in which Yushaʿ bin Nūn, due to his lesser spiritual degree, was not capable of partaking. Now Moses gathers together with al-Khaḍir, who warns him that he will not have patience with him because he possesses no knowledge of the hidden secrets of the acts that he was about to perform.[37]

As anticipated, Moses protests against al-Khaḍir's ruining a certain boat. Al-Khaḍir reminds him of his promise not to protest, and Moses says: "Blame me not for what I have forgotten." (Q 18:73) Moses also protests against al-Khaḍir's second act: "Have you killed an innocent person who had killed none. Truly you have committed a forbidden act." (Q 18:74) Later, al-Khaḍir explains to Moses that he killed the youth because his parents were believers and he would grow to torment them with his unbelief. Meanwhile, this truth was hidden from Moses's eyes and the divine commandment: "You shall not kill," pressed against his chances to keep his promise.[38] One might think that had Moses known the secret behind al-Khaḍir's act, he would not have protested. The problem is that even if he had known the truth about the youth, killing him would have destroyed the only evidence and justification for his act.[39] Thus al-Khaḍir's act was unequivocally unlawful, and Moses was facing an impossible test—a test that he was doomed to fail. On the one hand, he was ordered by God to pursue al-Khaḍir's knowledge that he bestowed on him from his own presence; on the other hand, he was ordered by the same God to observe the Law. In a sense, Moses finds himself in a situation similar to Satan's. On the one hand, Satan was ordered by God not to associate others with him; on the other hand, he was ordered to bow down to Adam.[40] It can be said that this predicament placed Satan at the limit between the traditionalistic understanding of God's commandment, which prohibits the believer from associating others with God, and his naturalistic understanding of the order that God appointed for his created existents.

This becomes clear from the examination of Satan's response to God's order: "(Allah) said: 'What prevented thee from bowing down when I commanded thee?' He said: 'I am better than he: Thou didst create me from fire, and him from clay.'"[41] In his interpretation of this verse, Abdullah ʿAlī says: "Notice the subtle wiles of Iblīs: his egotism in putting himself above men, and his falsehood in ignoring the fact that Allah had not merely made man's body from clay, but had given him spiritual form—in other words, had taught him the nature of things and raised him above the angels."[42] ʿAlī interprets Satan's rebellion in moral terms, as he attributes to him egotism and falsehood. At the same time, he mentions something that takes us to the real explanation of Satan's conduct, an explanation that is depicted in naturalistic terms. Satan thought that he was better than man because he was made of fire, the highest natural element, and man was made of earth, the lowest natural element.[43] Let us keep in mind that bowing is the form by which man prays to God in ritual prayer, which is called *ṣalāt* in Arabic and which means "connection" or "attachment." To bow down to Adam means to be in contact with him, something that Satan's natural logic forbids. Satan, however, ignores the naturalistic connection between man and himself through the quality of dryness that brings together earth and fire. He also ignores the spirit that attached itself to man, endowing him with the capacity to be taught the nature of things;[44] he ignores the spiritual implications of the naturalistic account of Adam's birth, as this is explicated in Ibn Ṭufayl's description of the natural formation of the human body:

> [I]n a depressed portion of a pocket of land[45] ... over the years, a mass of clay worked until hot and cold, damp and dry were blended in just the proper way

> and their strengths perfectly balanced. This fermented mass of clay was quite large, and parts of it were in better equilibrium than others and more suited for becoming human gametes. The midmost part was the best proportioned and bore the most perfect resemblance to the nature of man. The clay labored and churned, and in the viscous mass there formed what looked like bubbles in boiling water. In the very middle formed a tiny bubble divided in half by a delicate membrane and filled by a fine gaseous body, optimally proportioned for what it was to be. With it at that moment joined the Spirit which is God's in a bond virtually indissoluble according to the senses and reason. For it should be clear that this Spirit emanates continuously from God … It is analogous to the sunlight that constantly floods the earth.[46]

Entering the mystical stage, Ḥayy was able to bring to sophistication his liminal conception of the generation of spiritual life. Ḥayy learns that material mixtures, which are made of the four elements, suffer from lack of stability or balance as one element overwhelms the others. In this state, those mixtures are alive, but they are present only in low levels. There are mixtures the elements of which are counterbalanced and keep in check the force of each other. As a result, the form of the whole does not resemble the form of any of the elements taken singly; rather, it assumes a function that is the balanced outcome of the mutual counterbalancing activity of all the elements combined. Such a form does not suffer from opposition and dwells in a state of equilibrium. As equilibrium is reinforced, the mixture becomes more prepared to receive a higher form of life. Now the spirit of man, which resides in the heart, enjoys the most perfect equilibrium because it is finer than earth and water and denser than air and fire. Thus, it is situated at the limit between the opposing elements, and no opposition attaches itself to it. It does not move up or down and, in resemblance to celestial bodies and due to its circular form, it moves always around itself and around the center. Such spirit is alive to the highest possible degree.[47]

This liminal depiction of the manner of preparing matter for receiving the spiritual form is best accounted for by Ibn Sīnā. Davidson introduces Ibn Sīnā's account, which he gathers from a number of his works. According to Ibn Sīnā, the Active Intellect contains the imprints of the forms of the generated world by way of acting on these forms and bringing them from the state of potentiality, in which they exist in matter, to the state of actuality, as matter is prepared for receiving what belongs to it only potentially.[48] He explains a point that is especially important for understanding the liminal depiction of the meeting place between the naturalistic and traditionalistic accounts of the formation of life. According to Ibn Sīnā, the physical processes that enable matter to receive higher forms do not consist of merely preparing matter for receiving those forms but "equally as the removal of obstacles that prevented matter from receiving what was *rightfully its own*."[49] In a sense, the connection between matter and spirit is made essential and the boundaries between matter and form more flexible. Heavenly forces act by destroying the contrary qualities in the constituents of the mixtures of matter and those are drawn from a state of differentiation to a state of equilibrium. "To the degree that the mixture approaches 'the mean that has no contrary,' and comes to 'resemble the celestial bodies,' which contain no contrary qualities, just to such a degree, does it merit receiving an animating faculty from the incorporeal governing substance."[50] At the upper limit—that is, when matter reaches its highest point of preparation and becomes a perfect blend—it is then ready for receiving the human rational soul, which is distinguished from the animal and the vegetable souls in respect of the substantiality of its incorporeality.[51] According to Ibn Ṭufayl, matter at the upper limit forms a body that possesses the best aptitude for receiving light and, consequently, for reflecting it. This body reaches such a limit of perfection in self-reflexivity as it mirrors in itself the image of the sun—that is, as it becomes in its image. The human body in particular is apt for taking on the form of the spirit as indicated in the Prophet's words: "God created Adam in His own image."[52]

By commanding Satan to bow down to Adam, God was commanding him to bow down to what he had created in his own image. That is why Satan was rebuked with the words: "O Iblīs! What prevented you from bowing down to whom I created with my own hands?"[53] Now, for the rest of his history, Satan will dedicate himself to one mission: to prove that such a contact with the Godhead is actually impossible. Spirit will never come together with matter; man will never be in the image of God. Somehow, however, Satan was not living up to his own promise and with his own words, for even when he pledges to seduce humans, he pledges to seduce them all but a few "sincere servants."[54] In the Chapter of the Cave, al-Khaḍir is said to be one of God's sincere servants (*mukhliṣīn, ṣāliḥīn*). The reference is therefore for the saints (*awliyā'*), who are but a few, but who are the proof that a connection with the divine is still possible. They are proof that creation (of man in God's image) is possible.

I will conclude this part of the discussion with the third incident that took place in the encounter between Moses and al-Khaḍir, and that is al-Khaḍir's setting straight a wall that belonged to people who refused the travelers hospitality. Moses protests against this act by proclaiming that al-Khaḍir could at least exact a recompense for it. In his explanation, al-Khaḍir says that the wall belonged to two orphans whose parents were righteous, and that beneath it was buried a treasure, so out of mercy, God wished to preserve their treasure for them until they grew to maturity and dug it out.[55]

Both Suyūṭī and Ṭabarī say that a board of gold was buried under the wall. Both also say that knowledge was buried under the wall.[56] In a story so fraught with mystical implications, the connection should be discerned easily. As for the wall, Ian Netton counts it among the theologemes in the Chapter of the Cave. He defines a theologeme as "a basic unit of theological discourse which can also function as a sign."[57] The wall functions as a theologeme like the barrier that Dhū al-Qarnayn had established to protect the dwellers in the Land-of-the-Rising-of-the-Sun from Gog and Magog. Like the wall, the barrier is characterized as a mercy from God.[58] Those who are familiar with Ibn

ʿArabī's thought might be tempted to complete the sentence, so to speak, and think of the Qur'ānic description of the wall that separates hell and paradise, "within the nonmanifest side of which is mercy and before the manifest side of which is chastisement."[59] Indeed, Netton's interpretation of the occurrences in the Chapter of the Cave in great part is based on Ibn al-ʿArabī's chapter of Moses in *Bezels of Wisdom,* to which I turn now.[60]

MOSES IN *FUṢŪṢ AL-ḤIKAM*

As Moses took his people to the desert to be lost so they could be found as a renewed and reestablished nation, so Ibn Ṭufayl took his hero to an isolated island to establish him as a perfected saint possessing a purified human soul. Moses's may be considered a story about a new beginning, and in this respect, it resembles other scriptural stories of new beginnings. I have in mind the story of the Flood that brought salvation to Noah but damnation to humanity, and that can be compared to the drowning of Pharoah's people, which brought salvation to Moses's people and destruction to the Egyptians.

In his interpretation of the wisdom of laying Moses in the ark and casting the ark into the sea, Ibn al-ʿArabī says that the ark had the form (*ṣūrat*) of destruction in the manifest domain, whereas in the nonmanifest domain, it took the form of deliverance from slaughter (*qatl*).[61] Ibn al-ʿArabī uses here the term "form" as it is used by Ibn Ṭufayl to mean "function." The act of throwing the ark into the sea has two functions, just as the wall in Q 57:13 has two faces. One function applies to manifestation and conveys chastisement; the other applies to nonmanifestation and conveys mercy. Given that God's mercy encompasses everything (Q 7:156; 40:7), we should not depict the form of the nonmanifest as exclusive to the manifest form; rather, they must be depicted as the complementary halves that are brought together through the intermediary *barzakh.* In functional terms, the forms of the two faces of manifestation and nonmanifestation should be seen as interpenetrating each other as well as the whole that encompasses them: "Every intermediary is between two sides. If you like, you can say, 'The two sides have made manifest its property of intermediacy.' Or, if you like, you can say, 'The intermediacy has made manifest the property of the two sides.' This is the same as the knowledge of the Real through creation and of creation through the Real."[62]

Ibn al-ʿArabī says that the ark signifies Moses's humanity and that the sea stands for what he had acquired by means of the powers of sense perception, imagination, and rational consideration. God placed these powers in the soul as tools by means of which it directs the ark in which abides the *sakīna*[63] of the lord, his holy presence in the ark. Thus, although the spirit that governs the body is king and ruler, it governs it only by means of itself just as God governs the world only by means of the world, or, more precisely, by means of its form.[64] The form designates the Real's names and attributes, the meanings of which are to be found in the world. Ibn al-ʿArabī often cites the tradition:

"I was a treasure but was not known, so I loved to be known. Then I created the creatures and made Myself known to them, so they came to know Me,"[65] to explain the reason for the creation of the world. God creates with the Breath of the All-Merciful. The Breath of the All-Merciful carries all the forms of the cosmos, the names that God taught Adam and by them made manifest or differentiated what was nonmanifest or undifferentiated in the Breath.[66] Hence, the importance of Adam and the meaning of the tradition that God created Adam in his form. Adam became a spirit to which is subjected the higher and the lower domains of existence, and by which the supreme form of the level of the name Allah is perfected.[67] The name "Allah" is the encompassing name. It is the name that designates the intermediary being that is at the limit between creation and the Real, the first circle that is both Real and creation. In this encompassing circle, infinite circles become manifest. When this manifestation occurs, the first circle becomes nonmanifest: "When the circles become manifest, as many as they may be—and they never cease becoming manifest—the first circle, which gave new arrival to these circles, becomes hidden. It is neither known nor perceived, because each circle, whether near it or far from it, is in its form. Hence, concerning each circle, it is said, 'It witnessed it/it did not witness it.' This is an absent in a witnessed."[68]

The level of the name "Allah" is the level of nonmanifestation. But it is not merely the nonmanifestation that is the counterpart of manifestation; rather, it is the intermediary that brings together the nonmanifest Real and manifest creation. Because other essences are in its form, their manifestation becomes a manifestation that includes nonmanifestation. Perfect knowledge of the nature of the essence of the intermediation between the absent and the witnessed is preserved for the Real alone. The Perfect Man partakes in this knowledge because his essence resembles all the names, which are encompassed by the name "Allah." Other essences have knowledge, but theirs is less in perfection. The knowledge of the prophets, such as Moses, can be regarded as an approximation of the knowledge of the Perfect Man in the realm of the manifest. As for the knowledge of the saints, such as al-Khaḍir, it is an approximation of the knowledge of the Perfect Man in the realm of the nonmanifest. Let me quote at some length Qāshānī's following discussion of this subject:

> You should know that al-Khaḍir, peace be upon him, is in the form of Allah's name Nonmanifest and his station is the station of the spirit. To him belong sainthood, the secrets of the absent domain … and the science of essence and presence. That is why his tasting was limited to giving and gift-bestowing. God the All-Mighty said: 'We had bestowed on him mercy from ourselves and taught him knowledge from our own presence'(Q 18:65) … As for Moses, peace be upon him, he is in the form of Allah's name Manifest and his station is the station of the heart. To him belong the science of apostlehood and prophethood, and the Law that is based on commanding right and forbidding wrong … and the ruling according to the outward. That is why his miracles

were especially clear and manifest. God wished to bring Moses to a state of perfection by complementing the manifest revelation, which is related to prophethood, with nonmanifest unveiling according to the measure that he was capable of receiving from the sciences of sainthood. Moses stood before the people of Israel claiming that he had been the most knowledgeable man on Earth. God revealed to him that it was not he but "our servant at the Meeting-Place-Of-The-Two-Seas," meaning the sea of possibility and of necessity, or, the seas of manifestation and nonmanifestation, or, the seas of prophethood and sainthood. Moses felt shame of making his claim and asked God to allow for the companionship, so that [al-Khaḍir] might teach him what God had taught him from His own presence. Had he favored the companionship with Allah and received the science of sainthood from him [directly], Allah would have rid him of [the need of] going after al-Khaḍir. As the encounter occurred, discrepancy emerged due to the differentiation and the alterity between the manifest, regarded as such, and the nonmanifest, regarded as such, and parting occurred.[69]

We have seen that Ibn Ṭufayl places the spirit in the heart. What renders the heart fit for enclosing the spirit is its emptiness in particular. The spirit is the nonmanifest presence in the manifest heart exactly as the *sakīna*, the Lord's gift of mercy, is God's nonmanifest presence in the manifest ark. Al-Khaḍir possesses knowledge of the working of God's mercy, and due to this knowledge, he is capable of making liminal judgments—judgments that are situated at the limit between manifestation and nonmanifestation. That is why they seemed contrary to Moses's Law, which is situated within the limits of the manifest domain. But Moses's heart was exceedingly purified due to his constant search for the fire of truth[70] and his being constantly on the move, so that the task of complementing his control of the manifest domain with some tasting of the nonmanifest, according to his designated spiritual capacity, became expedient. Indeed, he seems to have possessed such a stern determination, as he declares that he will journey on until he reaches the Meeting-Place-Of-The-Two-Seas, the sea of possibility, manifestation, and prophethood, and the sea of necessity, nonmanifestation, and sainthood.

Now Moses makes a serious, inevitable mistake. When God informs him that he is not the possessor of perfect knowledge but al-Khaḍir, he hastens to associate perfect knowledge with a particular person and, accordingly, implores God to gather him together with the saint. He thinks in terms of taking what is given to him, and to this extent, he conforms to the ordinances of the science of the nonmanifest because nonmanifest knowledge is something that is for gift-giving. But he errs in thinking that the saint could actually present him with this gift, for it turns out that the knowledge of saints is extremely empty (indeed, the emptiest of all forms of knowledge), due to the immediate connection that places them face to face with their source of inspiration. This is why it was important for al-Khaḍir to remind him: "I did it not of my own accord."(Q 18:82) This is important because it sets a limit not only for knowledge of manifestation but also for knowledge of nonmanifestation, when this is cut off from its source and considered in the abstract. This is why it was important for Ibn Ṭufayl to indicate that knowledge of "witnessing, presence, and tasting" vanishes once it is given expression.[71] This is also why it was important for Ibn al-ʿArabī to emphasize al-Khaḍir's words: "I possess knowledge that you do not possess and you possess knowledge that I do not possess."[72] One might wonder what knowledge Moses possessed and al-Khaḍir did not. If knowledge was given to al-Khaḍir instantly and as a gift, what sense is there in saying that he *possessed* knowledge of anything? There is even a sense in which the knowledge that Moses possessed, which is knowledge of manifestation, is incomparably richer than al-Khaḍir's knowledge of nonmanifestation. Judged from the extreme viewpoint of mystics, the knowledge that Moses possessed might as well be denied all rights to be reckoned as such; but at least he possessed something. He could apply *this* rule to *this* case and come out with *these* judgments. The judgments might turn out to be false, but they will still be judgments. The fact that the spiritual meanings that descend onto the words become something else, something actually impossible as Ibn Ṭufayl says, does not prevent these meanings from descending. Manifest words are still the best, and perhaps the only carriers of knowledge and nonmanifest meanings cannot be tasted except in the manifest domain. Qayṣarī explains: "The *sakīna* abided by [the ark] because out of inner love, the real, universal, meanings kept moving till they arrived at the presence of witnessing and entered under the name Manifest. It is here that the wayfarer finds the meanings [embodied] in forms and finds peace ... That is why certitude and the science of tasting ... are possible only in the presence of the sensible. Through the intermediation of this presence, the world has become the farm of the hereafter and the *sakīna* of the lord."[73]

The emphasis in this passage is on love and motion, two crucial elements in Ibn al-ʿArabī's interpretation of the incident of the killing of the Egyptian by Moses. After killing the Egyptian, Moses fled from the people, saying: "I fled from you as I feared you." He did not say that he fled from them because of his love of safety and security. This is despite the fact that love rather than fear was the real reason behind the motion of fleeing.[74] This does not mean that Moses felt no fear. Fear was certainly there, applying to a definite form of action. But the function that the form of fear fulfilled was directed toward the relationship between Moses and other creatures, to be distinguished from the creative function of the form of love that directed Moses toward a relationship with his creator. This resembles the difference between the form of the relationship between Ḥayy and fire, which was based on fear, and which was weaker in affection and less illuminating than the form of the relationship of love. To recall, one of the things that Ḥayy loved about fire is that it constantly moved up toward the source that it resembled and which provided the light that was responsible for the beginning of life and motion.

Moses moved out of love for safety and security. As Qayṣarī says, love was the reason that the *sakīna* abided by the ark: the spiritual or nonmanifest meanings moved until they found peace in the manifest sensual domain. What Qayṣarī says next seems to be an antithesis to all mystical conventions: He explains that certitude and mystical tasting are possible only in the sensible or witnessed domain. This is strange because it is usually thought that sensible reality is a veil that hides and obstructs the spirit, and that spiritual achievement occurs only when the shackles that bind the mystic to the sensible world are disposed of. To consider his meaning more closely and examine more carefully the manner in which Ibn al-ʿArabī depicts the relationship between the nonmanifest and the manifest domains, let us look at the discussion that Ibn al-ʿArabī provides for the wisdom behind the slaughter of the male children in *Fuṣūṣ al-Ḥikam*: "The wisdom of the slaughter of the male children because of Moses was that the life of each boy killed because of him might revert to him as strength, since each one was killed as (potentially) being Moses. There was no ignorance in the matter, since the life of each boy killed because of him had to revert to Moses, each life being pure and innocent, unsullied by selfish aims and in the state of *Yea, indeed*. Moses was thus a fusion of each life taken in his stead."[75]

The day of "Yea, indeed" is the Day of the Covenant, when God turned to the souls in their state of purity and asked them whether he was their lord. The souls responded by saying "Yes we witness."(Q 9:172) In *al-Tajalliyāt*, Ibn al-ʿArabī mentions the state of Yea following a mention of the Doom of Arīn. The commentator Ibn Sawdakīn explains that Arīn is situated at the equator, where night and day are equal. In addition, he says that the Spring of Arīn is the spring of knowledge that is balanced in correspondence to the equilibrium that abides between day and night in that region. Osman Yahya points out that all the texts that are related to the Doom of Arīn, such as Ibn Ṭufayl's *Ḥayy*, refer to the myth of the birth of the first human being when he first appeared on the face of the Earth.[76]

Ibn al-ʿArabī establishes an interesting connection between the state of the soul at the Day of the Covenant and the state of purity characteristic of the souls of the children killed because of Moses. It is due to this purity, or emptiness, that the souls were especially strong. Notice how Ibn al-ʿArabī employs the example of the control that a little child exerts on an adult to explain his subtle meaning: "Do not you see how the child acts on the older person in a special way, so that the older person comes down from his position of superiority, plays and chatters with him, and opens his mind to him. Thus, he is under the child's influence without realizing it."[77] This observation is very deep indeed and deserves more attention than what I can provide here. The important point to notice now is related to the special power that the child possesses to move the adult despite his dependence on him. In this, there is what can be seen as an inversion of sorts, as the independent becomes dependent on the dependent,[78] and the reference is to the relationship between creation and the Real. Despite his immense richness and independence (*ghinā*), the Real needs creation to give manifestation to his love to be known. Creation makes the Real incline and move downwards, exactly as the adult moves downward in the direction of the child. The dependence that rules over his independence makes him move and descend. We can always say that it is actually the dependence of the independent on himself because the dependent, the world, is included in the independent, as there is nothing that the Real does not encompass. In this sense, we should speak about self-revelation rather than about revelation through the other because there is no other. Ibn al-ʿArabī, however, makes it clear that there is a difference between the Real's seeing himself through himself and seeing himself in the mirror of the world,[79] as the difference makes for the possibility of creating the world and the human being, who assists the Real in being known.

Staying in the same context of the discussion, Ibn al-ʿArabī brings two other subtle allusions. First, he refers to the tradition concerning the Prophet's exposing himself to the new rain and his saying that it is close in time to its lord.[80] He emphasizes that although the rain is an inanimate object, it moved the Prophet, the best of humans, and made him expose his head. In another allusion, Ibn al-ʿArabī compares human pregnancy and life formation to the life formation of plants. Ibn al-ʿArabī finds another instance of the combination of motion and water in the example of the earth that is moved and lives by the water, as in God's saying "*and it quivers* in its pregnancy, *and swells* in its bringing forth, and brings forth every joyous pair."[81] The reference is to Q 22:5, which describes the stages of conception and the formation of the human fetus and compares this with the formation of life from earth: "And (further), thou seest the earth barren and lifeless. But when We pour down rain on it, it is stirred (to life), it swells, and it puts forth every kind of beautiful growth in pairs."[82]

If there is a perfect description that brings the naturalistic and the traditionalistic accounts of birth together, then this is the one, for the beautiful growth in pairs is the work of polarity inherent in all that is given birth or is manifested from earth. Ibn al-ʿArabī compares this to the unity of the Real that becomes a multiplicity due to the multiplicity of the divine names, which is based originally on the duality of the names Manifest and Nonmanifest. This duality inherent in unity displays itself in all beings, as well as in their deeds. However, this bringing together of unity and duality or multiplicity comes in the subtlest form and is hidden from the eyes of most people, as it designates the paradoxical unity of the manifest and the nonmanifest, its very opposite. This subtlety is what the Qur'ān seeks to show by displaying to Moses acts that he once performed and that he seems to have forgotten: assisting the Midians in building a wall, which is repeated by al-Khaḍir's third act of rebuilding the wall; killing the Egyptian, which is repeated by al-Khaḍir's killing the youth; and finally, but coming first because it is first in the order of the history of Moses, the ship that resembles the ark that carried him to safety and that contained the lord's *sakīna*.

Ibn al-ʿArabī draws our attention to the Coptic derivation of Moses's name; for *mu* means water and *sa* means tree. "Thus he [Pharaoh] named him according to where he found him, since the ark stopped by the tree in the water."[83] This brings us back to Ibn Ṭufayl, whose traditionalistic account of Ḥayy's birth bears a close similarity to the biblical story, as both include a mention of the thicket of reeds and the crying of the child inside the basket.[84] Now the word that Ibn Ṭufayl uses for thicket is *ajimma*, which he uses again in his mention of the incident of the burning of fire in a thicket of reeds. The naturalistic birth of Ḥayy symbolizes the birth of the illuminated saint and is placed in parallel to the birth of Moses, the prophet. As we have seen, by applying the two accounts of naturalistic and traditionalistic births, Ibn Ṭufayl seeks to portray this prophethood-sainthood relationship in terms of complementarity, as he keeps revisiting the pointers that the two accounts contain and by this makes the connection tighter.

I wish to conclude this chapter with the following story, quoted by Aḥmad Amīn in *Ḥayy Ibn Yaqẓān by Ibn Sīna, Ibn Ṭufayl, and al-Suhrawardī*: "As Emelio Gomez was searching … for the versions in which the story of Alexander Dhū al-Qarnayn was mentioned in the Andalusian folkloric myths, he came by chance upon a manuscript entitled: The story of Dhū al-Qarnayn and the Statue and the King and his Daughter. He found in it several stories related to Alexander, one of which mentions how he arrived at an island called Arīn and found therein a statue with a writing on it … that tells the story of the owner of the statue and that is similar to the story of *Ḥayy Ibn Yaqẓān* in many respects. For he was also the son of a king's daughter, who cast him into the sea. The waves carried him to a distant isolated island. There a gazelle took care of him and he grew under her protection and began thinking and rationalizing."[85]

CHAPTER 9

Gilgamesh: The One Who Saw the Abyss

THE BUILDER OF THE GREAT WALLS AND THE MAN-AS-HE-WAS-IN-THE-BEGINNING

The *Epic of Gilgamesh* tells the story of the king of the Sumerian city of Uruk between 2700 and 2500 B.C.[1] In addition to Gilgamesh, the *Epic* mentions names of other heroes, the most central of which is Enkidu. As John Maier says, "Gilgamesh and Enkidu, like most heroes of myth, are breakers of barriers, pushing their way beyond normal limits."[2] Gilgamesh is depicted right at the opening of the story as a breaker of barriers even as he is erecting one. He is the builder of the great walls of Uruk, especially "its inner wall, which no work can equal,"[3] much like the Qur'ānic Dhū al-Qarnayn, who erected the great defense barrier to protect the people, "who scarcely understood a word," from Gog and Magog.[4] The esoteric aspect of the *Epic* becomes apparent upon observing the manner in which its author opens it by praising Gilgamesh's deep knowledge of the unseen and his stating that Uruk's wall foundations were laid down by the Seven Sages.[5]

Gilgamesh is depicted as a merciless king who oppresses the weak and does not allow the son to go with his father, the young woman to go with her mother, or the bride to go to her wedded husband.[6] This depiction seems to be at odds with the later depiction of him as most loving and a great mourner who almost wastes his soul away in agony over his friend's death. As his citizens had raised their bitter cry to the sky, the gods heard their lamentation. Anu, the sky god, called Aruru, the Great Mother who created humanity, and ordered her to create an image equal to Gilgamesh, so that the two may square off against each other and Uruk may have peace.[7] Thorkild Jacobsen provides an interesting interpretation of the gods' conduct as they, with a remarkable insight, divined that Gilgamesh's superior energy and enormous capacity set him apart from others and rendered him lonely so that a companion, his equal in potential, would fill his loneliness and balance his destructive forces.[8] Aruru formed an image of Anu, the god of the sky, in her heart,[9] and then she pinched off clay and tossed it into the wilderness; then Enkidu was born. "He was clothed in the clothing of … the cattle god. He fed with the gazelles[10] on grass; with the wild animals he drank at waterholes; with hurrying animals his heart grew light in the waters."[11] Jeffrey Tigay indicates that Enkidu was modeled on primordial man and quotes lines from a Sumerian text that represent a likely antecedent to the wild depiction of Enkidu.[12] John Maier observes that there is nothing negative about this (wild) description of Enkidu because the gods were often imaged as animals.[13] Andrew George debates the human versus divine orientation of the *Epic* and seems to be strongly in favor of the view that *Gilgamesh* "was more about what it is to be a man than what it is to serve the gods."[14] He identifies his position with that of William Morgan who discerns in the *Epic* a stark insistence on the significance of the human values and acknowledgment of human limitations, and he warns that we should not read it as myth. George says that ancient Mesopotamian mythical compositions display two basic characteristics or features as, on the one hand, the composition centers on the deeds of gods and, on the other, it takes as its objective the exploration of the features of the social or natural world. *Gilgamesh*, he insists, draws closer to explaining the human condition rather than mythical or religious origins. This is why he sees the myths brought in *Gilgamesh* as incidental to the *Epic* and emphasizes Morgan's depiction of it as "a document of ancient humanism."[15]

Enkidu was created in the image of the gods like Gilgamesh, who was two-thirds divine and one-third human.[16] As Gilgamesh troubled the citizens of his city and blocked the way of children to their parents and wives to their husbands, so Enkidu troubled the man-hunter in the wilderness and blocked his way to the watering place.[17] Maier remarks that the man-hunter stands as a mediating figure between the civilized city and the wilderness.[18] Hence, I suggest that by blocking his way, Enkidu was actually trying to block the way of connecting the two realms of reality, he and Gilgamesh being its two naturalistic and traditionalistic representations.

The man-hunter turns to his father and complains that Enkidu does not allow him to work. The description of his distress and the role that Enkidu took in augmenting it remind us of the Ḥayy of maturity, for when Ḥayy "saw any animal pursued by a wild beast, or entrapped in a snare … he took it upon himself to relieve it."[19] Ḥayy sought to free nature of its limitations, a freedom that meant only containment for civilized hunters, such as the hunter from Uruk. The hunter complained that Enkidu filled up the pits he dug, tore the traps he set, and allowed the beasts to slip through his hands.[20] His father had a ready solution for him: Enkidu must be hunted down by a love-priestess, a prostitute,[21] who will show him her beauty and make him, The-Man-As-He-Was-In-The-Beginning, know what a woman is.[22] Six days and seven nights Enkidu and the priestess made love. "The gazelles saw Enkidu, they started to run, the beasts of the field shied away from his presence. Enkidu had defiled his body so pure, his legs stood still, though his herd was in motion. Enkidu was weakened, could not run as before, but now he had *reason*, and wide understanding."[23]

This combination of priesthood and prostitution seems odd. Making love to the priestess rendered Enkidu impure, and how can imparting impurity be associated with religion? Notice that although the woman in Genesis is the one who urged Adam to eat the fruit of the Tree-Of-Knowledge-Of-Good-And-Bad, the critical act of temptation was attributed to the serpent. Consider also God's reaction to the sinful act: "The man has become like one of us, knowing good and evil; what if he now reaches out and takes fruit from the tree of life also, and eats it and lives forever."[24] As we shall see later in this chapter, the way to eternal life is blocked before man. The way to knowledge, however, is opened, and it commences with coupling with another human being. This coupling endows man with reason and understanding.

Tigay wonders how these emotional and rational shifts should have been brought about by intercourse and states that we can only speculate about this matter. He says, however, that it is possible that a week of intimate physical connection with a human being made Enkidu realize where he belonged, but that this was still not enough to explain the physical changes that he suffered and that made the gazelles run off upon seeing him.[25] Concerning the reaction of the gazelles, he remarks that this might be because he had now acquired a human odor.[26] Concerning the changes in his emotional and rational capacities, he refers the reader to some speculations based on "folklore motifs," to the effect that following intimate contact, qualities might be transferred from one being to another.[27] In what follows, I will suggest an explanation that is related to the speculations raised by Tigay on the basis of Ibn al-ʿArabī's thought.

INTERCOURSE AS AN ACT OF WRITING

As Chittick points out, according to Ibn al-ʿArabī, intercourse is an act of writing: "The 'Book' is the joining of meanings to meanings … [M]eanings join together by virtue of following the joining of the letters. This joining of letters is called 'writing.' Were it not for the joining of the spouses, there would be no marriage act. The marriage act is a writing."[28] On the basis of this merging of marriage and writing, Claude Addas interprets Ibn al-ʿArabī's vision in which he witnessed the celebration of his nuptial union with the stars of the sky and the letters of the alphabet.[29] She also provides an interesting interpretation to another vision that Ibn al-ʿArabī witnessed in the Earth that was created from the remainder of Adam's clay: "In that world I saw a sea of land as fluid as water, I saw stones … that attracted one another like iron and a magnet. When they came together, they could not come apart without someone intervening, just as when one takes the iron away from the magnet without the magnet being able to hold on. But if one fails to separate them, these stones continue to stick to one another at a set distance; when they are all joined, they have the form of a ship … When a boat is thus constructed, its passengers jump into the sea, and then they embark for wherever they wish."[30]

In Addas's interpretation, the ship resembles the classical Arabic poem and the stones resemble words. When words are joined together, they make up the poem, which carries spiritual meanings and provides a means for the possessor of gnosis to travel in the world of imagination.[31] The word for poetry in Arabic is *shiʿr*. It is related to *shuʿūr*, which means both feeling and knowing. Surely the development of the rational faculty is related to the development of the emotional capacity. Recall the major advancement that Ḥayy's emotional explosion upon his mother-doe's death caused in his logical capacity. Recall also that according to Fārābī's *Book of Letters*, poetry is regarded as the first or the primordial stage in the development of the human philosophical sciences, which development culminates in the invention of logic. Now, for Ibn al-ʿArabī, imagination is another name for the *barzakh*. Ibn al-ʿArabī sees in the *barzakh* the root of the logical capacity, as the essence of this capacity lies in coupling or tying together two premises and as the *barzakh* is the "tie between the two premises."[32] It is what yields syllogism, the logical proof that is based on triplicity: "Proofs [*dalīl*] are always triple in configuration—there is no escape from that: two terms [*mufrad*] and that which brings them together [*jāmiʿ*]. This is the third term [*wajh*] in every two premises that cannot be avoided if results are to be produced. 'Every *A* is *B*,' and 'Every *B* is *C*.' Hence *B* is repeated, and the proof that *A* is *C* is established. The comprehending term is *B*, since it is repeated in the two premises."[33] *B* is a comprehending term; it yields understanding because it joins both *A* and *C* and, in virtue of this joining, it provides for *A* yielding *C;* that is, it provides for giving birth in knowledge.[34]

What rendered Enkidu impure was the fact that he had become the locus of giving birth. Enkidu was made to adhere to his lovemaking woman, even as man was destined in Genesis to adhere to his wife and even as the sexual union that took place between him and the priestess was closer to fornication than to lawful marriage.[35] For six days and seven nights, Enkidu was in actual union with the priestess. The two lovemakers emerged to the gazelles as one unity. With their primitive faculties, animals observed this union in terms of weakness. Even animals "knew" that in sexual union, the male is weak because he is needy and receptive and the female is strong because she is needed and giving: "There is no creature in the world who is greater in power than the woman due to a secret that is not known except for he who knows the reason for creating the world and with what motion the Real brought it into existence and that it is the conclusion of two premises, as the subject of sexual intercourse is a seeker in need and the object of sexual intercourse is sought and enjoys the supremacy over the subject in need since desire prevails. Thus it has become clear to you the level that woman occupies among the existents."[36]

What is the secret that renders woman the strongest creature on Earth, and how is this related to the matter of the origination of the world? As we shall see, even after he loses some of his strength, Enkidu was still able to hold his own or even win[37] in the fight against Gilgamesh, "the pattern of strength."[38] And yet the woman weakened and subdued the one who won over the son of a lord[39] and reduced him to the status of an obedient slave. This brings to mind what Ibn al-ʿArabī says in the context of explaining the power that the child possesses and by virtue of which it moves the adult, despite the child's weakness and dependence on the adult. As we have seen, Ibn al-ʿArabī applies this to the relationship between the Real and creation, as creation makes the Real incline and descend to the world exactly as the adult inclines toward the child. What makes the Real incline to creation is the power of love, as the Real renders love for knowledge as the reason for creating the world.[40] Thus, through love, the Real is tied to the world. In a sense, love renders the Real humbled. Ibn al-ʿArabī insists, however, that it is not the beloved but love that humbles and subdues.[41] Likewise, it is not this or that specific woman that subdued Enkidu but a mysterious sort of love, a love for belonging and unity. I will use another passage by Ibn al-ʿArabī to explain the meaning of this point. The words depict his unique naturalistic stand, which seeks to establish unity not only between natural creatures but also between the natural and the divine:

> Man is related to the animal because animals possess sensation and to the plant because plants possess growth and nutrition and to inanimate things because of the non-existence of sensation in them. There is originally nothing in existence that is not related to some other thing, even as the lord and the creature are related and as the creature seeks the creator and the creator seeks the creature … All things in existence are intertied with an essential tying. Understand therefore what I have alluded to in relation to this tying since it reveals an immense matter … and since from it is known the meaning of the statement of he who states that the world is originated and he who states that it is eternal even as both parties agree that the world is possible-of-existence and that each part of it is originated.[42]

Existents are related by means of an intrinsic or natural relationship, which means that it is in their nature to be related. This rule applies to the Necessary-of-Existence, the creator who seeks the created world. We can say that the world is originated and also that it is eternal thanks to the unique mutual seeking, which brings all things together while maintaining their differences at the same time. The fact that, left to itself, the world is a nonexistent entity does not prevent the creator from being related to it. On the contrary, it makes it possible for the creator to manifest himself in it, as an image is manifested in a perfectly polished mirror.

Only man can use words. But animals can sense and man can seek sensation in the animal owing to the existence of the faculty of sensation in it. Man seeks plants because plants possess the capacities to feed and grow and those exist in man as well. The fact that inanimate things do not possess senses does not prevent man from being related to them. On the contrary, the nonexistence of sensation in the part of inanimate things is actually what makes man able to seek them, exactly as the nonexistence of the world is what makes the creator able to seek (manifestation in) it.

Once union had taken place between the priestess and Enkidu, Enkidu was able to belong to those who use words. Although animals were not able to use words, they were still able to sense that which they did not possess. The gazelles run off, not necessarily to separate from Enkidu, but rather for him to follow and seek them by what they had in common, the natural purity that endowed them with speed and swiftness. Enkidu's body, however, was impure. He could not run as fast anymore, and now that he was taught words, the priestess could proceed with her game of temptation, persuading the enlightened Enkidu to stop roaming the wilderness with animals and to come to the great city, where he could meet a great king and be introduced to the holy place of the gods.[43]

IN COMPANY WITH GILGAMESH

Although a fight with Gilgamesh is what was waiting for him, what seems to have been driving Enkidu to lend an ear to the temptation is that "[w]ith his heart's knowledge, he longs for a deeply loving friend."[44] Gilgamesh, who was destined to be Enkidu's other half, possessed a developed sense of imagination, which found expression in his dreaming capacity: "Last night, Mother, I saw a dream. There was a star in the heavens. Like a shooting star of Anu it fell on me. I tried to lift it; too much for me."[45] Gilgamesh tries to move the star, and the outcome is a ferocious fight with Enkidu. Enkidu wins the fight, but it was not the winning of a fight that he was after but rather the winning of a friend's heart. It became clear that he came not to overwhelm and conquer but to seek and unite. Gilgamesh praises Enkidu, but instead of filling him with pride and honor, his words sweep him with a strange sense of sadness mixed with love. "Enkidu stood there, listening to his words. They caused him to grow pale. He sat down, weeping; his eyes filled [with tears], his arms went slack, his strength left him."[46] Although Enkidu stands as an equal match for the mighty power of Gilgamesh, he is no match for the overwhelming power of love, and now that the burden was too much for him to bear, he found himself complaining like a little child who has lost a dear thing: "My strength has turned to weakness."[47]

According to Jacobsen, the following suggestion by Gilgamesh, that he and Enkidu set out to kill the terrible Humbaba, the guardian of the cedar forest, came as his response to Enkidu's state. What is needed is a strenuous adventure full of hardship.[48] But Enkidu, who has the better knowledge of the wilderness, expresses a serious worry concerning Gilgamesh's suggestion because he had known well Humbaba, "whose anger is the flood … and his breath is death."[49] His warning is to no avail, and his knowledge of the wilderness appoints him instead a companion and guard to his friend. As the two companions proceed toward the battlefield, they exchange mutual encouragement; each time one of them experiences weakness, the other is there to strengthen him until the battle is won and the ferocious Humbaba is defeated.

The next episode opens with the goddess Ishtar attempting to seduce Gilgamesh, who has purified and cleansed himself following the battle with Humbaba to become her lover and husband. Gilgamesh, however, does not bend to seduction, reminding Ishtar of the calamities that she had brought to her lovers, thus refusing, not without contempt, her offer.[50] Ishtar beseeches Anu to make the Bull of Heaven kill Gilgamesh, and Anu warns her: "If you ask me for the bull, for seven years the land of Uruk will harvest only chaff."[51] But Ishtar assures Anu that she has stored up grain for the people. The bull appears and another battle commences. One more time, Enkidu stands by his friend's side and together they slaughter the Bull of Heaven. He also does not forget, upon hearing Ishtar cursing Gilgamesh, to tear out the thigh of the bull and throw it in Ishtar's face. Joyful and victorious, the two companions wash away the blood from their bodies and embrace each other as they walk along.[52]

ENKIDU'S DEATH

This series of joys at wining battles terminates abruptly upon Enkidu's having a dream about the gods in council and a debate about the day of fate that must bring death to one of the heroes for having slain Humbaba and the Bull of Heaven. Enkidu is chosen.[53] Vexed and troubled, Enkidu directs a curse against the man-hunter and the temple prostitute, who had seduced him towards civilization and was responsible for his bitter fate. When the god Shamash heard his curse, he reproached him for cursing the woman who fed him with the food of the gods and gathered him together with his beloved friend.[54] His anger is abated and, as Maier remarks, when Enkidu is persuaded by Shamash, he is most like Gilgamesh, his double, who will become in his turn identical with Enkidu. As for Enkidu's becoming identical with Gilgamesh, perhaps he means that, like Gilgamesh, he learns to accept the facts of life, death being one of them. As for Gilgamesh becoming identical with Enkidu, he thinks that reference can be made to the fact that following Enkidu's death, Gilgamesh will turn into a wild creature and behave much like Enkidu behaved in the wilderness.

Enkidu lies down in the bed of death, complaining to his friend that some god must be angry with him for deciding his fate in the bed of death instead of on the battlefield. Gilgamesh assures him that all creatures will be mourning him: "[Y]our mother is a gazelle … raised by creatures with tails, and by the animals of the wilderness, with all its breadth. The paths going up to and down from the forest of cedars all mourn you: the weeping does not end day or night."[55] Now comes the part when Gilgamesh becomes identical with Enkidu: "And after you, I [will cover my body with unshorn hair]: I will put on a dog-skin [and roam the wilderness]."[56]

Active identification with Enkidu means also sharing with him the same fears, the strongest of which being fear of death. Does it matter whether we are going to die tomorrow or in a year from now, as we realize that a year from now and a night less than that, we will be standing in the same position, sharing the same fears and facing the same fate? Loss of relatives takes away from death its abstract import and invests it with a new concrete meaning, a meaning that reduces to nothingness the space of time between now and then and puts us face to face with the only phenomenon that he who witnesses it will never be able to see to the end of it. Fear of death will prove to be the master that taught

Gilgamesh the most important lessons in life, as it was responsible for teaching Ḥayy many wisdoms. On the way to confront Humbaba, Enkidu expresses his serious worries concerning their chances to defeat the monster. Gilgamesh reminds him, however, that only gods are immortal, while man's days are numbered. He reproaches him for fearing death despite his great strength, a strength that will make a name for him that lasts even as he falls in battle.[57] Now, after lying down for twelve days on his deathbed and as if to prove his friend's old advice futile, Enkidu reminds Gilgamesh how bitter his fate is, for he will not die falling in battle but in bed like a weak person.[58] Gilgamesh, the rationalist, resorts to another "argument" to prove his case. He reminds Enkidu of his origins: His mother is a gazelle and his home is the wilderness. Now that he will be gone, the animals of the plain will lament him. Meadows and rivers and the paths of the cedar forest will cry for him. The mourning will be total because those who knew him in his civilized state and witnessed his glorious deeds will also bewail him.[59] Finally, Gilgamesh, brother and lover, will weep for him in the wilderness "like a wailing woman, howling bitterly."[60]

But Enkidu dies, and with him all rational means of justification. As Jacobsen indicates, confidence was available to Gilgamesh when death was known to him only in the abstract. Now that Enkidu's death becomes a concrete fact, realization descends on him in its most naked reality and he refuses to believe.[61] He defines his state as a state of sleep and, as Ḥayy tried to call his mother-doe, he tries to call Enkidu. Then, again like Ḥayy, he comes to the heart but it does not beat. Then he knows, but he still refuses to believe. Like an eagle, he circles over his friend, "Like a lioness whose whelps are lost he paces back and forth."[62] "Six days and seven nights he wept over him until a worm fell out of his nose."[63] The body must now be emitting a terrible smell and Enkidu must rest in his grave, but Gilgamesh insists on having his image engraved in gold.[64] By doing this, Gilgamesh seeks to keep his friend's memory alive by arresting it in a golden body. But this was only another rational attempt by him to alleviate his own pain and make up for an unbearable loss and to fill in the emptiness that Enkidu's death has left in his heart.

THE QUEST FOR ETERNAL LIFE

This might sound strange, but considering the extraordinary love that Gilgamesh had for his friend and the mountains of sorrow that burdened his heart, one might wonder why he should seek eternal life rather than quick death. If there is an afterlife, then by departing from this world he can hope to join his friend. If there is not, then at least he can join him in his bitter fate, as total annihilation must be so sweet a relief for a heart as aching and burning as his. First, there is no doubt that Gilgamesh's desire for attaining eternal life was caused in part by a grave fear of death, and that this fear is what seems to be leading him to roam over the hills, as Enkidu once roamed the wilderness, and to reach to Utnapishtim, The-One-Who-Has-Found-Life: "Me! Will I too die like Enkidu?

Sorrow has come into my belly. I fear death; I roam over the hills. I will seize the road; quickly I will go to the house of Utnapishtim offspring of Ubaratutu. I approach the entrance of the mountain at night. Lions I see, and I am terrified. I lift my head to pray to the moon god Sin: for … a dream I go to the gods in prayer: ' … preserve me!' "[65]

Suddenly Gilgamesh, the mighty hero who brought Humbaba to grief and slew lions and was especially insulting to the gods, fears lions and has become truly needy, imploring the gods to preserve him. Notice, however, that Gilgamesh brought Humbaba to grief and slew lions *with* Enkidu.[66] Now Enkidu, with his love and even more with his death, makes Gilgamesh come to appreciate life better and fear most of losing it. Not only does death humble him, but it makes him realize the limitations of mortal humans compared to immortal gods. Now he acknowledges these limitations, but he is not yet ready to submit to them. With Enkidu, he was able to conquer everything and stand in the face of gods but not in the face of death. The adventure that he undertakes now is but a continuation of their adventures. Success in carrying out his mission means a victory not only for him but for Enkidu, as well as the mortal humanity that he represents. To conquer death is to revenge against the gods, the messengers that brought death on man. Gilgamesh sought life, but he feared death because he wanted to be such that the memory of his beloved lives forever and mortal man proves to be worthy of immortality again. As I will explain later in this chapter, this renders the story of the Flood an integral part of the tale of the encounter with Utnapishtim rather than an unskillful insertion in it, as Jacobsen thinks.[67]

Gilgamesh sets out on his journey. He comes to the twin peaks where a fearsome Scorpion-man guards the coming and going of Shamash, the sun. This sentry inquires about Gilgamesh's reasons for undertaking his arduous journey and warns him that no mortal has reached The-One-Who-Has-Found-Life.[68] But after hearing Gilgamesh's story, he decides to open the gate of the mountain for him. Gilgamesh enters now a place in which darkness is so thick that he can not see behind or ahead of him.[69] He proceeds for twenty-four hours and sees in bright light "the grove of stones … carnelian it bears as its fruit, [and] vines hang from it, good to see, leaves formed of lapis lazuli, the fruit it bears alluring to the eye."[70] Now he arrives at Siduri, the tavern-keeper, whose dwelling place is at the lip of the sea.[71] As in his encounter with the Scorpion-man, here he immediately mentions Enkidu, not forgetting to emphasize that the fate of *mankind* overtook him. He also says that he has roamed the wilderness, implying that he is doing what Enkidu used to do. Gilgamesh has acquired total identification with Enkidu, his other half, as seeking life for himself became the same as restoring life for him. Gilgamesh presses Siduri to show him the way to Utnapishtim but Siduri warns him that from the beginning of days no one has been able to cross the sea. And even if it can be crossed, then there are the waters of death.[72] Siduri leads Gilgamesh to Urshanabi, the boatman who will travel with him into the sea for a month and a half. The boat arrives at the waters of death, and after serious hardship, they are able to cross them.

THE ENCOUNTER WITH UTNAPISHTIM

The first thing that Utnapishtim teaches Gilgamesh is that permanence is not necessarily the ideal thing to seek.[73] Who would want to build a house or extend hostility between enemies, or for the rising of the river to last forever? "From the beginning there is no permanence. The sleeping and the dead, how like brothers they are! Do they not both make a picture of death. The-Man-As-He-Was-In-The-Beginning and the hero: [are they not the same] when they arrive at their fate?"[74] It is said in a Prophetic tradition that people are asleep, and that when they die, they wake up. It is also said in another tradition that sleep is the lesser or younger death.[75] Thus, sleep and death create the same picture of death, and man's life is but a dream in man's sleep. When a man dies, then we know that his dream has been exhausted. If man's life is a dream, what sense is there in talking about its permanence? The difference between The-Man-As-He-Was-In-The-Beginning (Enkidu) and the hero (Gilgamesh) is as irrelevant as the difference between a short dream and a dream that lasts longer. When both meet the same fate, what difference does it make which lasted longer?

Utnapishtim's words must have seemed unconvincing to Gilgamesh, and rightly so. "I look at you, Utnapishtim. Your features are no different than mine. I am like you … Your heart burns entirely for war-making. Yet there you are, lying on your back. Tell me, how did you stand in the Assembly of the Gods, asking for life?"[76] Maier states that Gilgamesh is astonished that Utnapishtim does not look different from him, although he lived before the Flood. As for the idea that his heart burns for battle although he is lying on his back, Maier says that there is perhaps a reference here to the contrast between the warriors as human heroes and the resting figures of the gods.[77] In my interpretation, Gilgamesh wants to tell Utnapishtim something like the following: I look at you, Utnapishtim. You speak about death as man's unavoidable fate and you, a man like me, have fought your battle and attained eternal life. It is only because your heart had attained what it desired that it is capable of resting. So put aside the wise advices and tell me a real story, the story of the war that you waged on death and how you had come to win it. In my opinion, this way of reading the lines makes the connection with the following story of the Flood tighter and casts doubt on Tigay's statement that the story is incidental to the main theme of the Epic.[78]

In the city of Shurippak, the gods assembled and fixed their minds on making the Flood. Their determination to annihilate the human kind was supposed to remain a secret. The god Ea, however, was determined to divulge the secret, and he invented a cunning trick to do so. He spoke to Utnapishtim, but not directly. Rather, he repeated the words of the gods from behind the wall of reeds. Ea urged him to abandon his riches, destroy his house, and build an ark that will contain the seeds of living things to deliver him through the deluge into secure land. Later, when Enlil reproaches the cunning Ea for connecting with humans, Ea is able to claim that he did not connect with them, but that it was the clever

Utnapishtim who discerned the gods' meaning.[79] Thanks to the existence of the wall of reeds, Ea can maintain that he did/did not seek humans, as al-Khaḍir was able to say that he did/did not do the things that Moses attributed to him. Utnapishtim explains to Ea a certain difficulty about having to account for building the ark, as his people will be "asking questions." The cunning Ea has a ready solution, though: Utnapishtim will tell his people that Enlil hates him and that he can dwell no longer among them. Therefore, he must go down to the Apsū (abyss) to live with Ea, who in return will rain all sorts of prosperities on them. For this purpose, an ark is to be constructed and put at his service. The ark will serve as a device of salvation for him but damnation for his people, in accord with Ibn al-ʿArabī's interpretation of the wisdom of putting Moses in the ark and throwing him into the sea.[80]

It took Utnapishtim seven days to build the ark. The hour of the Flood has come. Not only Utnapishtim's heart is filled with horror, but also the gods: "Ishtar cried out like a woman giving birth … The days of old are turned to clay since I spoke evil in the Assembly of the gods? How could I speak evil in the Assembly of the gods? How could I cry out for battle for the destruction of my people?"[81] As Ishtar took part in determining Enkidu's bitter fate, so she partakes here in determining the bitter fate of all humans. The goddess's words, "The days of old are turned to clay," are a reminder of Gilgamesh's words in mourning his friend: "Enkidu, the friend I love, has turned to clay."[82]

Ishtar pledges that she will never forget the terrible days of the Flood. In addition, she prevents Enlil from attending the offering because he brought about this calamity on her people without discussing the matter in the assembly of the gods. Now Enlil arrives and is furious because, according to his scheme, no man was meant to outlive the disaster. Ninurta informs him: "Who but Ea can create things? Ea knows all the Word."[83] Ea opens with a list of advices to Enlil on how he should handle the affairs of humans in future times, but he still insists: "I, *I* did not unhide the secret of the great gods. Utnapishtim the over-wise, a vision was shown to him; he heard the secret of the gods." Utnapishtim interrupts the story to require of Gilgamesh to think deeply about Ea's words.[84] Then he proceeds to tell him about Enlil's response to Ea's words. Enlil comes to Utnapishtim, takes his hand, and raises him and his wife from the ark. Then he praises them and declares that they shall be transformed to become like gods.

Two questions present themselves immediately: Why does Utnapishtim interrupt the narrative to demand that Gilgamesh think about Ea's words, and what is the explanation for Enlil's quick shift of mind upon hearing Ea's words? It turns out that the two questions are related. In Utnapishtim's words, there is an allusion, a drawing of the attention of Gilgamesh to the fact that although it was Ea who revealed the secret of the gods to Utnapishtim, the secret would not have been revealed had not Utnapishtim been there to receive the revelation. Thus, although there was a smell of pretension in Ea's denial of the charge directed against him, what he said was not completely inadequate. As a matter of fact, his words were so convincing that Enlil decided to lift Utnapishtim immediately to the level of the gods and to fix his dwelling place at the mouth of all rivers.[85] Gilgamesh must think about this because it seems that he came to receive from a person what a person should receive only from the gods. This is not to say that Gilgamesh was a man without achievements in the mystical way. Far from it, in fact: he came very close to mystical revelation, and the lesson that Utnapishtim had taught him will be engraved in his mind, never to be forgotten. Meanwhile, Gilgamesh has not fully grasped the allusion and there is need for an object lesson: "In your case, now, who will assemble the gods for you so that the life you seek you may discover? Test yourself! Don't sleep for six days and seven nights."[86] The assumption is that if Gilgamesh will not be able to conquer death's younger brother, then he has no chances of conquering death itself. And his failure was total because he fell into deep sleep even as he was sitting. Utnapishtim's wife asks him to touch the man so that he wakes up and goes home, but he reminds her of the nature of man, as Gilgamesh will deny that he had fallen asleep as soon as he is awakened. Thus, he asks her to bake a loaf of bread every day that Gilgamesh sleeps. When Gilgamesh is awake and makes the claim: "As soon as I was ready to fall asleep, right away you touched me and roused me,"[87] the condition of the loaves of bread will show his words to be false. Then, with a broken heart, he will say: "What can I do, Utnapishtim? Where can I go? … Death lives in the house where my bed is, and wherever I set my feet, there death is."[88]

Now Gilgamesh seems to have finally begun to understand. Once on his journey to Utnapishtim's place, as he dug wells and dressed in the skin of animals, he was reproached by Shamash for forsaking civilized life, and he replied: "I have lain down to sleep full many a time all the(se) years! (No!) Let my eyes see the sun."[89] But he can see now that he cannot fight death because death is an enemy that dwells within him. Utnapishtim asks Urshanabi to take Gilgamesh home. As the two were about to set out, Utnapishtim's wife convinces her husband to grant Gilgamesh a special gift. Utnapishtim acknowledges the great efforts that Gilgamesh invested in coming all the way to his place, and he announces that he will reveal to him a dear secret of the gods. A plant that bears the name The-Old-Man-Be-Made-Young can be found in the abyss, and Gilgamesh can eat it and become young again. Gilgamesh plunged deep into the abyss and came out with the plant. But instead of eating it immediately, he declares: "Urshanabi, this is the plant … by which a man can get life within. I will carry it to Uruk of the Sheepfold; I will give it to the elders to eat; they will divide the plant among them. I too will eat it, and I will return to what I was in my youth."[90] Maureen Kovacs sees in Gilgamesh's behavior a lack of faith in Utnapishtim because instead of eating the plant on the spot, he decides to test it on an old man first.[91] I doubt that this is a valid reading, even as his translation reads: "I will bring it to Uruk-Haven, and have an old man eat the plant to test it."[92] Rather than seeing in Gilgamesh's behavior an indicator of his lack of faith, it should be seen as an indication of the fact that he looks at himself as the carrier of a mission—the mission of fulfilling the dream of humanity to acquiring immortality.

Even his humble wish to rejuvenate a number of old people is denied to him. A snake appears and snatches the plant while he is bathing. Now, he turns to Urshanabi and, with a broken heart, complains that his toil and suffering ended in nothing. He concludes his journey with the following words: "Go up, Urshanabi, onto the walls of Uruk. Inspect the base, view the brickwork. Is not the very core made of oven-fired brick? Did not the seven sages lay down its foundation?"[93] Tigay points out that for the final editor of the *Epic,* the only lasting achievements of Gilgamesh were the building of the walls of Uruk and the wisdom that he gained on his journeys.[94] Tzvi Abusch aptly depicts the liminal character of Gilgamesh's achievements in the following words: "[Gilgamesh] learns to take pride in realistic if monumental creations, man-made structures whose extent may be limited by divine and natural spheres that surround and intersect the area of the city, but which manage, all the same, to draw together the human and the divine, the civilized and the natural."[95]

IN THE UNDERWORLD

The wisdom that Gilgamesh acquired on his journeys is exemplified in the last Tablet in the *Epic.* Notice that the mention of the building of the walls of Uruk opened the *Epic,* and with this, Tablet 11 is closed. This may convince us that Tablet 12 in Sin-Leqi-Unnini's version is not part of the Old Babylonian version. Tigay, for example, argues that Sin-Leqi-Unnini may have found the Tablet appropriate because of his special occupation as a priest and exorcist and his interest in the world of spirits.[96] At any rate, my special interest in including this part in my discussion is partially due to its resemblance to the account of the encounter between Ḥayy and the human society in Ibn Ṭufayl's work.

The Tablet opens with Gilgamesh's mentioning that he lost a certain drum and a beater to the underworld. Bold toward the gods as usual, he accuses them of having a heart that is not good. And, as usual, Enkidu offers his help in bringing his belongings from the underworld. Then Gilgamesh gives him some advice: "Do not put on a clean garment: it will mark you as a foreigner. Do not smooth your skin with sweet-smelling oil from the bowl: They will swarm and settle all around you. Do not throw the throwing-stick on the underworld; Those the throwing-stick hits will turn, unharmed, and menace you … Kiss not your beloved wife, nor strike the wife you hated; kiss not your beloved child, nor strike the child you hated. The song of the dead will snap around you."[97] Enkidu, however, did exactly what Gilgamesh advised him not to do, and he got trapped in the underworld. Gilgamesh turns to the gods to ask for their help in rescuing his friend. Only Ea, "whose words make what never was before," responded by turning to Nergal and asking him to open a hole in the ground so that Enkidu's ghost emerges from the underworld and tells its ways to his friend.[98]

Enkidu's ghost emerges. To remind us of what had transpired earlier in the *Epic,* Enkidu asks Gilgamesh to sit and weep because his body has been eaten by vermin and filled with dirt.[99] Then Enkidu throws himself to the earth, explaining the fate of humans. He says that the one who has begotten one son lives under the wall, weeping bitterly, perhaps reminding us of the prostitute as Enkidu's curse touched her.[100] The one with two sons lives in a brick house and eats bread; the one with three sons will drink water from deep wells; the one with four sons, his heart rejoices; the one with five sons will live in the king's palace; the one with six sons will be truly proud. As for the one with seven sons, he will be "like a man close to the gods."[101]

When Shamash urged Enkidu to bless the prostitute, even as he cursed her, he decrees: "May the mother of seven be abandoned [for your sake]."[102] The mother of seven has a husband who is like a man close to the gods. Thus, there is a reference here to the condition of the prostitute when she is touched by Enkidu's blessing. The underworld, which is nothing but our world, is therefore the place of the manifestation of Enkidu's blessing /curse, the blessing /curse of The-Man-As-He-Was-In-The-Beginning, in actual reality, including the seven levels between the curse and the blessing, according to the number of sons begotten to the receiver of what he deserves. But the sons are not meant to be merely the sons of the flesh. Instead, each son designates a degree of wisdom, as seven degrees of wisdom enable one to become immortal, like gods and those who have been given life.

Ibn Ṭufayl divides Ḥayy's story into seven stages. In the seventh, Ḥayy arrives at unification with the divine. Then he meets Absāl, who warns him against engaging himself with human society. But he does not listen to the warning. He encounters people and casts his wisdom at them, as Enkidu threw his throwing-stick at the people of the underworld. But his wisdom does not affect them. Instead, they turn and put his life in jeopardy. From this, Ḥayy learns a valuable lesson: that the ways of the underworld, the world of humans, are convoluted, and that he should never kiss the son that he loves or strike the son that he hates. He learns that one should not serve wisdom in old skins because those who will be filled with it will blame the wine and the server and forget about themselves.

CHAPTER 10

The *Tale of Bulūqiya* between Ibn al-ʿArabī and *Gilgamesh*

THE TALE OF ḤĀSIB KARĪM AL-DĪN

There was once a great sage in Greece whose name was Daniel. Wisdom he had been given, but not a son to inherit it. The sage prayed to God to grant him a son, and God was quick to answer. He carnally knew his wife and she became pregnant.[1] The sage went on a sea journey, and his ship was ruined and his books were lost except for five leaves, which he laid in a box. As he felt his days were numbered, he turned to his wife, saying that after his death, she will give birth to a male child, whom she should call Ḥāsib Karīm al-Dīn and to whom she should give the five leaves. Upon reading them and conceiving their meaning, he will become the most knowledgeable man of his time.

But Ḥāsib did not fare well in school or in learning any sort of trade, and his mother sent him to the mountains to work with the woodcutters. The sequence of events leads to Ḥāsib's imprisonment in a well. As a reminder of Joseph's story, the woodcutters, who used Ḥāsib to fill their vessels with the honey that he had found in a well and then imprisoned him therein, told his mother that he had been devoured by the wolf.[2] In the well, a great scorpion fell down on Ḥāsib from a hole that proved to be an entrance to a vast gallery ending with a door of black iron with a silver padlock that held a golden key. As it will become clear later in this chapter, the door was a symbol for the entrance to the World of the *Barzakh*.

Upon opening the door, Ḥāsib saw a great lake and a hill of green emerald. On the hill was a golden throne, studded with all sorts of gems, and chairs made of silver, gold, and emerald. Next he saw huge serpents sitting on the chairs. One of the serpents approached him, bearing on its back a tray of gold holding a serpent that shone like crystal. Her face was human, and she spoke with eloquent tongue. She informed Ḥāsib that she was the queen of the serpents and asked him to relate his story to her. When he finished telling his story, the serpent-queen assured him that only good things should happen to him, meaning that she would help him go home, but she would like him to stay longer so that she may tell him her wondrous story with Bulūqiya.[3]

THE QUEST FOR THE PLANT OF LIFE

There was in the city of Cairo a just and knowledgeable king of the Banū Isrā'īl. The king had a son called Bulūqiya. After his father's death, Bulūqiya ruled justly, and his subjects lived in ease and harmony. It happened that one day, he found a casket of gold in one of his father's treasures. He opened it and found a book in which there was a mention of Muḥammad and that he shall be sent in the latter days and shall be the master of all humans. Bulūqiya's heart burned with love and longing for Muḥammad, and he was determined to leave his kingdom and roam the world until he gathered together with him. He took off his fine clothes and put on a gown made of goat's hair, and then he set out on foot toward Syria.

As we can see, the reason that Bulūqiya undertook his journey is the same reason that made Gilgamesh undertake his. In both cases, the reason has to do with the quest for love mixed with the longing for eternal life. Notice also that in both cases, kings are involved, and that the manner in which they abandon their riches and fine clothes and acquire the dressing gown of wanderers to set out on a long and critical journey is described in almost identical terms.[4] One of the necessities of mystical quests for knowledge, such as the one that Gilgamesh and Bulūqiya took upon themselves to initiate, is that the seeker quit riches. The possessor of riches is a prisoner who is possessed by what he possesses: "The Prophet, the possessor of perfect unveiling said: 'The possessors of riches are imprisoned,' and he who is imprisoned is delimited. But he who is destitute has no riches to delimit or imprison him, so he is not delimited by this delimitation of the possessors of riches."[5]

Bulūqiya arrives at Syria and walks to the seashore. There, he sails in a ship that takes him to an island. On the island, he sits to rest under a tree and is overcome by sleep. When he wakes up, he sees serpents the size of date palms singing the praises of Muḥammad. One serpent approaches him and inquires about his story. Then she informs him that Muḥammad's name is inscribed on the gate of Paradise and that the serpents love him because all that had been created was created for his sake.[6] When Bulūqiya hears the serpent's words, his love for Muḥammad becomes even stronger. He leaves the serpents and reaches another island, where he finds the serpent-queen. She listens to his story and asks him to carry her salutation to Muḥammad in case he gathers together with him.

Now Bulūqiya sets out to Jerusalem, where ʿAfān, the master of religious and spiritual sciences, dwells. ʿAfān had come upon a book that reads: "He who wears our lord Solomon's ring will rule over men and Jin[7] and birds and beasts and all creatures."[8] He also found in a certain book that "when Solomon died they laid him in a coffin and crossed the Seven Seas. As for the ring, no man or Jin could pluck it from our lord Solomon's finger and no navigator could cross the Seven Seas that they crossed with his coffin." In yet another book he found that "there was a certain herb, which if one squeezes it and anoints with the juice his feet he will be able to walk upon the surface of any sea without wetting his soles. And none could obtain this herb unless he had the serpent-queen with him."[9]

In both *Gilgamesh* and *Bulūqiya* is a warning that the heroes' destination is unreachable; and in both, their efforts prove to be in vain.[10] This is not to belittle the value of the attempt, but rather to emphasize the great effort that they exerted in breaking many barriers, even as they fell short of breaking the ultimate barrier between mortality and immortality. Notice the resemblance between what is said in ʿAfān's report and Urshanabi's warning to Gilgamesh: "Do not let your hand touch the waters of death."[11] The objective of Gilgamesh's journey was to reach the dwelling place of Utnapishtim, The-One-Who-Found-Life. In the Islamic tradition, this is al-Khaḍir. The following is Ibn al-ʿArabī's report of one of his encounters with al-Khaḍir. Notice what he says at the conclusion: "I was in the port of Tunis, on a small boat at sea, when I was gripped by pain in the stomach. While the other passengers slept I went to the side of the boat to look out at the sea.[12] Suddenly, in the light of the moon which on that particular night was full I caught sight of someone in the distance who was coming towards me walking on the water. As he drew level with me he stopped and lifted one foot while balancing on the other; I saw that the sole of his foot was dry. He then did the same with his other foot, and I saw the same."[13]

Bulūqiya finds ʿAfān and relates his story to him. When ʿAfān hears about the serpent-queen he almost loses his mind: "Take me to the serpent-queen and I will make you see MuḤammad. The time of Muḥammad is far indeed but if we take hold of the serpent-queen we carry her in a cage and we go to the mountain. As we pass the plants and as long as she is with us they will speak and inform us of their virtues.[14] For I have found in my books that there is a certain plant that bears such a description. If we take the serpent-queen she will lead us to it. When we find it we express it and extract its juice and release the serpent. We anoint our feet with the juice and cross the Seven Seas. Then we reach the burial-place of our lord Solomon and take the ring off his finger and rule even as he ruled … Then we enter the Sea of Darkness and drink the Waters of Life and Allah will keep us alive for the end of time to gather together with Muḥammad."[15]

ʿAfān does not reveal the secret behind the serpent-queen's capacity to make plants speak as humans. Perhaps the secret has its roots in *Gilgamesh,* as the serpent in the *Epic* had consumed the plant of rejuvenation and as a result, she came to acquire extraordinary capacities. The resemblance becomes stronger as we examine the conclusion of Ḥāsib's story, where the serpent-queen meets the fate that was appointed for her since the beginning of time, to die when Ḥāsib returns home and enters the public bath. She bids Ḥāsib to have her body cooked and divided into three pieces. The king will consume one piece and be healed of a lethal sickness. His minister will eat another piece and die.[16] And he, Ḥāsib, will eat the third piece and see the Seven Heavens and all that is therein to the

Lotus-Tree-Of-The-Limit. His sight will penetrate Earth, and he will see all that it contains. In an instant, he will become versed in all the arts, such as chemistry and medicine, in addition to the magical arts, such as the art of transforming metals into gold. The body of the serpent-queen proves to be a source of life and knowledge: life because she rejuvenated the king's body and knowledge because she rejuvenated Ḥāsib's soul and rendered it as pure as it was in the very beginning, when souls had enjoyed a perfect state of witnessing before the fall sealed their spiritual eyes and planted forgetfulness in their once-wakeful hearts. It seems certain to me that Ibn al-ʿArabī was familiar with *Bulūqiya*. Recall his mention of the plants that speak when one passes them in his imaginal visit to the World of the *Barzakh* in Chapter 8 of the *Futūḥāt*.[17] As Ibn al-ʿArabī says in this chapter, only visitors to this world are possessors of knowledge 1 (that is, knowledge of the essences of things) and knowledge2 (that is, knowledge of their manifestations in the world).[18] In Chapter 310 of the *Futūḥāt*, Ibn al-ʿArabī speaks about a certain revelation that results in the acquistion of many knowledges and that is caused by a striking (between the shoulders as in the Prophet's case) or a consideration (through question and answer): "In a similar way, someone opens his eyes and with one glance perceives everything from the Earth to the sphere of the constellations."[19] Likewise, Bulūqiya came to witness in an instant what is in heaven (that is, the science of essences), and what is on Earth (that is, the natural sciences).

ʿAfān and Bulūqiya manage to deceive the serpent-queen and lock her in a cage. The serpent wonders about the sons of Adam and the strange reward that they store for those who can inflict harm upon them but choose not to. But Bulūqiya assures her that he will release her as soon as he achieves his goal. Bulūqiya and ʿAfān find the plant and take the serpent back to where they captured her. There, they release her as they promised, and now the serpent asks the companions about the purpose of taking the plant. They tell her that it is to reach Solomon's burial place and take his ring. The serpent says: "How an impossible thing you have asked for! No taking of the ring is possible … It is Allah's gift to Solomon by which gift he distinguished him [from all humans] … You should instead obtain The-Plant-That-He-Who-Eats-It-Shall-Not-Die, since this will be better for you … When they heard her words they repented a great deal and set out in their way."[20] The serpent goes back to her winter dwelling place in the mountain Qāf, which encircles the world, whereas ʿAfān and Bulūqiya cross the Seven Seas while applying the juice to their feet. They come to an island on which they see a stream of running water and a soaring mountain of green emerald. They find that the soil of that island is made of musk, which is a reminder of Ibn al-ʿArabī's mention of one of the worlds of Earth, whose soil is made of musk as well.[21] The two companions finally arrive at Solomon's burial place. As they try to pluck the ring from his finger, a huge serpent appears and blows fire that turns ʿAfān to ashes. Bulūqiya is saved and is found weeping bitterly upon remembering the warning of the serpent-queen.

THE MYSTICAL DIMENSION

A sequence of events commences as Bulūqiya crosses the Seven Seas. After crossing the first sea, he comes to an island that is much like the Garden of Eden, whose soil is saffron and whose gravel is carnelian. In this, there is a reminder of what Ibn al-ʿArabī says in Chapter 8 of the *Futūḥāt*: "Among its Earths there is no Earth that was fairer in my eyes or that suited my temperament more than the Earth of saffron. Of all the peoples of the other Earths I had never seen a people whose souls were subtler than theirs or who were more welcoming to their guest … One of its miracles … is that you pick one of its fruits and the time you pick it is the time of its regeneration. None but the witty perceives its renewal."[22] In this, there is direct reference to the Qur'ānic depiction of the fruits of the Garden of Eden as neither picked nor forbidden. It is not by accident that the inhabitants of the Earth of saffron are depicted as possessing the subtlest of souls. It is because the food that nourishes them, like the Earth that they inhabit, is most subtle.

Bulūqiya crosses the second through the fifth seas and comes to a small island: "Its soil and mountains are like crystal. In it there are the veins from which gold is made and trees bearing flowers in gold-like color … As the flowers wither under the sun they fall on the ground and gather under the rocks to become the elixir and to be used for making gold."[23] Compare to Ibn al-ʿArabī's description of the Earth whose soil is made of musk, in which he saw a "land of red malleable gold. In it there are trees all gold bearing golden fruits. A person would take an apple or some other fruit and eat it to find that it possesses an indescribably delicious taste and a delicate scent. I saw that the size of these fruits was so tremendous that were a single fruit to be placed between Earth and sky it would hide the sky from people's sight or upon Earth and it would surpass it by many-old. And yet a person encloses it with this familiar hand due to its gracefulness and air-like subtlety."[24]

Bulūqiya crosses the sixth sea and comes to another island, the description of which brings to mind the first account of Ḥayy's birth: "He saw two mountains covered with a large number of trees. The fruits of these trees are like the heads of humans hanging by the hair."[25] Bulūqiya proceeds to cross the seventh sea, and he comes upon yet another island and walks on it for hours. He finds an apple tree and stretches his hand to pick one of its fruits, and suddenly a huge person cries out and warns him: "You are the son of Adam and your father had forgotten the covenant that he made with his lord and ate of the tree."[26] The sequence of events leads Bulūqiya to the mountain Qāf. There he meets a great angel, who explains to him that mountain Qāf encircles the world. He also informs him that the roots of all the worlds are in his grasp, so whenever God wishes to make an affair arrive newly in the world, he commands him and he carries out the command without making the slightest shift from his fixed place.[27]

After leaving the angel, Bulūqiya walks toward the west, where he comes upon two persons, one with the semblance of a lion and the other of a bull. They were sitting and guarding a certain door. He inquires about the door and what is within it, but they deny that they possess knowledge of it and explain to him that none may open the door but the archangel Gabriel. So Bulūqiya prays to God, and God "commanded Gabriel to descend to Earth and open the door of the Meeting-Place-Of-The-Two-Seas so that Bulūqiya may enter and see what was within it … Bulūqiya saw a vast sea half salt and half fresh, encompassed by two mountains made of red carnelian. Bulūqiya proceeded toward the mountains whereon he saw angels occupied with praising and hallowing the lord. He inquired about the sea and the two mountains and the angels said: 'This place is situated under the Throne and this sea provides for all the seas in the world. As for us, we divide the waters and drive them to the lands, the salt to the salt land and the fresh to the fresh land. As for the two mountains, God created them to contain the waters.'"[28] This is a straightforward reference to the mention of the *barzakh* in the Qur'ān. The presence of the *barzakh* in Chapter 8 of the *Futūḥāt* is most vivid, as it is mentioned twice and the example of the two seas is discussed at length.[29] It is also clear that the sea under the Throne provides for the seas in the world, not in terms of corporeality but rather in terms of essence; it provides the essences or the fixed entities of saltwater and freshwater. The essences do not intermingle and, as a result, the salt corporeal water and the fresh corporeal water, which are in their image, do not intermingle as well.

After relating his story to the angels, Bulūqiya anoints his feet with the juice and sets out upon the face of the sea. On his way, he encounters a good-looking youth who salutes him. Then he sees the four archangels in their way to cast into hell a huge dragon that had appeared in the East. Next, Bulūqiya comes to an island where he finds a good-looking youth sitting between two tombs weeping and mourning. This will be the beginning of the story of Janshāh.

At this point, Ḥāsib interrupts the serpent-queen's story and beseeches her to bring him to the surface of the Earth. As a matter of fact, this was not the first time that Ḥāsib pleads for help. On a previous occasion, the serpent-queen explains to him the reason for her reluctance to carry him to the surface of the Earth: "You should know Ḥāsib Karīm al-Dīn that once you emerge to the surface of the Earth you will go to your people and enter the public-bath. As soon as you will have finished bathing I die, since this will be the cause of my death. Ḥāsib said: 'I swear I will never enter the public-bath as long as I live, and when I must I will wash my body at home.' The serpent-queen responded: 'Even if you swear with hundred oaths I will not believe you and this thing will never pass. You should know that you are the son of Adam and that a convenant with you is good for nothing. For your father Adam made a covenant with God and violated it even as God had fermented his clay for forty days and made the angels prostrate themselves to him.'"[30]

This description of the lack of faith in man finds its parallel in Utnapishtim's counsel to his wife: "A man who is trouble will give you trouble."[31] More interesting is the serpent-queen's prophecy that the moment that Ḥāsib washes in the public bath will be the time of her death. As we can see, the connection has nothing to do with the physical act of washing, or else there will be no sense in Ḥāsib's promise to wash his body (privately) at home. In my opinion, the connection has to do with the symbolic significance of washing in a public bath (that is, washing in common with other members of the community), as this draws the person away from the realm of the esoteric. The connection gains in symbolic depth as we consider the affinity that there is in religious and mystical traditions between washing in (cold) water and acquiring knowledge. For example, it is said in the name of a famous Jewish mystic: "As far as attaining [mystical knowledge and experience] is concerned, there is nothing more necessary and needful for man than to immerse himself in water."[32] Also, it is said concerning the same mystic that he used to immerse himself in cold water even though he was suffering from a certain disease and was not supposed to do so.[33] The reason for bathing in cold water is explained by Ibn al-ʿArabī: "Because of the heat we have mentioned that is found when the angel casts [revelation into the heart]. God's messenger used to say at the opening of every prayer [*ṣalāt* in Chittick] and in most states, 'O God, wash us with snow,' 'with cold water,' or 'with hail.' All three of these are cold things through which the heat of revelation is counterbalanced, for it burns."[34]

As it turns out, when Ḥāsib comes back to his community, he eventually does wash in the public bath, which leads to the serpent-queen's death as prophesized. In *Gilgamesh,* we find the parallel to this in the story of Enkidu, who "knew neither people nor homeland … He fed with the gazelles on grass; with the wild animals he drank at waterholes; with hurrying animals his heart grew light in the waters."[35] It is at the watering place that the hunter found Enkidu, and with the help of the harlot, he was able to subdue him and to seduce him toward civilization and turn him from The-Man-As-He-Was-In-The-Beginning into a man who lives in public. This will be the cause of his death. Enkidu was primitive but pure. This is why it was said that following his cohabitation with the harlot, he became impure. But then it was said that his rational soul was broadened. His intuitive soul, The-Soul-As-It-Was-In-The-Beginning, became seriously delimited, though. He could then fight monsters and challenge gods, but he could not become the child of nature that he once had been. The moment he mated with the harlot was the moment his death was fixed, even as Gilgamesh thought, with his developed rationalized mind, that his fate could be altered or at least postponed.

The serpent-queen reminds Ḥāsib of the treacherous nature of man, but he and the other serpents continue to beseech her to release him. Finally, she succumbs and requests of one of her serpents to carry him to the surface of the Earth. Assured of returning home, he wanted now to hear the end of Janshāh's story—the story of the young man whom Bulūqiya found sitting between two tombs—and listened to his strangest adventures. The serpent-queen then relates to him the end of Janshāh's story, which connects with the end of Bulūqiya's. After hearing Janshāh's long and sad story, Bulūqiya leaves him and walks until he arrives at a great sea. He sets out upon its water and comes to an island, the description of which removes all doubts that Ṣūfī thought is at the heart of the tale. This island is visited by saints (*awliyā'*) and poles (*aqṭāb*), who come to it each Friday and stay therein as God's most welcome guests. Then Bulūqiya sees al-Khaḍir, who bids him to hang on to him. With one single step, he makes it all the way to Cairo. Let me conclude this chapter by completing the quotation that I brought above from Addas's *Quest for the Red Sulphur*, and which describes Ibn al-ʿArabi's witnessing of al-Khaḍir's walking on water without wetting his soles: "After that he spoke to me in a language which is unique to him; he then took his leave and went off in the direction of the lighthouse which stood at the top of a hill a good two miles away. It took him three paces to travel the distance."[36]

Conclusion

I have used Ibn Ṭufayl's *Ḥayy Ibn Yaqẓān* to present a liminal reading of the story of Islamic philosophy. This reading revolves around two accounts of Ḥayy's birth, naturalistic and traditionalistic, and attempts to construct a unitary concept of the nature of the relationship between the two accounts. I have attempted to show the manner in which Ibn Ṭufayl develops this unitary concept by employing a carefully deliberated analysis of the tenets of philosophical naturalism and a clever manipulation of and subtle allusions to religious contents.

Those who read *Ḥayy* for the first time get the impression that, with the exception of the introduction of the work, the description of Ḥayy's witnessing of the transcendent essences, and the encounter with the human society, the work is one continuous depiction of rationalistic presentation and logical elaboration. Hence, Hourani's view that the main aim of the work is to assert the possibility of the soul's unaided assent to Truth and Hawi's overlooking of its mystical import seem to be justifiable. Even Gauthier's argument that the concluding part of the work, which deals with the problem of the harmony between philosophy and religion, is its most important part is based on the impeccability of its logical plan. Hence, reservations against Hourani's and Hawi's views, provided those can be sustained, also must hold in relation to Gauthier.

My main objection to the rationalistic depiction of Ibn Ṭufayl's work, as well as works of other thinkers, is that they fall short of distinguishing between the form of the thinker's argument and the drive that sets his argument in motion and dictates its presentation. I think this shortcoming lies behind the reflection of certain scholars on Plato as a mystical antagonist: "But the difference between Plato and the mysticism that has attached itself to his philosophy is essential. Plato's aim is to take the reader by steps, with as severe a logic as the conversational method permits, to an insight into the ultimate necessity of Reason."[1] Plato states explicitly, however, that the essence of truth cannot be delivered by words and that illumination occurs only at the limit of rational discourse when arguments are exhausted and conversations are brought to a halt and the mind is flooded with light.[2] Moreover, Plato says that when it comes to the enquiry concerning real things or the essences, the power of reason becomes unable "to aid the man who has not an inborn affinity with the subject."[3] In this, there is a reminder of the role that Ibn Ṭufayl assigns to the inborn nature that is called *fiṭra* and the distinction that he draws between it and quick-wit, which he identifies with the formal or logical capacity. This means that for Plato, as well as for Ibn Ṭufayl, the part of rational argument that bears logical fruit is situated between a beginning that is tied to an inborn affinity and an end that is unbound by the limits of its formal presentation.

The light of illumination is the driving force that employs rational argument as a tool to achieve mystical ends, as Ḥayy in Ibn Ṭufayl employs fire and the mind in Plato employs the eye to see.[4] Failing to be aware of this compels us to consider the possibility that our thinkers contradict themselves, not in relation to this or that argument, but rather in relation to a major methodological principle and a declaration that they make with the utmost solemnity to the effect that rational deliberation is or can be delimiting. Notice how Huntington Cairns seems to be unaware of this, as he attempts to turn Plato's dialectical moves in *Parmenides*, which are destined in my opinion to drawing mystical ends, into a blind adherence to rationalistic argumentation: "And he never hesitates to submit his own ideas to the harshest critical scrutiny; he carried this procedure so far in the *Parmenides* that some commentators have held that his own doubts in this dialogue prevail over his affirmations. But the beliefs of mystics are not products of critical examination and logical clarification; they are, on the contrary, a series of apprehensions, flashes, based on feeling, denying the rational order."[5] Neither Plato nor Ibn Ṭufayl denies the rational order. And yet this does not prevent them from fixing limits for rational consideration. In doing so, they abide by the dictates of reason itself because apart from acknowledging the limitations inherent in the very nature of the rational faculty, the possessor of reason will never be able to transcend its fixed limit and, by means of that, ascend to a higher level of intellection: "Hardly after practicing detailed comparisons of names and definitions and visual and other sense perceptions … at last in a flash understanding of each blazes up, and the mind, as it exerts all its powers to the limit of human capacity, is flooded with light."[6]

Similarly to Cairns, Abū al-ʿAlāʿ Afīfī claims that "mystics have no philosophical system or a fixed doctrine." However, he thinks that Ibn al-ʿArabī is an exception because "he has a definite philosophical doctrine of pantheism."[7] Although I have reservations about ʿAfīfī's identification of Ibn al-ʿArabī's thinking with pantheism, I do think that there is some sense in saying that he is an exception to the rule.[8] It is true that Ibn al-ʿArabī often emphasizes the limitations of rationalistic thought. However, as Chittick explains: "As a human faculty *ʿaql* (reason) almost always implies restriction and confinement, though on occasion the Shaykh will employ the term in a sense which suggests that it has transcended its limitation and become identical with the heart."[9] As a matter of fact, reason implies restriction and confinement not almost always, but absolutely. In this, however, Ibn al-ʿArabī finds its benefit: "This is the benefit of reason … for reason delimits its possessor, not allowing him to enter into that which is improper. That is why it is called 'reason,' from 'fetter.'"[10]

A sound judgment comes from a person who possesses reason and who is able to discern its limits. Ibn Ṭufayl and Ibn al-ʿArabī saw, in failing to be aware of this, the source of the limitation of theologians and philosophers alike. In dealing with the problem of the origination of the world, Ibn Ṭufayl demonstrates how it is possible to use this rational limitation to ascend to a higher level of intellection. The work of balance is apparent here. The opposing arguments do not cancel out; rather, they balance and complement and, in this sense, reinforce each other. The knower, who transcends the two opposing rationalistic stands, perceives this as an act of intellectual self-transcendence. Then, as if in a state of intoxication, he opens his mouth to loudly condemn rationalistic thinkers and the categorical confines with which they have chained themselves, as if they were held captive in a Platonic cave from which he, Ibn Ṭufayl, had managed to emerge. Fearing that *they* would be mistaken for an unqualified reference to the philosophers or to philosophy itself,[11] Ibn Ṭufayl knew that balance was called for one more time and, with Qur'ānic verses, uttered a severe condemnation of people "who had taken for their God their own desire (*hawa*) and passion (*shahwa*)."[12] According to Ibn al-ʿArabī: "God created the faculty named 'reason,' placing it within the rational soul to stand opposite natural passion when passion exercises control over the soul by diverting it from the occupation proper to it as specified by the lawgiver."[13] Chittick explains that the role that reason plays in opposing passion was especially important in medieval Islamic moral and spiritual teachings,[14] and that for Ibn al-ʿArabī, natural passion in itself is not a bad thing because its existence is crucial for the continuation of life. But the very existence of the rational faculty, which decides between right and wrong, renders passion a negative human condition.[15] Although the human being is a natural creature, humans are distinctive in that they possess souls that are endowed with a rational faculty. Insofar as the human soul employs its reason in controlling its passions, it is free morally. Insofar as it employs its reason in producing correct intellectual rulings, it is free intellectually. As it exaggerates its rationalistic tendencies, it finds itself trapped by the very passion that its rational faculty was destined to control; for now it is involved in accumulating intellectual riches in the form of rational arguments and seeks to defend whatever it possesses against nothing but another rational soul that is trapped in the same predicament. The outcome is endless, pointless conflict. There is no Hegelian salvage to be anticipated here, and our thinkers seem to have realized when it becomes crucial to get right to the point. The Idea can never be defined by reason because, like Ibn al-ʿArabī's *barzakhī* limit, it is what defines.[16] It can never be captured with words because, as Ibn Ṭufayl says, once it is joined to words, its truth is altered.[17] It is like the new creation that Ibn al-ʿArabī witnessed on Earth, and that is discerned only by the possessor of the state, who has become one with it, and similarly to the manner in which Ibn Bājja's knower becomes one with his object of knowledge.

For Ibn Bājja, this act of (intellectual) identification is actualized through rational or theoretical deliberation. For Ibn Ṭufayl, however, this sort of identification must be empty, an identification with a dead product. That is why it was important for him to name his hero "Living Son of the Wakeful." As the spirit of light, which is from God's Command never ceases to flow on the world to create life,[18] so must the living remain wakeful to receive it. Light flows constantly on the world and enjoys a permanent presence in it. Thus, the state of the living must be the state of the present or the moment (*al-ān*), which is the essence of time. However, as Aristotle says, the moment cannot exist as this or that or as any definite part of time. Rather, it belongs to the absent domain. Thus, the living must be absent even as he is present, as Ibn Sīnā says in *Ishārāt*; and this was the state of the Sleepers in the Cave mentioned in Aristotle and the Qur'ān. The living must remain wakeful because forgetfulness, which abides in sleep (the lesser death) and death (the greater death), is an especially threatening enemy, and one against which the living must always be on guard. When death approached Enkidu, the child of nature who was seduced toward civilization, he was terrified. Gilgamesh, the builder of Uruk's unmatched walls, however, reminded him of the great deeds that he had performed and the fame, name, and glory that he had gleaned. Enkidu refused to be consoled. His state resembled that of Ghazālī, who fell prey to agony when his books were taken from him. But then he had to be reminded that there was no point in possessing words that could be forgotten. Now that his very life was vanishing, Enkidu could not care less about the great deeds that he had accomplished. His deeds had become like words written in a book, defenseless as their author is no more.[19]

In the scholarship, it is believed that Islamic philosophers were, after all, only interpreters of Aristotle, and that they never swerved from the path of rationalism that he set up for philosophy. This, scholars say, is true not only in relation to Fārābī, who stated explicitly that with Aristotle, philosophy had reached a state of perfection, but also in relation to Ibn Sīnā, whose mystical works were shunned as insignificant; Ibn Ṭufayl, whose claim for illuminationism was interpreted as a cunning maneuver to attract audiences to his work; and, of course, Ibn Rushd, whom scholars had presented as divinizing Aristotle.

In this work, I have attempted to show that although the outward form of their argument is inevitably rationalistic, as it is drawn mainly from the works of Aristotle, the inward form, which drove it and determined the sort of liminal philosophical mysticism to follow from it, owes much to Plato's unique trend of mysticism. In the process, I have come to realize that Aristotle himself is not immune from the influence of Plato's mysticism, as his depiction of the nature of time and the infinite reveals.[20] In this sense, it would not be totally incorrect to say that the story of Islamic philosophy might be read as a rationalistic endeavor to understand what Aristotle, Plato's disciple, had perfected.

Ibn al-ʿArabī said that both Aristotle and al-Ashʿarī would have agreed with him, if he had rectified their argument.[21] Now whether by Aristotle is meant the historic Aristotle or the author of *Uthūlūjiya*, namely, Plotinus, the general tendency is to think that for Islamic thinkers, the views of the philosophers and those of the Ashʿarite theologians on the notion of creation are in total disagreement. And yet Ibn al-ʿArabī thought that he was capable of harmonizing their views. This is the declaration of the greatest of Islamic mystics. Surprisingly, it is also the declaration of Ibn Rushd, who "can rightly be reckoned as the staunchest exponent of the thesis of an eternal universe."[22] In my previous book, I discussed Whitehead's statement that the purpose of philosophy is to rationalize mysticism.[23] I consider this book as another attempt to achieve this purpose. However, as I emphasized there, I wish to emphasize here that I am not attempting to depict the activity of rationalizing mysticism in *finalized* terms but rather as a constant *activity* of finalization. This is why I find it useful to modify Whitehead's statement by saying that the purpose of philosophy is to rationalize mysticism and to mystify rationalism. I hope that with the use of Ibn Ṭufayl's philosophical story and Ibn al-ʿArabī's mystical insights, as well as the crucial contributions of other ancient and medieval thinkers, I have succeeded in making a humble contribution to achieve this purpose.

Notes

INTRODUCTION

1. Abū Naṣr Muḥammad al-Fārābī was born in 870 in Fārāb, Turkistan, and studied in Baghdad where he remained for more than forty years. He was a scientist, philosopher, and musician. Among his important works are *al-Madīna al-Fāḍila (The Virtuous City)* and *Risāla fi al-'Aql (Epistle on the Intellect)*. He died in 950 in Damascus. In the Islamic intellectual tradition al-Fārābī received the title "The Second Teacher", which indicates his serious influence on this tradition.

2. Muḥammad Ibn al-'Arabī was born in 1165 in Murcia, Spain. At the age of 35 he left Andalusia for good and lived in several places in the East including Egypt, Arabia, and Asia Minor. In 1223 he settled in Damascus where he died in 1240. Hundreds of works are attributed to him about 150 of which are extant. His most important works are *al-Futūhāt al-Makkiyya (Meccan Revelations)* and *Fuṣūṣ al-Ḥikam (Bezels of Wisdom)*. Since the end of the Twelfth century Ibn al-'Arabī became the most influential thinker in the Islamic intellectual tradition, inspiring a whole history of original interpreters of his mystical philosophy from Ṣadr al-Dīn al-Qunawī (d. 1274) to Dawūd al-Qayṣarī (d. 1350) all the way to Abd al-Ghanī al-Nābulsī (d. 1731) and 'Abd al-Qādir al-Jazā'irī (d. 1883).

3. Abū Ḥāmid al-Ghazālī was born in 1058 in Ṭūs. He received his education in Nishapur and Baghdad, where he also taught. In 1096 he left his teaching duties to become a wandering ascetic. He died in 1111 in Ṭūs. His most important books are *Iḥyā' 'Ulūm al-Dīn (Revival of the Sciences of Religion)* and *Mishkāt al-Anwār (Niche of Lights)*. Some scholars express the view that with his *Tahāfut al-Falāsifa (The Incoherence of the Philosophers)* Ghazālī brought about the end of Islamic philosophy that Ibn Rushd desperately attempted to rescue with his *Tahāfut al-Tahāfut (The Incoherence of the Incoherence)*. This view is severely limited as it is based on a narrow rationalistic conception of philosophy and the false belief that Islamic philosophy ended with Ibn Rushd. There can be no doubt, however, that Ghazālī was a major factor in establishing a mystical synthesis in the Islamic intellectual tradition between philosophy and theology. Abū 'Alī Ibn Sīnā was born in 980 in a village near Bukhāra. He received his religious and scientific education at a young age but was seriously troubled by Aristotle's

Metaphysics, which he could not understand till he read a short commentary on it by Fārābī. He worked in the service of several rulers and was incarcerated by one of them in a fortress. It is believed that during this period he wrote his mystical recitals. Ibn Sīnā was also a physician and wrote the famous *Canon of Medicine*. His most important philosophical work is *Shifā' (Healing)*. Ibn Sīnā died in 1037 and was buried in Hamadān. Ibn Sīnā is considered one of Islamic greatest thinkers of all times and had a considerable influence on the development of later Iranian philosophers.

4. Abū al-Walīd Muḥammad Ibn Rushd was born in 1126 in Cordoba to a family of legal judges. He was a philosopher, physician, and jurist. Among his works are his famous commentaries on Aristotle's philosophy and Plato's *Republic*, and his *Tahāfut al-Tahāfut (The Incoherence of the Incoherence*). He died in 1198 in Morocco.

5. Sāmī Ḥāwī, *Islamic Naturalism and Mysticism: A Philosophical Study of Ibn Ṭufayl's Ḥayy bin Yaqẓān* (Leiden: E. J. Brill, 1974), 3-4 (Hereafter cited as INM).

6. I think his failure to take this declaration seriously stands behind his rather apologetic statement that "our author's views *may* not emerge from this enquiry as completely original, but the attitude and spirit which spur them are of lasting significance to both Islamic culture and philosophy in general." Ibid., 4.

7. INM, 11.

8. INM, 56, 268.

9. INM, 56.

10. INM, 15, 243, 256.

11. INM, 254, 178, 251, 23. That Ibn Ṭufayl can be considered an existentialist is stated in Ibid., 240, 247.

12. INM, 230.

13. INM, 251, 26-28.

14. INM, 27.

15. William Chittick, *The Self-Disclosure of God: Principles of Ibn al-Arabī's Cosmology* (Albany: State University of New York Press, 1998), 253 (Hereafter cited as SD).

16. SD, 253. Ibn al-ʿArabī, *al-Futūḥāt al-Makkiyya.* 4 vols. (Beirut: Dār Sādir, 1968), 2, 30: 12-17, emphasis mine (Hereafter cited as FUT).

17. Aristotle, *The Basic Works of Aristotle*, ed. Richard McKeon (New York: Random House, 1970), *Metaphys.,* 5. 17, 1022a (*Basic Works* hereafter cited as BWA).

18. SD, 80; FUT, 4, 146: 11-12.

19. FUT, 3, 518.

20. FUT, 2, 47: 29.

21. FUT, 2, 30: 8-10.

22. FUT, 2, 47: 30.

23. SD, 65; FUT, 3, 405: 3-5.

24. SD, 64.

25. FUT, 3, 393. Andrey Smirnov explains in what sense bewilderment can be positive and the bewildered can be said to possess knowledge. He brings Ibn al-ʿArabī's statement in *Bezels of Wisdom* that bewilderment is caused by the multiplication of the One in the facets and correlations. Then he explains that multiplication is not just epistemological but also ontological, as the bewildered (*ḥā'ir*) moves in the whirlpool (*ḥīra*) of life and the universal order and possesses realization of this movement: "*Ḥayra*

is the movement between the two opposites which presuppose each other and make sense only in conjunction; this is why the movement from one to the other is endless since those two opposites can *be* only together, and by this constant transition from the one to the other the Universal Order is constituted." The two opposites are the two faces of reality, the faces of manifestation and nonmanifestation. *Ḥayra* consists of a constant transition-movement between the two faces and the ability of the realizer to place any being in this manifestation-nonmanifestation transition-movement. Andrey Smirnov, a paper presented at the international conference *Sufism, Gnosis, Art* (Seville, November 2004).

26. Muḥyiddīn Ibn al-ʿArabī, *Fuṣūṣ al-Ḥikam*, ed. Abū al-ʿAlā Afīfī (Beirut: Dār al-Kutub al-ʿArabī, 1946), 200 (Hereafter cited as FUS).

27. Ibn al-ʿArabī, *Kitāb al-Tajalliyāt*, ed. Ayman Ḥamdī (Cairo: al-Hai'a al-Miṣriyya li-al-Kitāb, 2002), 28. Commenting on this story, Ḥamdī says: "In this there is an allusion to the seekers of knowledge. The seekers use themselves in their spiritual struggle in purifying themselves until they become like mirrors that are the locus of the manifestation of what faces them-the Names of the Real." Ibid. Notice the resemblance between this story and the Greek myth of Medusa.

28. SD, 159; FUT, 4, 73: 2-3.

29. SD, 159; FUT, 4, 72: 33.

30. Abū Bakr Ibn Ṭufayl, *Ḥayy Ibn Yaqẓān*, ed. Fārūk Saʿd (Beirut: Dār al-Āfāq al-Jadīda, 1980), 119 (Hereafter cited as THA).

31. THA, 235.

32. Muḥammad al-Jābirī, *Ishkāliyyāt al-Fikr al-ʿArabī al-Muʿāṣir* (Beirut: Markiz Dirāsāt al-Waḥda al-ʿArabiyya, 1989), 36.

33. Muḥammad al-Miṣbāḥī, "al-Jābirī wa-al-Ḥulum al-Muzdawaj bi-al-ʿAqlaniyya," in *al-Turāth wa-al-Nahḍa: Qira'at fi Aʿmāl Muḥammad ʿAbid al-Jābirī*, ed. Kamāl ʿAbd al-Laṭīf (Beirut: Markiz Dirāsāt al-Waḥda al-ʿArabiyya, 2004), 183-4.

34. Ibid., 207.

35. See discussion of Ibn al-ʿArabī's view on skepticism in my "Plato and Ibn al-ʿArabī on Skepticism," *Journal of the Muhyiddin Ibn Arabi Society* 30 (2001): 19-35.

36. Abū Bakr Muḥammad Ibn al-Ṣāyigh was born in 1085 in Saragossa. He was a poet, philosopher, and scientist. His philosophical works are badly organized and several of them are incomplete. His influence on Ibn Ṭufayl is apparent, especially his *Governance of the Solitary* and *Contact between the Active and the Human Intellect*. He died in 1138 in Morocco.

37. Stephanie Dalley, *Myths from Mesopotamia: Creation, The Flood, Gilgamesh and Others* (Oxford: Oxford University Press, 1989).

CHAPTER 1. THE FILE OF ILLUMINATIONIST PHILOSOPHY AND THE PURPOSE OF WRITING *ḤAYY*

1. Following Dimitri Gutas, I avoid the use of "Oriental" for *mashriqiyya*. See Dimitri Gutas, "Avicenna's Eastern ("Oriental") Philosophy: Nature, Contents, Transmission," *Arabic Sciences and Philosophy* 10 (2000): 159, n. 1.

2. Ibn Sīnā draws a distinction between the asceticism and the worship of the gnostic (*ʿārif*) and the nongnostic. In contrast to the nongnostic, who employs his

asceticism and worship as a means of trading what belongs to the hereafter with what belongs to this world, the gnostic practices his asceticism and worship as a means of subjugating his estimative and imaginative faculties by orienting them to the side of the Real, away from the side of the illusionary world. The gnostic adjusts his faculties to his inner secret (*al-sirr al-bāṭin*), which reveals the Real by adhering to the constant illumination of the Real's light. Ibn Sīnā, *al-Ishārāt wa-al-Tanbīhāt*, ed. Sulaymān Dunyā, 4 vols. (Cairo: Dār al-Maʿārif, 1960), 1: 801–2.

3. See relevant discussion in Muḥammad al-Jābirī, *Naḥnu wa-al-Turāth* (al-Dār al-Bayḍā': Markiz al-Thaqāfa al-ʿArabī, 1985), 115–19; George Ṭarābīshī, *Naqd Naqd al-ʿAql al-ʿArabī: Waḥdat al-ʿAql al-ʿArabī al-Islāmī* (Beirūt: al-Sāqī, 2002), 127–39.

4. Ibn Sabʿīn, *Budd al-ʿĀrif*, ed. George Kattūra (Beirūt: Dār al-Andalus, 1978), 116.

5. Ibid., 37. Ibn Rushd, on the other hand, criticized Ibn Sīnā for failing to rise to the level of logical proof, thus placing him in the same category as Ghazālī: "It has become clear to you that neither the arguments that he [Ghazālī] ascribed to the theologians in relation to the origination of the world are sufficient to rise to the level of certainty and proof nor, for that matter, the arguments that he ascribed to the philosophers [Ibn Sīnā] in this book are sufficient." Ibn Rushd, *Tahāfut al-Tahāfut*, ed. Aḥmad Shams al-Dīn (Beirūt: Dār al-Kutub al-ʿIlmiyya, 2001), 33.

6. For a discussion of the figure of Hermes and his influence on Islamic esoteric thought, see John Walbridge, *The Wisdom of the Mystic East: Suhrawardī and Platonic Orientalism* (Albany: State University of New York Press, 2001), 17–50.

7. Shihāb al-Dīn Yaḥyā al-Suhrawardī, *al-Talwīḥāt al-Lawḥiyya wa-al-ʿArshiyya*, in *Majmūʿa fī al-Ḥikma al-Ilāhiyya*, 16 vols., ed. Henry Corbin (Istanbul: Maṭba ʿat al-Maʿārif, 1945), 1: 111–12.

8. Ibn Sīnā describes *Shifā'* as "the great book that contains a detailed exposition of all the principal sciences, including the science of music." See ʿAbd al-Raḥmān Badawī, *Arisṭū ʿinda al-ʿArab* (Kuwait: Wakālat al-Maṭbūʿāt, 1978), 121.

9. THA, 113.

10. Ibid.

11. Gutas, "Avicenna's Eastern ("Oriental") Philosophy," *Arabic Sciences and Philosophy* 10 (2000): 160–61.

12. Ibid., 160. For more on Ibn Ṭufayl's "misinterpretations" and "misrepresentations," see Dimitri Gutas, "Ibn Ṭufayl on Ibn Sīnā's Eastern Philosophy," *Oriens* 34 (1994): 230–37.

13. Ibid., 232–33.

14. Gutas, "Avicenna's Eastern ("Oriental") Philosophy," 161.

15. Ibid., 162–63.

16. Tarabishi, *Naqd Naqd al-ʿAql*, 38.

17. Ibid., 39.

18. Ibid.

19. This denial of Ibn Sīnā's illuminationism is stated somewhat humorously by Gutas: "A pertinent example is provided by the astonishment exhibited by Ch. Jambet, Corbin hierophant, who could not believe how anyone could deny (as I did), against the entire Iranian tradition, that Avicenna was a mystic and illuminationist." Gutas,

"Avicenna's Eastern (Oriental) Philosophy," 163. See also Gutas, "Ibn Ṭufayl on Ibn Sīnā's Eastern Philosophy," 165n.22.

20. Ibid., 161. Emphasis added.

21. Simon Ockley, *The Improvement of Human Reason Exhibited in the Life of Hai Ebn Yokdhan* (New York: Georg Olms Verlag, 1983), 17.

22. The translation is Gutas's with slight variations. Gutas, "Avicenna's Eastern ("Oriental") Philosophy," 160–61.

23. Ibid., 161–62.

24. His use of "unity" in the subtitle of the book is ambiguous given his frequent reference to what he sees as the total dependence of the minds of Arabic philosophers in general, and Ibn Sīnā and Ibn Rushd in particular, on Aristotle. He demonstrates this dependence with his favorite chessboard example: Arabic commentators of Aristotle moved like pawns on a chessboard in a game whose rules were set by Aristotle, and as faithful apprentices who would never break the rules of the master. Tarabishi, *Naqd Naqd al-'Aql*, 38–39, 94, 109, 135.

25. Especially in Jabiri's three works: *Naḥnu wa-al-Turāth* (al-Dār al-Bayḍā: al-Markiz al-Thaqāfī al-'Arabī: 1985); *Naqd al-'Aql al-'Arabī: Takwīn al-'Aql al-'Arabī* (Beirūt: Markiz Dirāsāt al-Waḥda al-'Arabiyya, 2002); *Naqd al-'Aql al-'Arabī: Bunyat al-'Aql al-'Arabī Dirāsa Taḥlīliyya Naqdiyya li-Nuẓum al-Ma'rifa fi al-Thaqāfa al-'Arabiyya* (Beirūt: Markiz Dirāsāt al-Waḥda al-'Arabiyya, 1990).

26. Tarabishi, *Naqd Naqd al-'Aql*, 140–41.

27. Ibid., 156.

28. Ibid., 219. This serves as a reminder of Gutas's claim that the difference between Ibn Sīnā's *Shifā'* and Eastern philosophy is but a difference in style, by which he means that the difference is insignificant.

29. Ibn Rushd, *Faṣl al-Maqāl fī Taqrīr mā bayna al-Sharī'a wa-al-Ḥikma min al-Ittiṣāl*, ed. Muḥammad al-Jābirī (Beirūt: Markiz Dirāsāt al-Waḥda al-'Arabiyya, 2002), 96.

30. The word *philodoxers* is my translation of *mutafalsifa*: those who occupy themselves with philosophy but who are unfit for the occupation. It is a term that Plato uses to distinguish philosophers, who know things as they are in themselves, from those who know things for how they appear. Plato, *The Collected Dialogues*, ed. Edith Hamilton and Huntington Cairns, (Princeton: Princeton University Press, 1994), *Republic*, 5: 480 (*The Collected Dialogues,* hereafter cited as TCD). Eric Voegelin introduces Plato's distinction between philosophers and philodoxers as one of three important "pairs of concepts" that Plato employs in *Republic*: justice/injustice, philosopher/philodoxer, and truth/falsehood. Voegelin says that in developing these pairs of concepts, Plato continues the tradition of the mystic-philosophers, "who experienced truth in their resistance to the conventions of society" Eric Voegelin, *Order and History*, 3 vols. (Baton Rouge: Louisiana State University Press, 1957), 3: 63. Voegelin's next words are worth quoting: "We have philosophers in English, but no philodoxers. The loss is in this instance peculiarly embarrassing, because we have an abundance of philodoxers in reality; and since the Platonic term for their designation is lost, we refer to them as philosophers. In modern usage, thus, we call philosophers precisely the persons to whom Plato as a philosopher was in opposition. And an understanding of Plato's positive half of the pair is today practically impossible, except by a few experts, because we think of philodoxers

when we speak of philosophers." (Ibid., 65.) In my opinion, Ibn Ṭufayl's distinction between real and pseudo-philosophers extends beyond any limited reference to the person of this or that philosopher or period of time.

31. THA, 235. Q 17:45 reads: "When you recite the Qur'ān we place an invisible veil between you and those who believe not in the hereafter." In *al-Jam'*, Fārābī says: "His [Aristotle's] famous letter to Plato, in which he responded to the latter's blaming him for composing books and arranging the sciences and publishing them, is sufficient for [demonstrating] our case…for in it he says: 'Even as I have written these sciences down together with the wisdoms contained in them, I have arranged them in such a manner that none but those who are worthy of them could attain them and I have presented them with such an expression conceived only by those who are their rightful offspring.'" Abū Naṣr al-Fārābī, *al-Jam' bayna Ra'yay al-Ḥakīmayn*, ed. Albīr Naṣrī Nādir (Beirūt: Dār al-Mashriq, 1968), 85. Ibn al-'Arabī attributes the following tradition to the Prophet: "Do not bestow wisdom on other than its folk, lest you wrong it, and do not hold it back from its folk, lest you wrong them." SD, 159.

32. Tarabishi, *Naqd Naqd al-'Aql*, 249.

33. THA, 209.

34. This is an allusion to Q 3:41. For an elaborate discussion of Ibn Ṭufayl's use of the terms "symbol" (*ramz*) and "hint" (*ishāra*) and their roots in the Islamic intellectual tradition, see J. Christoph Burgel, "Symbols and Hints: Some Considerations Concerning the Meaning of Ibn Ṭufayl's *Ḥayy Ibn Yaqẓān*," in *The World of Ibn Ṭufayl: Interdisciplinary Perspectives on Ḥayy Ibn Yaqẓān*, ed. Lawrence L. Conrad (Leiden: E. J. Brill, 1996), 115–22.

35. Ibid., 115.

36. Tarabishi, *Naqd Naqd al-'Aql*, 293. See discussion in Ibn Rushd, *Faṣl al-Maqāl*, 98.

37. Ibn Rushd, *The Incoherence of the Incoherence*, 2 vols., trans. Simon Van Den Bergh (Oxford: Oxford University Press, 1954), 1: 281. The words in italics are my translation of *lā huwa illā huwa*, rendered by Van Den Bergh as *There is no reality besides Him.*

38. Ibid., 1: 215.

39. Ibn Rushd, *Faṣl a-Maqāl*, 119.

40. Ockley, *Improvement of Human Reason*, 158.

41. Ibid., 140. Word in Arabic added.

42. A version of Aristotle's statement is repeated by Fārābī in *al-Jam'*. See n.31 above. The words attributed to Aristotle signify the power of language, which is depicted by the famous Ṣūfī al-Tirmidhī al-Ḥakīm as "both revealing and concealing." See Sara Sviri, "Words of Power and the Power of Words," *Jerusalem Studies in Arabic and Islam* 27 (2002): 212–13.

43. THA, 111.

44. THA, 110.

45. Consider the following statement by the Mu'tazilite Qāḍī 'Abd al-Jabār: "Unification (*tawḥīd*) in Arabic signifies that by which a thing is made one, as moving signifies that by which a thing is moved and blackening signifies that by which a thing is blackened. The statement that the thing is one is not a true statement unless the thing

is one indeed. It is therefore like affirmation (*ithbāt*), which in Arabic implies finding. They say: 'You affirmed it in the paper,' meaning that you made it exist in the paper. It is employed in stating the existence of the thing. They say: 'Someone affirms things' meaning that he states their existence, since were they not to exist his statement would not be true." Qādī', Abd al-Jabār, *Sharḥ al-Uṣūl al-Khamsa*, ed. 'Abd al-Karīm 'Uthmān (Cairo, 1965), 128.

46. Here are Ibn Ṭufayl's words: "Because it is a thing of infinite extent, comprehending all things in itself but is not comprehended by any." Ockley, *Improvement of Human Reason*, 12.

47. THA, 205.

48. Tarabishi, *Naqd Naqd al-'Aql*, 14.

49. Jabiri, *Naḥnu wa-al-Turāth*, 165.

50. Ibid., 49.

51. Ibid., 49–50.

52. Tarabishi, *Naqd Naqd al-'Aql*, 100.

53. Ibid., 38–39, 94, 109, 135.

54. 'Abd al-Raḥmān Badawī, *Aristū 'Inda al-'Arab* (Kuwait: Wakālat al-Maṭbū'āt, 1978), 6.

55. Ibid., 7.

56. 'Abd al-Raḥmān Badawī, *al-Aflāṭūniyya al-Muḥdatha 'inda al-'Arab* (Kuwait: Wakālat al-Maṭbū'āt, 1977), 1.

57. 'Abd al-Raḥmān Badawī, *al-Muthul al-'Aqliyya al-Aflāṭūniyya* (Cairo: Maṭba'at Dār al-Kutub al-Maṣriyya 1947), 13–14.

58. Ibn Sīnā, *Letter to al-Kiyā*, in 'Abd al-Raḥmān Badawī, *Aristū 'Inda al-'Arab* (Kuwait: Wakālat al-Maṭbū'āt, 1978), 121, 121n.3. Ibn Sīnā's words, translated by Gutas: "I commented clearly on the difficult passages in the original texts up to the end of *Theologia Aristotelis*, despite the fact that *Theologia* is somewhat suspect, and I talked about the oversights of the commentators." Gutas, *Avicenna and the Aristotelian Tradition*, 63–64.

59. Fārābī, *al-Jam' bayna Ra'yay al-Ḥakīmayn*, 105–6.

60. Badawi, *al-Muthul*, 15. A similar characterization of Arabic and Persian intellectuals is provided by Fritz Meier: "The principal achievements of Islamic intellectual life are not so much to be thought in the ideas and insights growing out of inner vision as in logical analysis. Proof of this may be found in the numerous works that break down language, traditions, nature, and art into their atoms and define the character of the whole on the basis of its composition." Fritz Meier, "The Mystery of the Ka'ba: Symbol and Reality in Islamic Mysticism," in *The Mysteries: Papers From the Eranos Yearbooks*, trans. Ralph Manheim (New York: Pantheon Books, 1955), 151.

61. Ibid., 45.

62. Ibid. One might wonder what prevents Badawi from regarding the author of PS as a follower of Ibn al-'Arabī, given the special reverence that he displays towards him. It seems that Badawi, who has already distinguished the Platonism of our anonymous author from all known forms of Platonism (illuminationist, Neoplatonic), fears to fall into inconsistency because he seems to consider Ibn al-'Arabī as a thinker who is heavily influenced by Neoplatonism.

63. In *Tārīkh al-Ḥukamā'*, Qifṭī says: "This man, Flūṭīn, had a distinguished name. He was dwelling in the land of the Greeks and he interpreted some of Aristotle's works." David Santalana comments that the Flūṭīn that Qifṭī mentions cannot be identified with Plotinus because Plotinus provided no interpretations of Aristotle's works. David Santalana, *al-Madhāhib al-Yūnāniyya fī al-ʿĀlam al-Islāmī*, ed. Muḥammad Jalāl Sharaf (Beirūt: Dār al-Nahḍa al-ʿArabiyya, 1981), 87. Santalana adds that Shahrastānī did not mention Plotinus by name but dedicated a separate chapter for a certain philosopher whom he called "al-Shaykh al-Yūnānī." He also brings Shahrastānī's statement that al-Shaykh al-Yūnānī employed symbols and proverbs in his writings. For example: "your mother is merciful but impoverished and unstable, whereas your father is young but generous and providing [forms for matter]." Ibid., 88.

64. See, for example, Ibn Rushd, *Talkhīṣ Kitāb al-Qiyās*, ed. Muḥammad Qāsim (Cairo: al-Ḥayāt al-Maṣriyya al-ʿĀmma li-al-Kitāb, 1983), 139–40.

65. Ibn Rushd, *Talkhīṣ al-Āthār al-ʿUlwiyya*, ed. Jamāl al-Dīn al-ʿUlwī (Beirūt: Dār al-Gharb al-Islāmī li-al-Kitāb, 1994), 145–46. It is important to bear in mind that Aristotle's *Metaphysics* was not considered by philosophers, such as Fārābī, as consisting of divine science, although this can be considered as constituting part of it. Metaphysics is a universal science to compare with other sciences that are particular, and the god of *Metaphysics* is not the god of theology but the principle of all things. See Therese-Anne Druart, "al-Fārābī, Emanation, and Metaphysics," in *Neoplatonism and Islamic Thought*, ed. Parviz Morewedge (Albany: State University of New York Press, 1992), 128. Ibn Sīnā holds the same view. See discussion in Reza Akbarian, "The Fundamental Principles of Ibn Sīnā's Ontology," *Transcendent Philosophy* 2 (2001): 60.

66. Ibn Rushd, *Talkhīs Kitāb al-Qiyās* 139–40.

67. Tarabishi, *Naqd Naqd al-ʿAql*, 133.

68. Ibn Rushd, *The Incoherence of the Incoherence*, 1: 281.

69. In *Uthūlūjiya*, Aristotle (Plotinus) describes an incident in which he takes off his body and all that is in the outside to (re)enter the inside of his soul. There, he becomes knower, knowledge, and the known and sees a shining light that renders him bewildered because no tongue can express it[s nature] or ear bear its description. See ʿAbd al-Raḥmān Badawī, *Aflūṭīn ʿinda al-ʿArab* (Kuwait: Dār al-Maṭbūʿāt, 1977), 22.

70. Ibn Rushd, *al-Kashf ʿan Manāhij al-Adilla fī ʿAqā'id al-Milla*, ed. Muḥammad al-Jābirī (Beirūt: Markiz Dirāsāt al-Waḥda al-ʿArabiyya, 1998), 101.

71. ʿAbdullah Yūsuf ʿAlī, *The Meaning of the Holy Qur'ān* (Beltsville, MD: Amana Corporation, 1989), 127n.347 (hereafter cited as MHQ).

72. Qur'an, 3: 7.

73. THA, 218, 222.

74. Ockley, *Improvement of Human Reason*, 226.

75. THA, 228.

76. Ockley, *Improvement of Human Reason*, 158.

77. THA, 234. Commenting on the *Revelation of the Fiṭra (tajallī al-fiṭra)* in Ibn al-ʿArabī's *Tajalliyāt Ilāhiyya,* an anonymous commentator explains that *fiṭra* signifies a state that is related to "the existence that is the spring of the good and all the additional benefit, which is indicated by the Prophet's saying that each new born is born according to the *fiṭra*, meaning the *fiṭra* that is related to the good. In this respect man adhered to

guidance." See *Kashf al-Ghāyāt fī mā Iktanafat ʿalayhi al-Tajalliyāt*, in Ibn al-ʿArabī, *al-Tajalliyāt al-Ilāhiyya*, ed. Muḥammad ʿAbd al-Karīm al-Nimrī (Beirūt: Dār al-Kutub al-ʿIlmiyya, 2002), 77. Ibn Sawdakīn explains that in its external existence, the soul of man inclines away from this guidance because its lordly nature inclines toward unlimitation. Out of love for the Real, some people control the tendencies of their nature, while others find themselves unable to do so, which is why the law is needed to restrict and contain these tendencies, Ibid., 77–78.

78. A similar description of the logical structure of Ibn Ṭufayl's work is provided by Lenn Goodman, *Ibn Ṭufayl's Ḥayy Ibn Yaqẓān* (New York: Twayne, 1972), 58 (hereafter cited as THY).

79. Lawrence I. Conrad, "Through the Thin Veil: On the Question of Communication and the Socialization of Knowledge in *Ḥayy Ibn Yaqẓān*," in *The World of Ibn Ṭufayl: Interdisciplinary Perspectives on Ḥayy Ibn Yaqẓān*, ed. Lawrence I. Conrad (Leiden: E. J. Brill, 1996), 240.

80. Ibid, 248. Conrad mentions Lenn Goodman and Sami Hawi as advocators of Hourani's view. Hourani elaborates on his position in "The Principal Subject of Ibn Ṭufayl's *Ḥayy Ibn Yaqẓān," Journal of Near Eastern Studies*, 15 (1956), 45–46.

81. Ibid., 242–43. Conrad establishes point 2 on the basis of an argument by Hillel Fradkin, "The Political Thought of Ibn Ṭufayl," in *Islamic Theology and Philosophy: Studies in Honor of George Hourani*, ed. Michael E. Marmura (Albany: State University of New York Press, 1984), 254–55.

82. THY, 61. Goodman says that *Ḥayy* builds on Ibn Sīnā's "Floating Man" thought experiment. See Lenn Goodman, "Ibn Ṭufayl," in *History of Islamic Philosophy*, ed. Seyyed Hossein Nasr and Oliver Leaman, 2 vols. (Routledge: New York, 2001), 1: 315.

83. THY, 61.

84. THA, 128.

85. Conrad, "Through the Thin Veil," 249, 258.

86. Ibid., 265.

87. Ibid., 265.

88. Ibid., 264.

89. THA, 199.

90. Conrad, "Through the Thin Veil," 254.

91. Ibid., 248.

92. Ibid., 249.

93. Ibid., 251.

94. Ibid., 254.

CHAPTER 2. THE INTRODUCTION

1. I think this must be the case even if the reference is to a real person; why should a reference to a real person exclude mystical considerations? Introducing Plato's *Republic*, Eva Brann points to the risks in the way of immediately coming to grips with the dialogue as the writer's social and cultural conditions are injected between him and

his work: "Is it not possible for a writer to be so deep, so original in the strong sense, that he can be defined neither from, nor even against, his social setting?" Eva Brann, *The Music of the Republic: Essays on Socrates's Conversations and Plato's Writings* (Philadelphia: Paul Dry Books, 2004), 90.

2. THA, 106.

3. Edward Lane, *Arabic-English Lexicon*, 8 vols. (Beirūt: Librairie du Liban, 1980), 2:637 (hereafter cited as AEL).

4. Ibid., 2:637.

5. *Ḥamīm* means also "hot water." Ibid., 2:635.

6. Ibid., 4:1704.

7. For example, Lane interprets *muṣāfāt* and *ṣafā'* as: "Reciprocal purity or sincerity of mind, or of love, or affection, or of brotherly affection; or pure, or sincere, reciprocal love." Ibid., 4:1703–4.

8. THA, 125. Compare this with Fārābī's words in *al-Jam'*: "He [Aristotle] says in his famous book *Uthūlūjiya*: "As I often retreat into myself it happens that I set my soul apart from my body to become an incorporeal spiritual substance. Then I enter into my soul and withdraw from everything else to become knowledge, the knower, and that which is known combined." Fārābī, *al-Jam' bayna Ra'yay al-Ḥakīmayn*, 109. As Classen points out: "For the mystic writer the book becomes a mirror of herself which she holds up for herself and her soul, and which then serves as a purifying agent in the presence of God." Albrecht Classen, "Flowing Light of the Godhead: Binary Oppositions of Self and God in Mechthild von Magdeburg," *Studies in Spirituality* 15 (2005): 79–97.

9. THA, 106.

10. Ibid.

11. 'Alī Muḥammad al-Jurjānī, *al-Ta'rīfāt* (Beirūt: Maktabat Lubnān, 1969), 132.

12. Jabiri, *Bunyat al-'Aql al-'-Arabī*, 288.

13. AEL, 3:885.

14. *'Ilm al-tawḥīd mubayinun li-wujūdihi wa-wujūduhu mufāriqun li-'ilmihi.* Abū al-Qāsim al-Qushayrī, *al-Risāla al-Qushayriyya* (Cairo: Sharikat Maktabat wa-Maṭba'at Muṣṭafā al-Bābī al-Ḥalabī, 1940), 147.

15. Ibid., 34.

16. THY, 152.

17. "Hence, they say that the Ṣūfī is the son of the moment, meaning that he acts in accord with the dictates of his time". See, Qushayrī, *Risāla*, 34.

18. THA, 106.

19. Qushayrī, *Risāla*, 141.

20. THA, 211.

21. See AEL, 5:2013 on *'ilm*, 5:2138 on *'urf.*

22. According to Lane, *khabbartuhu* means: "I informed him, or told him, of such a thing; or acquainted him with such a thing; or made him to know the internal, or real, state of such a thing." AEL, 2:695.

23. THA, 106–7. "Taught the discipline of the mind and the good qualities of the soul" is Lane's interpretation of *addabathu*. AEL, 1:34.

24. William C. Chittick, *The Heart of Islamic Philosophy: The Quest for Self-Knowledge in the Teachings of Afḍal al-Dīn Kāshānī* (Oxford: Oxford University Press, 2001), 30.

25. THA, 115.

26. I wish to draw the reader's attention at this point to the skeptics' argument in relation to the authenticity of Ghazālī's authorship of *Niche*. The argument relies on the observation that in this work, Ghazālī develops an explicit conception of the universe in harmony with Neoplatonic thought, of whose exponents he was severely critical. See, for example, William Montgomery Watt, "A Forgery in al-Ghazālī's *Mishkāt?*" *Journal of Royal Asiatic Society of Great Britain and Ireland* (1949): 5–22. A useful summary of the debate over this subject can be found in Buchman's introduction to his translation of *Niche*. David Buchman, *al-Ghazālī: The Niche of Lights* (Provo, UT: Brigham Young University Press, 1998), xxvii–xxxi. One particular statement that Buchman brings and that is related to our discussion is Abū al-ʿAlāʿAfīfī's that the *Niche* exerted an influence on illuminationist philosophers, such as Suhrawardī and Mulla Sadra, being one of the earliest treatises to equate knowledge of God systematically with the illumination of the heart by divine light. "If he is correct," says Buchman, "then al-Ghazālī's effect on Islamic philosophy was not just destructive but also formative." Ibid., xxii. He must be correct, if Ibn Ṭufayl's most explicit acknowledgment of Ghazālī's influence on his thought is to be taken seriously.

27. Ghāzalī: *The Niche of Lights*, 1–2.

28. Ibid., 17–18.

29. Ibid., 18.

30. To draw the reader's attention to the distinction between Ṣūfīs who belonged to the camp of intoxication (*ahl-al-sukr*), including figures such as Shiblī, Abū Yazīd al-Basṭāmī, and Ḥallāj, and ṣūfīs who belonged to the camp of soberness (*ahl-al-ṣahw*), such as Junaid and Ghazālī.

31. According to one interpretation, Ṣūfī is derived from *ṣafā*', which when "said of wine or, beverage, or of water, or of a thing," means "It was, or became clear, limpid, or pure." AEL, 4:1703.

32. Qushayrī, *Risāla*, 140. Thus, the claim (for Truth) seems to be a characterization not only of the possessors of *shaṭaḥāt* but of all Ṣūfīs, without exception. This is because all Ṣūfī are, in a sense, possessors of a claim for Truth, and all ṣūfīs seem to be destined, in the final account, to fail to amount to the absolute signification of their name.

33. Ghāzalī, *Niche*, 14.

34. THA, 211–14.

35. THA, 212.

36. Q 24:35 reads: "Allah is the Light of the heavens and the earth. The parable of His Light is as if there were a niche and within it a lamp enclosed in glass. The glass as it were a brilliant star lit from a blessed tree. An olive, neither of the East nor of the West whose oil is well-nigh luminous though fire scarce touched it. Light upon light! Allah doth set forth parables for men and Allah doth know all things." MHQ, 877.

37. Ghazālī, *Niche*, 1.

38. Ghazālī is aware of the version of the tradition that mentions seventy thousand veils instead of seventy. See Ghazālī, *Niche*, 44.

39. THA, 214.

40. Ghazālī, *Niche*, 44.

41. THA, 115. Notice that Ibn Ṭufayl says that he arrived at his illuminative knowledge by combining Ghazālī's and Ibn Sīnā's teachings. The view that Ghazālī's main object of criticism was Ibn Sīnā's philosophy has been challenged by Jules Janssens, "al-Ghazālī's *Tahāfut*: Is It Really a Rejection of Ibn Sīnā's Philosophy?" *Journal of Islamic Studies* 12 (2001): 1–17.

42. THA, 114.

43. THY, 101. For example, Ghazālī attacks the theologians in the *Deliverer from Error* but identifies his position with the Ashʿarite theologians in *Incoherence*. See Ghazālī, *al-Munqidh min al-Ḍalāl*, ed. ʿAlību Milḥim (Beirūt: Dār wa-Maktabat al-Hilāl, 1993), 27–28.

44. THA, 108; Ibn Sīnā, *al-Ishārāt wa-al-Tanbīhāt*, ed. Sulaymān Dunyā, 4 vols. (Cairo: Dār al-Maʿārif, 1957), 4:828–35. Notice the similar manner in which Suhrawardī depicts the mystical experience. Shihāb al-Din Yaḥyā al-Suhrawardī, *Kitāb al-Talwīḥāt al-Lawḥiyya wa-al-ʿArshiyya*, in *Majmūʿa fī al-Ḥikma al-Ilāhiyya*, 1: 113–14.

45. Compare with what Plato says in TCD, *Letter 7*, 344 b: 4–10. Majid Fakhry has noticed the resemblance between Ibn Sīnā's and Plato's allegorical expressions, which "reveal an obvious preoccupation with the problem of philosophical expression," and "a spirit of dissatisfaction with the discursive forms of philosophic exposition and the urge to transcend or bypass them." Majid Fakhry, *A History of Islamic Philosophy* (New York: Columbia University Press, 2004), 161. Compare also with what is related in Ibn Sīnā's treatise *On Destiny*. Upon returning to Ispahan, Ibn Sīnā meets with a friend who is convinced that Truth can be reached through the exchange of arguments. They exchange a long and hopeless argument on the theme of destiny, hopeless because the arguments exchanged ended in an impasse and led to no change in destiny. The friends had to be silent. "It is now, out of the depths of this silence, on the threshold of inmost consciousness, that the person of Ḥayy Ibn Yaqẓān suddenly presents itself." Henry Corbin, *Avicenna and the Visionary Recital*, trans. William R. Trask (London: Routledge and Kegan Paul, 1960), 154.

46. Qushayrī, *Risāla*, 34–35.

47. See the passage quoted previously from Ibn Sīnā's *Ishārāt*. Ibn al-ʿArabī says that the people of the Way use the term *waqt* (time) "to designate the reality of the instant—that which you are in and upon in the present time, and that is the Order of Being between two non-existents." Cited from *Futūḥāt* in Stephen Hirtenstein, "Aspects of Time and Light," *Journal of the Muḥyiddīn Ibn al-ʿArabī Society* 6 (1987): 46.

48. Qushayrī, *Risāla*, 33–34.

49. This is a reminder of al-Khaḍir's warning to Moses in the Chapter of the Cave.

50. Corbin, *Avicenna and the Visionary Recital*, 141.

51. See Ibn Sīnā, *Ishārāt*, 4:838.

52. Corbin, *Avicenna and the Visionary Recital*, 204.

53. Ibid., 214.

54. Ibid., 215–16.

55. Ibid., 208.

56. Ibid., 218–19.

57. Ibid., 218.

58. Ibn Sīnā, *Ishārāt*, 4:791–92.

59. Corbin notes that the recital indicates some traces of alchemical symbolism, which accounts for the reality of the operations performed by the adapter as a way of projecting his inner truth into spiritual manifestation. Corbin, *Avicenna and the Visionary Recital*, 209.

60. John Walbridge, *The Leaven of the Ancients: Suhrawardī and the Heritage of the Greeks* (Albany: State University of New York Press, 2000), 124.

61. Ibid., 175.

62. Ibid., 138.

63. Bayhaqī, for example, states that in contrast to Plato, who was abstinent, Ibn Sīnā was extremely fond of wine and sexual excess. Kiki Kennedy-Day, who cites his testimony, says that when hearing such testimonies, one should doubt their historical accuracy. Kiki Kennedy-Day, *Books of Definition in Islamic Philosophy: The Limits of Words* (London and New York: Routledge Curzon, 2003), 88.

64. See discussion in Corbin, *Avicenna and the Visionary Recital*, 124–25.

65. Ibid., 224.

66. Ibn Sīnā, *Ishārāt*, 4:797.

67. Compare with THA, 123.

CHAPTER 3. THE NATURALISTIC ACCOUNT OF ḤAYY'S BIRTH

1. In my previous book, I expressed my criticism of Abū al-ʿAlāʾ Afīfī's interpretation of Ibn al-ʿArabī's doctrine on the basis of pantheism. Salman Bashier, *Ibn al-ʿArabī's Barzakh: The Concept of the Limit and the Relationship between God and the World* (Albany: State University of New York Press, 2004). Alfred Ivry points out that Ibn Ṭufayl's brand off mysticism is unclear, and that although it appears to be pantheistic, it "veers of into theosophical constructions." 5. Alfred L. Ivry, "The Utilization of Allegory in Islamic Philosophy," in *Interpretation and Allegory*, ed. Jon Whitman (Leiden: E. J. Brill, 2000), 169.

2. INM, 104.

3. Ibid., 104.

4. Ibid.

5. As noted by Conrad, the interest that Hawi shows in the mystical dimension of *Ḥayy* is far from what seems to be implied by the title of his book. He confines his treatment of this dimension to a partial discussion in chapter 8 of his book, and even there, the discussion is heavily judgmental. For a treatment of this dimension, Conrad refers the reader to a Ph.D. dissertation by Hillel G. Fradkin. However, he notes that Fradkin's work does not seem to be based on any philosophical thinking beyond that of Ibn Ṭufayl himself. Lawrence I. Conrad, "Introduction: The World of Ibn Ṭufayl," in *The World of Ibn Ṭufayl: Interdisciplinary Perspectives on Ḥayy ibn Yaqẓān* (Leiden: E. J. Brill, 1996), 16.

6. INM, 90. Hawi says that traditional scholarship has neglected the philosophical and scientific themes in Ibn Ṭufayl's work, partially due to its interest in Neoplatonic

or mystical aspects or its preoccupation with his attempt to establish harmony between philosophy and Islamic religion. Sami Hawi, "An Islamic Naturalistic Conception of Abiogenes: The Views of Ibn Ṭufayl," *Islamic Culture* 49 (1975): 22. Shortly after saying this, he describes Ibn Ṭufayl as a mystic and the aim of his naturalism as "taking the results of experimentations and rational inference as a point of departure for all philosophical speculation and leaving open the possibility of achieving knowledge of transempirical entities." Ibid., 24.

7. See William C. Chittick, *The Ṣūfī Path of Knowledge: Ibn al-ʿArabī's Metaphysics of Imagination* (Albany: State University of New York Press, 1989), 203. For example, the author of *ʿAwārif al-Maʿārif* says that he wrote a book against "Greek turpitudes" and that, with the help of God, he personally obliterated ten volumes of Ibn Sīnā's *Shifāʾ*. Herman Landolt comments that even philosophical ṣūfīs of Ibn al-ʿArabī's school made it a point to distinguish themselves from the philosophers. Herman Landolt, "Suhrawardī's 'Tales of Initiation,'" *Journal of the American Oriental Society* 107 (1987): 479–80.

8. See Ibn Rushd, *al-Kashf*, 117.

9. THA, 25–26.

10. Zakariyya al-Qazwīnī, *Athār al-Bilād wa-Akhbār al-ʿIbād* (Beirūt: Dār Ṣādiq, 1960), 33.

11. Remke Kruk, "Ibn Ṭufayl: A Medieval Scholar's Views on Nature," in *The World of Ibn Ṭufayl: Interdisciplinary Perspectives on Ḥayy ibn Yaqẓān*, ed. Lawrence I. Conrad (Leiden: E. J. Brill, 1996), 81.

12. Ibid., 73. THA, 131, 146.

13. THA, 111. Some give to the substance that is used in alchemical transmutations, the elixir, the color of sulphur. Others describe it as a red powder. In general, the substance was considered unreal. See Jehane Ragai, "The Philosopher's Stone: Alchemy and Chemistry," *Alif* 12 (1992): 60. For a general account of works on alchemy in Islam, see Julius Raska, "Alchemy in Islam," *Islamic Culture* 36 (1962): 30–36.

14. Consider the heavily laden Ṣūfī tone of Qazwīnī's narration and the detailed anecdotes that he provides of things that happened to or were said by famous Ṣūfīs such as Nūr al-Dīn al-Jīlī, Abū Yazīd al-Basṭāmī, Abū Bishr al-Ḥāfī, Abū al-Qāsim al-Junaid, Ibrāhīm bin Adham, Abū Saʿīd Ibn Abī al-Khair, Abū al-Futūḥ Shihāb al-Dīn al-Suhrawardī, Abū Ḥāmid al-Ghazālī, Maʿrūf al-Karakhī, and others.

15. All the Ṣūfīs mentioned by Qazwīnī in the preceding note are located in the fourth zone.

16. THY, 104.

17. Suhrawardī provided a simple explanation for this point: "Warmth comes from the rays not from the sun itself; for were heat due to the sun separately what is higher up should become warm more quickly than what is lower down, which is not the case." See Shihāb al-Din Yaḥya al-Suhrawardī, *The Book of Radiance: A Parallel English-Persian Text*, ed. Hossein Ziai (,Costa Mesa California: Mazda Publishers, 1998), 21.

18. THA, 121.

19. Bernd Radtke, "How Can Man Reach the Mystical Union? Ibn Ṭufayl and the Divine Spark," in Lawrence I. Conrad, *The World of Ibn Ṭufayl: Interdisciplinary Perspectives on Ḥayy ibn Yaqẓān* (Leiden: E. J. Brill, 1996), 194. Therefore, Chittick's

view must be qualified. Chittick brings Ibn al-ʿArabī's statement that unaided wise thinkers are able to grasp the divine origin of the cosmos, and he comments that his narrative is "slightly reminiscent of *Ḥayy Ibn Yaqẓān*." Then he says, "In the manner of many Muslim philosophers, Ibn Ṭufayl thought that the rational perception of philosophers could achieve the same level of knowledge as the revelation given to the prophets. Ibn al-ʿArabī disagrees vehemently, as he makes clear throughout his works." William Chittick, *Imaginal Worlds: Ibn al-ʿArabī and the Problem of Religious Diversity* (Albany: State University of New York Press, 1994), 128.

20. Conrad, "Introduction: The World of Ibn Ṭufayl," 31.

21. Vincent J. Cornell, "Ḥayy in the Land of Absāl: Ibn Ṭufayl and Ṣūfism in the Western Maghrib during the Muwaḥḥid Era," in Lawrence I. Conrad, *The World of Ibn Ṭufayl: Interdisciplinary Perspectives on Ḥayy ibn Yaqẓān* (Leiden: E. J. Brill, 1996), 164. For further discussion of this subject, see Lloyd Ridgeon, "Aziz Nasafī's Six Ontological Faces," in Ian Richard Netton, *Islamic Philosophy and Theology* (Routledge: London, 2007), 3: 360; William C. Chittick, "Ibn ʿArabī," in *Islamic Philosophy and Theology*, ed. Ian Richard Netton (Routledge: London, 2007), 4: 129–30; Mohammed Rustom, "Is Ibn al-ʿArabī's Ontology Pantheistic?" *Journal of Islamic Philosophy* 2 (2006): 64–67. Harvey Hames ascribes the individualistic trend in Ibn al-ʿArabī's ṣūfism to the fact that ṣūfīs in the West were not institutionalized, as was becoming fashionable in the East. Harvey J. Hames, "A Seal Within a Seal: The Imprint of Ṣufism in Abraham Abulafia's Teachings," *Medieval Encounters* 12 (2006), 159.

22. The truffle is a kind of fungus that grows underground; it is also called in Arabic "the fat of the earth" and "the small-pox of the earth." AEL, 7: 2629.

23. Ibn al-ʿArabī, *ʿUqlat al-Mustawfiz*, in *Kleinere Schriften des Ibn al-ʿArabī*, ed. H. S. Nyberg (Leiden: E. J. Brill, 1919), 93–94.

24. In *al-Tadbīrāt al-Ilāhiyya,* Ibn al-ʿArabī says: "I saw that man is one such fruit among others, growing and feeding and then coming to his end as they grow and feed and come to their end. From him benefits are drawn as they are drawn from them. He diminishes and grows old as they do, and dies as they die. Then we saw him being born as they are born. Then seeds might be taken from him as they might be taken from a fruit to be sown and to turn into plants that bring forth fruits that resemble them." Ibn al-ʿArabī, *al-Tadbīrāt al-Ilāhiyya fī Iṣlāḥ al-Mamlaka al-Insāniyya*, in *Kleinere Schriften des Ibn al-ʿArabī*, ed. H. S. Nyberg (Leiden: E. J. Brill, 1919), 107.

25. THA, 151.

26. Truffles, for example.

27. Remke Kruk, "Ibn Ṭufayl: A Medieval Scholar's Views on Nature," 80. For details on the date palm as a symbol and object of religious worship in the ancient medieval world, see ʿĀtif Jūda Naṣr, *al-Khayāl: Mafhūmuhu wa-Waẓāʾifuhu* (Cairo: al-Sharika al-Maṣriyya li-al-Nashr-Longman, 1997), 108–12. For a description of the element of continuity between the chains of existents, see Ikhwān al-Ṣafāʾ, *Rasāʾil Ikhwān al-Ṣafāʾ*, ed. Khair al-Dīn al-Zarkalī (Cairo: al-maṭbaʿa al-ʿArabiyya, 1928), 3: 138–39.

28. THA, 198.

29. Remke Kruk, "Ibn Ṭufayl: A Medieval Scholar's Views on Nature," 87.

30. Ibid., 88.

31. Ibid., 89.

32. Ibid.

33. TCD, *Charmides* 156d8-e7.

34. FUT, 1, 126: 22. Part of the chapter is translated by Henry Corbin, *Spiritual Body and Celestial Earth: From Mazdean Iran to Shi'ite Iran*, trans. Nancy Pearson (London: I. B. Tauris, 1990), 135–43.

35. THA, 123.

36. FUT, 1, 126: 30–33.

37. Qazwīnī, *'Ajā'ib al-Makhlūqāt wa-Gharā'ib al-Mawjūdāt*, ed. Fārūk Sa'd (Beirūt: Dār al-Āfāq al-Jadīda, 1993), 304–5. Pablo Beneto Arias points out that Qazwīnī met Ibn al-'Arabī in 1232 and described him as an excellent man of wisdom. He also brings a tale that Qazwīnī had heard from Ibn al-'Arabī. According to this tale, there was a date palm that had bent so much over the middle of the street that people wished to cut it down, and they decided to do it the following day. That night, Ibn al-'Arabī saw the tree complaining to the Prophet concerning the people's intention. He laid his hand on it and it became straight. See Pablo Beneto Arias, "A Summary of the Life of the Prophet by Ibn al-'Arabī and the Miracle of the Palm Tree of Seville," *Journal of the Muḥyiddīn Ibn 'Arabī Society* 30 (2001): 93. Notice also that in describing the figure of the Sage in *Ḥayy Ibn Yaqẓān,* Ibn Sīnā says that his figure was not bent, and no signs of old age were to be found in him.

38. FUT, 1, 126: 33–127: 1.

39. FUT, 1, 127: 12–14.

40. For a discussion of the notion of fixed entities, see William C. Chittick, *The Self-Disclosure of God* (Albany: State University of New York Press, 1998), xx, 29–33, 50–52; and *The Ṣūfī Path of Knowledge*, 83–85.

41. Recall Qazwīnī's earlier description of the Island of Women.

42. FUT, 1, 128: 1–10.

43. FUT, 1, 128: 19.

44. Ibn al-'Arabī says that compared with the fruits of the World of Barzakh, the fruits of the Garden of Paradise are considered inferior. FUT, 128: 3.

45. MHQ, 1411.

46. MHQ, 1399.

47. FUT, 1, 128: 23–27.

48. *Masraḥ* means "a place of pasturage or a place into which beasts are sent forth in the morning to pasture." I use the term "theatre" because I think that Ibn al-'Arabī's words warrant this use.

49. FUT, 1, 127: 2–3.

50. This brings to mind Ibn Ṭufayl's example of the mirror that reflects on itself and burns everything else. THA, 125.

51. Simon Van Den Bergh indicates that state (*ḥāl*) is regarded by the theologians as a meaning (*ma'nā*) that is intermediate between reality and unreality, and that *ma'nā* can mean "idea" in the Platonic sense. Van Den Bergh, *Incoherence of Incoherence*, 2: 3 n.6.

52. FUT, 1, 130: 26–29.

53. SD, 18.

54. FUT, 1, 128: 19.

55. Thus, in Lane: *"a'tabiru al-ḥadīth, I judge by comparison with what has been transmitted by tradition* from the Prophet; meaning I interpret a dream according to what has been transmitted by tradition, like as I do according to the Kuran; as when a crow is interpreted as meaning an unrighteous man." AEL, 5: 1937.

56. FUT, 1, 551: 3–9. See brief discussion of Ibn al-'Arabī's Platonic understanding of the interpretation (*taw'īl*) of the Qur'ān in James Morris, "Ibn 'Arabī and his Interpreters Part 2: Influences and Interpretations (Conclusion)," *Journal of the American Oriental Society* 107 (1987): 102n.75.

57. Ignaz Goldziher, *Introduction to Islamic Theology and Law*, trans. Andras and Ruth Hamori (Princeton: Princeton University Press, 1981), 152, 155.

58. H. A. R. Gibb and J. H. Kramers, (eds.) *Shorter Encyclopaedia of Islam* (Leiden: E. J. Brill, 1974), 146. Ibn al-'Arabī states that he adhered to no specific school of law. See Ibn al-'Arabī, *Dīwān*, ed. Nawāf al-Jaraḥ (Beirūt: Dār Sādiq, 1999), 433.

59. Jabiri, *Bunyat al-'Aql al-'Arabī*, 296, 297, 374.

60. For a comprehensive discussion of Ibn al-'Arabī's mystical view of the significance of the heart, see James Winston Morris, *The Reflective Heart: Discovering Spiritual Intelligence in Ibn al-'Arabī's Meccan Illuminations* (Louisville: Fons Vitae, 2005), 17–91. See also the discussion in Luce López-Baralt, "Saint John of the Cross and Ibn 'Arabī: The Heart or Qalb as the Translucid and Ever-changing Mirror of God," *Journal of the Muḥyiddīn Ibn al-'Arabī Society*," 28 (2000): 71–81.

61. I say "poets" and not "poetry" because I think that rather than poetry itself, what is condemned in Q 26:224–26 and Q 36:39 is the use that poets make of it to say things that are untrue. Indeed, were Ibn al-'Arabī to disagree with this explanation, he would not have produced hundreds of poems and insisted on opening the chapters of his *Futūḥāt* with lines of poetry in which he saw hidden the keys for understanding their meanings. See the discussion of the poetic aspect of Ibn al-'Arabī's writings in Ralph Austin, "Ibn al-'Arabī-Poet of Divine Realities," *Muḥyiddīn Ibn 'Arabī: A Commemorative Volume*, ed. Stephen Hirtenstein and Michael Tiernan (Rockport, MA: Element, 1993), 181–89. For more on the common characteristics of poetry and the text of revelation, see 'Abdullah Saeed, "Rethinking 'Revelation' as a Precondition for Reinterpreting the Qur'ān: A Qur'ānic Perspective," *Journal of Qur'ānic Studies* 1 (1999): 96. For a similar discussion of Ibn al-'Arabī's "condemnation" of *shaṭḥ*, see Pierre Lory, "The Symbolism of Letters and Language in the Work of Ibn 'Arabī," *Journal of Muryiddīn Ibn 'Arabī Society* 23 (1998): 39–40.

62. SD, 316; FUT, 4, 25: 24–25.

63. TCD, *Critias*, 111e-3–5.

64. Ibid., 109c–d 2.

65. TCD, *Republic*, 3, 414c–e 5.

66. Ibid., 3, 415a.

67. Ibid., 415c5.

68. The severest criticism against Plato in this regard has come from Karl Popper, *The Open Society and Its Enemies*, 2 vols. (London: Routledge, 1966), 1: 31–56.

69. See TCD, *Rep.* 7, 521 a3.

70. TCD, *Republic* 3: 415b1.

71. Ibid., 3: 415 c.

72. Ibid., 3: 414d-5.

CHAPTER 4. THE TRADITIONALISTIC ACCOUNT FROM THE END

1. THA, 217.

2. THA, 218.

3. THA, 219.

4. THA, 232.

5. See TCD, *Rep*. 509d–516b.

6. See TCD, *Rep*. 511e.

7. THA, 218.

8. This is Voegelin's version of Plato's depiction of the significance of dialogue in the Digression to the *Theaetetus,* 170b. Eric Voegelin, *Order and History*, 3 vols. (Baton Rouge: Louisiana State University Press, 1957), 3: 12. Plato's words are the following: "But there is one thing about them; when you get them alone and make them explain their objections to philosophy, then, if they are men enough to face a long examination without running away, it is odd how they end by finding their own arguments unsatisfying." TCD, *Theaetetus* 177b:1–5.

9. See previous note.

10. The term *hawā*, which is one of the designations for love, means also inclination and falling. Compare this with Ibn al-ʿArabī's analysis of Moses's fleeing from the Egyptians in *Fuṣūṣ al-Ḥikam* in Chapter 8.

11. THA, 221–22.

12. THA, 222.

13. THA, 223.

14. See THY, 35.

15. THA, 225–26.

16. See Malson's discussion of the development of the verbal capacity of wolf children in Lucien Malson and Jean Itard, *Wolf Children: The Wild Boy of Aveyron*, trans. Edmund Fawcett, Peter Ayrton, and Joan White (London: NLB, 1972), 40–41, 44–47, 55.

17. THY, 189n.72.

18. Notice that the nature of God's attributes was one of the problems that occupied Absāl's mind upon his arrival to Ḥayy's island.

19. See the discussion in Jābirī, *Naqd al-ʿAql al-ʿArabī: Bunyat al-ʿAql al-ʿArabī*, 42. See also Jalāl al-Dīn al-Ṣuyūṭī, *al-Muzhir fī ʿUlūm al-Lugha wa-Anwāʿiha*, ed. Muḥammad al-Mawlā and Muḥammad Ibrāhīm (Dār Iḥyā' al-Kutub al-ʿArabiyya, 1:6–8.

20. Goodman renders *min amr Allah* as "about God." THY, 160.

21. Qur'ān 3:190 reads: "Surely in the creation of the heavens and the earth and the alternation of the night and the day signs for those who have hearts." Chittick renders *albāb*, which I render as "hearts," as "kernels." SD, 9, 218. *Ulū al-albāb* should

probably be rendered as "those who possess understanding," which accords with the Arabic identification of the heart as the seat of comprehension.

22. The mention of the "friends of God who know neither fear nor grief" occurs in Q 10:62. The mention of believers in general who "know neither fear nor grief" occurs in Q 2:38, 62, 112, 262, 274; 5:69; 6:48; 10:62; 43:68; 46:13. It is interesting that Q 2:62; 5:69 assure not only Jews and Christians of relief from fear and grief but also Sabians, also mentioned in Q 22:17.

23. THA, 226.

24. In Ṣūfī terminology, Ḥayy possessed *ʿayn al-yaqīn,* while Absāl possessed *ʿilm-al-yaqīn*. See Khwaja ʿAbdul Ḥāmid, "The Philosophical Significance of Ibn Ṭufail's *Ḥaiy Ibn Yaqẓān," Islamic Culture* 22 (1948): 66.

25. For a discussion in Ghazālī of the notion of the resemblance between the phenomenal world and the invisible world and the need for interpretation (*taʾwīl, taʿbīr*) for understanding the things that are said in reference to the invisible world by means of metaphors that relate to this world, see Kojiro Nakamura, "Imām Ghazālī's Cosmology Reconsidered with Special Reference to the Concept of *Jabarūt,*" *Studia Islamica* 80 (1994): 32–34. Nakamura's discussion makes a reference to Plato's Parable of the Cave and compares Plato's world of ideas with Ghazālī's invisible world or the world of *malakūt*. Ibid., 34.

26. SD, 273. FUT, 2, 66: 33–67: 1–6.

27. Ibid., 273.

28. Q 42:52 reads: "And we have also sent the spirit to you by our command when you had no knowledge."

29. THY, 106–7.

30. Abraham Melamed, *The Philosopher-King in Medieval and Renaissance Jewish Political Thought*, ed. Lenn E. Goodman (Albany: State University of New York, 2003), 58–59.

31. Ibid., 59.

32. THY, 209. Ibn Ṭufayl makes a clever use of the term *silsila*, which means a chain and also a circle made of parts of iron or some other metal that are connected to one another. See AEL 4: 1397, 1398. Although they can move, the movement of those who are dazzled by the sun is limited, as if within the confines of a circle. In *Metaphysics*, Aristotle says: "Perhaps, too, as difficulties are of two kinds, the cause of the present difficulty is not in the facts but in us. For as the eyes of bats are to the blaze of the day, so is the reason in our soul to the things which are by nature most evident of all." BWA, *Metaphysics*, a 1: 993b 5–11. It might be the case, therefore, that Ibn Ṭufayl is referring here to Aristotle. See THY, 221n.211. It is highly possible, however, that the reference is to Plato's Parable of the Cave, according to which the illuminated philosopher, who makes his way back to the cave, is required to follow a ruthless process of habituation among prisoners who do not show any understanding of his situation. And if he tries to explain his state, "would he not provoke laughter, and would it not be said of him that he had returned from his journey aloft with his eyes ruined and that it was not worthwhile even to attempt the ascent? And if it were possible to lay hands on and kill the man who tried to release them and lead them up, would they not kill him?" TCD, *Rep*. 517a 5–9.

33. THA, 210.

34. Simon Ockley, *Improvement*, 129.

35. THA, 110.

36. It is true that we have the testimony of the historian ʿAbd al-Wāḥid of Marrakesh that Ibn Ṭufayl composed works on natural and metaphysical philosophy, including *Ḥayy* and an essay on the soul that he had seen in his own hand (which might be Ibn Bājja's *Risāla fī Ittiṣāl al-ʿAql bi-al-Insān*), and that he devoted his last days entirely to the study of metaphysics. See THY, 4. However as Marakūshī indicates, Ibn Ṭufayl was an especially central intellectual figure in the court of the Commander of the Faithful. (Ibid.) Thus, any major philosophical work other than *Ḥayy* that he might have written should have been preserved.

37. Sami Hawi, "Philosophus Autodidactus: Lineage and Perspective," 202.

38. THY, 4. Hence, I agree with George Sarton, who says that although the idea behind *Ḥayy* is not Ibn Ṭufayl's invention, he was nevertheless "the first to exploit it with sufficient completeness" and was, in this sense, the real creator of it. George Sarton, *Introduction to the History of Science*, 2 vols. (Baltimore: Carnegie Institution of Washington, 1931), 1: 356.

CHAPTER 5. THE ORIGINATION OF THE WORLD

1. Fārābī, *al-Jamʿ Bayna Ra'yay al-Ḥakīmayn*, 78. Erwin Rosenthal points out that *al-Jamʿ* was an attempt to establish harmony not only between the views of Plato and Aristotle, but between revelation and philosophy. Erwin I. J. Rosenthal, "The Place of Politics in the Philosophy of al-Fārābī," *Islamic Culture* 29 (1955): 159. Miriam Galston argues that Fārābī's attempt to establish harmony between the two philosophers is based on practical rather than merely theoretical considerations that are related to defending philosophy against the claims of revealed religion and the attacks of Muslim theologians. Miriam Galston, "A Re-examination of Fārābī's Neoplatonism," in *Islamic Philosophy and Theology* (Routledge: London, 2007), ed. Ian Richard Netton, 2: 131. The problem of the origination/eternity of the world was a major divide between the theologians and the philosophers—so much so that Ghazālī dedicated a quarter of his *Incoherence* to discussing it.

2. THY, 5.

3. Fārābī, *al-Jamʿ*, 86.

4. Ibid., 105, 107.

5. Ibid., 106.

6. TCD, *Timaeus*, 29a8. See discussion of the difference between Plato's depiction of creation in *Timaues* and the Neoplatonic depiction of creation in relation to the status of the forms in Emil L. Fackenheim, "The Possibility of the Universe in al-Fārābī, Ibn Sīnā, and Maimonides," in *Islamic Philosophy*, 12 vols., ed. Fuat Sezgin (Frankfurt: Institute for the History of Arabic-Islamic Science, 1999), 9: 391.

7. Fārābī, *al-Jamʿ*, 101.

8. For more on the reference to Ibn al-ʿArabī as Son of Plato, see Franz Rosenthal, "Ibn ʿArabī between 'Philosophy' and 'Mysticism,'" *Oriens* 31 (1988): 204.

9. THA, 211.

10. Ibn Ṭufayl's depiction of the nature of the essences is similar to Ibn al-ʿArabī's paradoxical characterization of the nature of images in mirrors: "Imagination is neither existent nor nonexistent, neither known nor unknown, neither affirmed nor negated. A person who sees his image in the mirror knows decisively that he has perceived his form in some respect and that he has not perceived his form in some other respect. Then if he says: 'I saw my form I did not see my form,' he will be neither a truth teller nor a liar. What is then the truth of the perceived form? The form is negated and affirmed, existent and nonexistent, known and unknown. God manifested this truth to the servant as a sign so that he realizes that once he has become incapable of recognizing the truth of this affair [the truth of the liminal nature of the image], although it is an affair of this world, then he knows that he is even more incapable in relation to the knowledge of its Creator." FUT, I 304: 22–32.

11. BWA, *Phys.*, 3. 4, 202b: 1–7.

12. Ibid., 203a: 1–6.

13. Antonio Capizzi, *The Cosmic Republic: Notes for a Non-Peripatetic History of the Birth of Philosophy in Greece* (Amsterdam: J. C. Gieben, 1990), 51.

14. BWA, *Phys.*, 3. 4, 204a: 5–6.

15. Ibid., 3, 5, 206a: 20–26.

16. Ibid., 206a: 29–30. The phrase "In its full completion" here means "in actuality." See also *Metaphys*. 11, 10, 1066b: 11–12.

17. BWA, *Phys.*, 3. 6, 206a: 10–11.

18. Aristotle says: "But we apprehend time only when we have marked motion, marking it by 'before' and 'after,' and it is only when we have perceived 'before' and 'after' in motion that we say that time has elapsed.... When we think of the extremes as different from the middle and the mind pronounces that the 'nows' are two, one before and one after, it is then that we say that there is time." BWA, *Phys.*, 4. 10, 219a: 22–30.

19. See *Phys.*, 3. 6, 206a; *Metaphys.*, 9. 6, 1048b: 8–18. For further discussion of the problem in the context of Islamic theological debates, see Harry Wolfson, *The Philosophy of the Kalām* (Cambridge: Harvard University Press, 1976), 412.

20. BWA, *Metaphys*. 5, 16, 1021b: 12–14; *Metaphys*. 9, 3 1047a: 30.

21. BWA, *Phys*. 3. 6, 207a: 10–12

22. Ibid., 206a: 27–28.

23. Ibid., 206a: 30.

24. Ibid., 206a: 20.

25. Ibid., 206a: 30.

26. Ibid., 206a: 31–35.

27. For a general discussion of the challenges that Aristotle's conception of time posed to Islamic philosophers in dealing with the problem of creation, see Lenn Goodman, "Time in Islam," in *Islamic Philosophy and Theology*, ed. Ian Richard Netton (Routledge: London, 2007), 3: 15–38.

28. THA, 166.

29. THA, 137–38.

30. Herbert A. Davidson, *Alfarabi, Avicenna, and Averroes on Intellect: Their Cosmologies, Theories of the Active Intellect, and Theories of Human Intellect* (Oxford: Oxford University Press, 1992), 99.

31. Ibid.

32. Ibid.

33. This concept will be discussed in greater detail in chapter 7.

34. This should alert us to a different reading of the insistence of Islamic philosophers on paying such special attention to Aristotle's concept of motion, for acknowledging and even exaggerating the idea that the world is a place of motion is crucial for affirming a motionless divinity.

35. THA, 166. Lane renders *khāṭir* as an idea bestirring itself in the mind or a thing coming at random into the mind. AEL, 2: 705.

36. See the discussion in Wolfson, *Philosophy of the Kalām*, 414–15.

37. Simon Van Den Bergh, *Averroes' Tahāfut al-Tahāfut (The Incoherence of the Incoherence)*, 2 vols. (Oxford: Oxford University Press, 1954), 1:10.

38. Ibid., 8–9.

39. Ibid., 10.

40. Ibn Sīnā, *Ishārāt*, 3: 114–15.

41. THA, 111.

42. THA, 171.

43. İNM, 227 (italics mine).

44. According to the thesis in Kant's first antinomy, the world has a beginning in time and is limited in space. According to the antithesis, the world has no beginning and no limits in space. See Norman Kemp Smith, *Immanuel Kant's Critique of Pure Reason* (New York: St. Martin's Press, 1965), 396–97.

45. INM, 228.

46. Ibid., 229 (italics mine).

47. "He was no longer troubled by the dilemmas of creation versus eternity, for either way the existence of a non-corporeal Author of the universe remained unscathed, being neither in contact with matter nor cut off from it, neither within nor outside it—for all these terms … are merely predicates of the very physical things which he transcends." THY, 133.

CHAPTER 6. THE SHADOW OF FĀRĀBĪ

1. Abū Naṣr al-Fārābī, *Kitāb al-Ḥurūf*, ed. Muḥsin Mahdī (Beirūt: Dār al-Mashriq), 1970, 155 (hereafter cited as KH). Part of this work has been translated by Muḥammad ʿAlī Khālidī in *Medieval Islamic Philosophical Writings*, ed. Muḥammad ʿAli Khālidī (Cambridge: Cambridge University Press, 2005), 1–26. Khālidī uses Mahdī's edition, which has the passages numbered so that it is easy for the reader to compare with the Arabic edition. Khālidī's translation will be hereafter cited as BL.

2. Miriam Galston points out that Fārābī's *Book of Letters* contains the most explicit statement concerning the limits of human knowledge. She indicates, however,

that no such statement is to be found in Fārābī's commentaries on Aristotle's *Rhetoric*, a work that contains much of the account of the arts in *Book of Letters*, and that his account of Aristotle's thought in *Philosophy of Aristotle* supports the position that philosophy was still an active search for truth in Aristotle's time. Miriam Galston, "The Theoretical and Practical Dimensions of Happiness as Portrayed in the Political Treatises of al-Fārābī," in *The Political Aspects of Islamic Philosophy: Essays in Honor of Muḥsin S. Mahdī*, ed. Charles E. Butterworth (Cambridge: Harvard University Press, 1992), 123.

3. Paul Walker suggests a reading that "seems to recognize the true rank of a supreme philosopher as someone who can be none other than a religious prophet." Paul E. Walker, "Philosophy of Religion in al-Fārābī, Ibn Sīnā, and Ibn Ṭufayl," in *Reason and Inspiration in Islam: Theology, Philosophy, and Mysticism in Muslim Thought*, ed. Todd Lawson (London: I. B. Tauris, 2005), 92.

4. Hillel Fradkin, "The Political Thought of Ibn Ṭufayl," in *The Political Aspects of Islamic Philosophy: Essays in Honor of Muḥsin S. Mahdī*, ed., Charles E. Butterworth (Cambridge: Harvard University Press, 1992), 235.

5. In *Taḥṣīl al-Sa ʿāda*, Fārābī says that human beings live in groups by nature (*fiṭra*), and that is why man is called a political animal. Fārābī, *Taḥṣīl al-Sa ʿāda*, ed. Jaʿfar Āl Yāsīn, (Beirūt: Dār al-Andalus, 1981), 61–62.

6. THY, 57–58.

7. KH, 2.

8. THA, 138.

9. THA, 144–45.

10. BL, 1; KH, 131.

11. KH, 131.

12. KH, 132.

13. See AEL, 4: 1559. *Sha ʿara* also means "He said, or spoke, or gave utterance to poetry; spoke in verse; poetized; or versified." AEL, 4: 1559. In his account of the development of the human sciences, Fārābī regards poetry as one of the earliest means of conveying knowledge.

14. THA, 134.

15. KH, 132.

16. BL, 3; KH, 133; words in Arabic added.

17. *mā amkanahu waṣfuhu mimmā shāhadahu ʿinda al-wuṣūl.*

18. THA, 218.

19. This is what led Hawi to emphasize the rationalistic aspect of Ibn Ṭufayl's book and strongly argue for it as a philosophical treatise rather than a symbolic romance. See INM, 25–32.

20. BL, 4–5; words in Arabic added.

21. BL, 4.

22. Q 7: 172.

23. BL, 5.

24. Ibid.

25. THA, 129.

26. *ʿUhūdihi* is the plural of *ʿahd*, which means pledge or vow. *Maʿhūd* means familiar, known. *ʿAhd* also means covenant or agreement.

27. As we are going to see shortly, *aʿyān* is the designation that Fārābī gives to sensible existents.

28. THA, 226. That Ḥayy was able to speak in a short time is a clear indication of his quick-wit. In a sense, he resembles the first human being, who possessed superior intellectual capacities. The words in italics allude to Q 2:31, which emphasizes the superiority of Adam over the angels, "And he taught Adam all the names. Then he placed the things before the angels and said: 'tell me the names of these if you are correct. They said 'Glory to you, we know not except for what you have taught us. You are the possessor of knowledge and wisdom.'"

29. BL, 6–7; words in Arabic added.

30. THA, 148.

31. This accords with Fārābī's account of the development of the sciences and the teaching of the domination of humans over the animal kingdom in religion.

32. THA, 148.

33. THA, 150.

34. THA, 149.

35. THA, 151.

36. MHQ, 801.

37. MHQ, 880–881.

38. BL, 11. The phrase "Relative to the time uttered" is Khālidī's translation of *bi-al-iḍāfa ilā zamān al-nuṭq*.

39. AEL, 1: 251. According to Lane, the difference between *balāgha* and *faṣāḥa* is that "the latter is an attribute of a single word and of speech and of the speaker; but the former is only an attribute of speech and the speaker." AEL 1, 251.

40. KH, 12.

41. KH, 146.

42. THY, 69.

43. KH, 152.

44. BWA, *Topics*, 1, 100a 8–14.

45. BWA, 1, 100b 19–22.

46. Ibid., 1, 12, 105a, 16–19. Notice that in the definition of reasoning, Aristotle says that through reasoning, things come about *necessarily* from other things, which explains why reasoning is more forcible than induction.

47. TCD, *Rep.*, 7, 532a, 4–13.

48. TCD, 7: 533a 13–21.

49. TCD, *Symposium*, 210 e15–b.

50. BWA, *Topics*, 1, 12, 105a, 17–18.

51. TCD, *Rep.*, 7: 534b 5.

52. The concluding part of Ibn Ṭufayl's story is destined to teach us what will become of the philosopher as he decides to break his silence and communicate to the followers of religion the truth of the dependence of their religion on perfect philosophy.

Fārābī seems to be aware of the reason that may have convinced the original founder of religion to remain silent about this. See Muhsin Mahdi, "Alfarabi on Philosophy and Religion," *Philosophical Forum* 4 (1972): 7.

CHAPTER 7. THE SHADOW OF IBN BĀJJA

1. Abū Bakr Ibn Bājja. *Ittiṣāl al-ʿAql bi-al-Insān*. In *Rasā'il Ibn Bājja al-Ilāhiyya*. Ed. Majid Fakhry (Beirūt: Dār al-Nahār, 1968), 157 (hereafter cited as IAI). Ibid., 157. Compare with THA, 138, 144.

2. Ibid., 158. Compare with THA, 131.

3. Ibid., 158–59. Compare with THA, 143, 151.

4. Ibid., 159–60.

5. Ibid., 159. THA, 159;

6. Ibid.

7. THY, 124.

8. Ibid.

9. The full implications of the mystical characteristics of the nature of nature (the form and the soul), however, are still hidden from Ibn Bājja. Compare with Ibn al-ʿArabī's *barzakhī* depiction of the soul. See SD, 270–71. Compare also with Mullā Ṣadrā's conception of the soul: "For Mullā Ṣadra, it is not a question of the soul moving across an immutable *barzakh* or barrier between the apparently mutually exclusive existential modes of immateriality and bodliness, createdness and eternity, but rather for Ṣadra, the soul itself is the *barzakh*—a moving *barzakh* that traverses the various modes of being through its own process of transformation." Maria Massi Dakake, "The Soul as *Barzakh*: Substantial Motion and Mullā Ṣadrā's Theory of Human Becoming," *Muslim World* 94 (2004): 107–8.

10. Reading *mundhu tufuhima dhālika al-maʿnā* instead of *mundhu tafahama dhālika al-maʿnā*. In the latter reading, reference is made to a person who comprehends the meaning.

11. IAI, 172–73.

12. IAI, 160. More on the intermediary imaginal forms will be discussed later in this chapter on.

13. Ibid.

14. IAI, 160n.5.

15. Davidson, *Alfarabi, Avicenna, and Averroes on Intellect*, 35.

16. Ibid., 36.

17. IAI, 166.

18. As Davidson points out, Plotinus employed a metaphor that was frequently used in Arabic literature, one that depicts the state of the soul in relation to the cosmic intellect. According to this metaphor, the soul functions as a mirror that reflects images sent to it when it is properly situated toward the higher world. Davidson, *Alfarabi, Avicenna, and Averroes on Intellect*, 25.

19. IAI, 167.

20. IAI, 168–69.

21. Davidson, *Alfarabi, Avicenna, and Averroes on Intellect*, 21, 26.

22. TCD, *Rep.*, 514e7–515c2. The prisoners are only aware of the reality of the shadows, so it might be misleading to say that they think of the shadows as identical to real things.

23. TCD, *Rep.*, 515a3–7.

24. Eva Brann points out that the *Republic* is a dialogue, a conversation, and that "the author wants us as soon as [we begin reading it] to *join* in, to be converted from passive perusal to active participation, to be drawn in among the other silent 'interlocutors.'" Eva Brann, *The Music of the Republic*, 88.

25. TCD, *Rep.*, 515c7–10.

26. Ibn Bājja says, "Blindness is a bad thing. Without light our eyes are blind. The difference between walking with light and walking in darkness is known by itself, so also the situation of the ignorant, who possesses no knowledge of a thing. To know a thing is to acquire knowledge of its predicated concept. To judge now and then that certain individuals come under a certain concept resembles walking." IAI, 168. Q 6:122 reads, "Can he who was dead to whom we gave life and a light whereby he can walk amongst men be like him who is in the depths of darkness from which he can never come out?" MHQ, 329–30. As Ibn Bājja says in *Risālat al-Wadā'*, "He who sees in the light avoids things that he likes to avoid and comes close to things because he likes to come close to them, whereas the situation of the person who 'sees' in the darkness is opposite to that, since he might avoid what he is seeking and run away from what he desires." Ibn Bājja, *Risālat al-Wadā'*, in *Rasā'il Ibn Bājja al-Ilāhiyya*, ed. Majid Fakhry (Beirūt: Dār al-Nahār, 1968), 138.

27. TCD, *Rep.*, 515e1–4.

28. TCD, *Rep.*, 515e6–516a–b2.

29. TCD, *Rep.*, 517b7–8–c5.

30. This is a free interpretation of his words: *fa'amma al-ṣuwar al-jismāniyya fa'innaha tufīd al-wujūd al-mushār ilayhi wa-huwa aqṣar al-wujūdāt.*

31. Ibn Bājja, *Tadbīr al-Mutawaḥḥid*, in *Rasā'il Ibn Bājja al-Iāhiyya*, ed. Majid Fakhry (Bairūt: Dār al-Nahār, 1968), 77.

32. IAI, 160.

33. Ibn Bājja, *Tadbīr al-Mutawaḥḥid*, 50.

34. Ibid., 77.

35. For the description of the prisoners in the cave as lacking any sense of past, future and, consequently, present time, see Thomas Wheaton Bestor, "Plato's Semantics and Plato's Cave," *Oxford Studies in Ancient Philosophy* 14 (1996): 36–37.

36. Ibn Bājja, *Tadbīr al-Mutawaḥḥid*, 88.

37. See the opening lines of Aristotle's *Metaphysics*. *Insān al-'ayn* also called *nāẓir* (seer).

38. Ibn Bājja, *Tadbīr al-Mutawaḥḥid*, 87.

39. Ibid., 50.

40. Ibid., 94. This is a major characteristic of the Platonic form, which is depicted as permanent and fixed. It can be the case that Ibn Bājja's depiction of this feature of fixity (*thubūt*) had exerted some influence on Ibn al-'Arabī's characterization of the fixed entities (*a'yān thābita*).

41. Ibid., 93. Compare with TCD, *Phaedo*, 102d–3b.

42. Ibid., 94.

43. Ibid.

44. Ibid., 95.

45. Ibid., 96.

46. THA, 110. Goodman has an interesting explanation of Ibn Bājja's reservation against the ṣūfīs' reliance on their mystical subjective experience as this distances them from the attainment of the spiritual forms. See Lenn Goodman, "Ibn Bājja," in *History of Islamic Philosophy*, eds. Seyyed Hossein Nasr and Oliver Leaman, 2 vols. (Routledge: New York, 2001), 1: 301–2.

CHAPTER 8. THE TRADITIONALISTIC ACCOUNT FROM THE BEGINNING

1. The reference is to Q 18:17.

2. THA, 121–23.

3. THY, 61.

4. THY, 61.

5. MHQ, 711.

6. THA, 142–43. In mystical symbolism, fire reflects the desire of the mystic to return to his origin through the mystical ascent as the love of return burns in his heart. See Morteza Aghatehrani, *Khājah Naṣīr al-Din Ṭūsī on the Meta-Mysticism of Ibn Sīnā* (Ann Arbor, MI: UMI Dissertation Services, 1999), 75. To learn more about the intermediary or *barzakhī* nature of fire, see Chittick, *Imaginal Worlds*, 26.

7. Goodman renders the first sentence in this passage as: "A fire broke out one day by friction in a bed of reeds." THY, 115. Ockley, who seems to adhere to a more literal interpretation of the text, renders the sentence as: "It happened that by collision a fire was kindled among a parcel of reeds or canes." Ockley, *Improvement*, 51. "Happened" and "chanced" are the two translations for *ittafaqa,* according to AEL, 8: 1057.

8. BWA, *Phys.* 36, 6, 198a, 6–10.

9. Catarina Belo, "Ibn Sīnā on Chance in the *Physics* of *As-sifā'*," in *Interpreting Avicenna: Science and Philosophy in Medieval Islam*, ed. Jon McGinnis with the assistance of David C. Reisman (Leiden: E. J. Brill, 2004), 26.

10. Ibid., 29, 32.

11. Ibid., 36.

12. Donald Coggan, *The Revised English Bible* (Oxford: Oxford University Press, 1989), *Proverbs*, 1, 7.

13. BWA, *Metaphys.*, 1, 2, 982b12–13.

14. See Plato's depiction of the form of the Good in TCD, *Rep.* 517c2–5. I cite this to remind the reader that Ibn Ṭufayl refers to Ibn Bājja's *Ittiṣāl al-ʿAql bī al-Insān*, in which the latter makes a direct reference to the Parable of the Cave.

15. TCD, *Rep.*, IV, 434e 6–435a 1–4.

16. THA, 226.

17. Aristotle, *Physics*, trans. Hippocrates G. Apostle (Bloomington: Indiana University Press, 1973), 4. 11, 218b: 21–34.

18. Ibid., 4, 11, 219a: 23–24.

19. Ibid., 4, 11, 219b: 3.

20. In the margin of the Arabic text of Aristotle's *Physics,* it is noted that this town is thought to be Ḥarrān. Aristotle, *al-Ṭabī'a*, trans. Isḥāq bin Ḥunayn, 2 vols., ed. 'Abd al-Raḥmān Badawī (Cairo: al-Dār al-Qawmiyya, 1964), 414.

21. AEL 4: 1346.

22. Ibid., 1347.

23. Aristotle, *Ṭabī'a*, 435.

24. Ibid., 416.

25. THA, 191.

26. Ibid.

27. Aristotle, *Ṭabī'a*, 407.

28. Ibid., 435.

29. THA, 195.

30. Aristotle, *Ṭabī'a*, 435.

31. Qushayrī, *Risāla*, 34.

32. THA, 205.

33. According to Ṣuyūṭī, *ḥiqba*, which is rendered here as "years," designates seventy years. Jalāl al-Dīn al-Ṣuyūtī, *al-Dur al-Manthūr fī al-Tafsīr al-Ma'thūr*, 8 vols. (Beirūt: Dār al-Kutub al-'Ilmiyya, 1983), 4: 417. See also Abū Jarīr al-Ṭabarī, *Tafsīr al-Ṭabarī*, 12 vols. (Beirūt: Dār al-Kutub al-'Ilmiyya, 1992), 8: 246.

34. Q 7:160 reads: "We directed Moses by inspiration, when his (thirsty) people asked him for water: 'Strike the rock with thy staff.' Out of it there gushed forth twelve springs." MHQ, 391. See also Q 2:60.

35. See Ṭabarī, *Tafsīr*, 8: 253; Ṣuyūṭī, *al-Dur*, 4: 417.

36. MHQ, 727.

37. Ṭabarī explains: "You will not have patience with me since I act according to a nonmanifest knowledge that I had been taught by God and you know only things that are manifest." Ṭabarī, *Tafsīr*, 8: 256.

38. In the Bible, this commandment follows the commandment: "Honour your father and your mother, so that you may enjoy long life in the land which the Lord your God is giving to you." *Revised English Bible, Exodus*, 20:12. In the Qur'ān, this commandment follows immediately the divine decree not to associate others with God, which is placed as the highest of decrees. Q 17:23 reads: "And your Lord had decreed that you worship none but him, and that you be kind to your parents."

39. As 'Ali b. Abī Ṭālib was making a speech in which he mentioned his companions, Yazīd b. Muljam was heard saying: "I shall relieve them of you." His companions informed him of what he had said, but he refused to take action, saying: "He has not killed me yet so you must leave him in peace." His companions said: "You know him and you know his intentions, why not kill him then?" He responded by asking: "How can I kill my killer?" Abū al-'Abās al-Mubarrad, *al-Kāmil fī al-Lugha wa-al-Adab*, ed. Ḥanā al-Fākhūrī, 2 vols. (Beirūt: Dār al-Jīl, 1997), 1: 181.

40. Satan's refusal to bow down to Adam is mentioned in Chapter of the Cave, Q 18:50.

41. MHQ, 347.

42. Ibid.

43. Peter Awin brings Ṭabarī's and Ibn Kathīr's interpretation as follows: Iblīs employed analogy (*qiyās*) in inferring that he must be a superior being because fire is superior to clay: "Through this reasoning process Iblīs becomes the first creature to leap headlong into the abyss of *qiyās*. His analogy and its seemingly logical conclusion hardened his heart to God's command and lured him to his destruction." Peter J. Awin, *Satan's Tragedy and Redemption: Ibīs in Ṣūfī Psychology* (Leiden: E. J. Brill, 1983), 36.

44. This is confirmed by Bayḍāwī's interpretation brought in Awin, *Satan's Tragedy and Redemption*. Ibn al-'Arabī says in Chapter 325 of the *Futūḥāt* that due to this intermediation by means of dryness, Adam was closer to Satan than humans who descended from him because they were made of water, which opposes fire absolutely as it is cold and wet, whereas fire is dry and hot. See the discussion in Angelika al-Masri, "Imagination and the *Qur'ān* in the Theology of 'Oneness of Being,'" *Arabica* 47 (2000): 527–28.

45. This literally means "belly of earth."

46. The translation is cited from THY, 106–7, with a slight variation.

47. THA, 187–88

48. Davidson, *Alfarabi, Avicenna, and Averroes on Intellect*, 80.

49. Ibid. Ṭaghrā'ī employs a similar argument to establish the possibility of turning low metals to gold and directs it against Ibn Sīnā. See 'Abd al-Raḥmān Ibn Khaldūn, *Muqaddima* (Beirūt: Dār al-Turāth al-'Arabī, n.d.), 527.

50. Davidson, *Alfarabi, Avicenna, and Averroes on Intellect*, 80.

51. Ibid. As Fakhry points out, Ibn Sīnā attempted in his theory of the formation of the soul, which includes the formation of the human life as well as the human knowledge, to combine the naturalistic interpretation, which establishes a connection between matter and spiritual form, and the theological interpretation, which rejects a naturalistic interpretation that is incompatible with the notion of the creation of the soul by a divine command. Majid Fakhry, "The Arabs and the Encounter with Philosophy," in *Philosophy, Dogma, and the Impact of Greek Thought in Islam* (Brookfield,VT Variorum, 1994), 13.

52. THA, 124–25.

53. Q 38:75.

54. Q 17:62; 38:82–83; 15:39–40.

55. Q 18:82.

56. Ṣuyūṭī, *al-Dur*, 4: 425, 431–32; Ṭabarī, *Tafsīr*, 8: 254, 268.

57. Ian Richard Netton, "Towards a Modern *Tafsīr of Sūrat al-Kahf*: Structure and Semiotics," *Journal of Qur'ānic Studies*, 2 (2000): 77.

58. Ibid., 76.

59. SD, 221. See pages 225 and 227 for additional references in the same work to Ibn al-'Arabī's employment of the verse.

60. See Ian Richard Netton, "Theophany as Paradox: Ibn 'Arabī's Account of *al-Khaḍir* in His *Fuṣūṣ al-Ḥikam*," *Journal of the Muḥyiddīn Ibn 'Arabī Society* 11 (1992), 11–22.

61. FUS, 199.

62. Chittick, SD, 232.

63. *Sakīna* is mentioned in Q 2:248: "And their prophet said to them that a sign of his kingdom is that there shall come to you the ark (*tābūt*) in it *sakīna* from your Lord . . . " I used the word *sakīna* in its Arabic form (meaning "stillness," "tranquility," or "calmness"), because it is clear to me that Ibn al-ʿArabī wants with it not the ordinary literal meaning, but what it designates in mystical usage. ʿAfīfī explains: "Most probably he wants another meaning close to the meaning of the word *sakīna* in its religious and philosophical Jewish usage. It is true that there is no agreement among the Jewish thinkers on the meaning of *sakīna* but it implies for them the meaning of the divine presence among the Israelites as it is also used as a synonym for the name God. It also was understood as an intermediary between God and the created world and as the Holy Spirit." FUS, 294. For more about the notion of *shekhinah* in Jewish mystical and philosophical traditions, see Peter Schäfer, *Mirror of His Beauty: Feminine Images of God from the Bible to the Early Kabbalah* (Princeton: Princeton University Press, 2002), 86–117.

64. Ibid., 198.

65. SD, 70.

66. Ibid., 70.

67. FUS, 199.

68. SD, 232. In this, I find a striking reminder of Ibn Ṭufayl's depiction of the essence of the encompassing circle that is neither identical nor different from the Real, as the other essences that proceed from the first circle and enjoy the nature of intermediary images are mirrored reflections of it.

69. ʿAbd al-Razzāq al-Qāshānī, *Sharḥ Fuṣūṣ al-Ḥikam* (Cairo: al-Maṭbaʿa al-Maymāniyya, n.d.), 295.

70. See SD, 111. Q 20:10 reads: "Behold, he saw a fire: So he said to his family, 'Tarry ye; I perceive a fire; perhaps I can bring you some burning brand (*qabas*) therefrom, or find some guidance at the fire.'" MHQ, 766–767; also Q 27:7. Notice that *qabas* is the word used by Ibn Ṭufayl.

71. THA, 110.

72. FUS, 206.

73. FUS, 258.

74. Ibn al-ʿArabī, *Fuṣūṣ al-Ḥikam*, 204. For a useful discussion of the theme of love in the Chapter of Moses, see Jane Clark, "Universal Meanings in Ibn ʿArabī's *Fuṣūṣ al-Ḥikam*: Some Comments on the Chapter of Moses," *Journal of the Muḥyiddin Ibn ʿArabī Society*, 12 (2005) 105–29. In the final passage of her article, Clark says that emphasis on mercy "makes Ibn ʿArabī's compassionate insight almost Christic in its scope."

75. Ibn al-ʿArabī, *The Bezels of Wisdom*, trans. R. W. J. Austin (New York: Paulist Press, 1980), 251–52. As Nettler points out, for Ibn al-ʿArabī, the children are "part of the collectivity of Adam's emerging descendants who universally make the covenant with God for humanity." See the discussion in Ronald L. Nettler, *Ṣūfī Metaphysics and Qurāʾnic Prophets: Ibn ʿArabī's Thought and Method in the Fuṣūṣ al-Ḥikam* (Cambridge, UK: The Islamic Texts Society, 2003), 28–29.

76. Ibn al-ʿArabī, *al-Tajalliyāt al-Ilāhiyya*, ed. Osman Yahia (Tehran: Danshkahi, 1988), 97. Ibn al-ʿArabī says that at the Spring of Arīn, he encountered the youth who was the counterpart of the angel Gabriel. See Steven Hirtenstein, *The Unlimited Mercifier: The Spiritual Life and Thought of Ibn ʿArabī* (Oxford: Anqa Publishing, 1999), 93.

77. Austin, *Bezels of Wisdom*, 252.

78. As Nettler points out, this inversion of sorts determines a relationship between Moses's soul and his body, the Real and creation, in terms of a complementarity of lower and higher forces that is organized by the lower's control of the relationship. Nettler, *Ṣūfī Metaphysics and Qur'ānic Prophets*, 34–35.

79. "For the seeing of a thing, itself by itself, is not the same as its seeing itself in another, as it were in a mirror." Austin, *Bezels of Wisdom*, 50.

80. *Qarību ʿahdin birabbihi*. The word *ʿahd* also means covenant.

81. Austin, *Bezels*, 254.

82. MHQ, 822.

83. FUS, 200.

84. "[Moses's mother] conceived and bore a son ... Unable to conceal him ... she got a rush basket for him, made it watertight with pitch and tar, laid him in it, and placed it among the reeds by the bank of the Nile." *The Revised English Bible, Exodus*, 2:1.

85. Aḥmad Amīn (ed.), *Ḥayy bin Yaqẓān li Ibn Sīnā wa Ibn Ṭufayl wa al-Suhrawardī* (Cairo: Mu'assasat al-Khānjī, 1958), 13. Now it is not a human being that will find the child but an animal, and not any animal, but the most striking symbol in Arabic poetry for love and swift motion. For the Arabs, the gazelle symbolized love, beauty, and health. It is also described as possessing strong sight and a developed sense of wariness. See Kamāl al-Dīn al-Damīrī, *Ḥayāt al-Ḥayawān al-Kubrā*, 2 vols. (Beirūt: Dār al-Fikr, n.d.), 2: 102–6.

CHAPTER 9. GILGAMESH: THE ONE WHO SAW THE ABYSS

1. The opening line of the *Epic* reads: "The one who saw the abyss I will make the land know; of him who knew all, let me tell the whole story." John Gardner and John Maier with the assistance of Richard A. Henshaw, *Gilgamesh* (New York: Alfred A. Knopf, 1984), 57: line 1 (hereafter cited as G).

2. G, 21.

3. G, 57.

4. Q 18:93–98.

5. G, 57:19. For mentions of the number seven, see G, 91:4–5; 93:6–7;152:51–52; 156:103–4;128:45; 177:9–10; 212:4–5; 236:127–78; 239:156–57; 241:199; 245:228; 250:307; 266:114–16.

6. G, 67.

7. G, 68:30–32.

8. Thorkild Jacobsen, *The Treasures of Darkness: A History of Mesopotamian Religion* (New Haven, CT: Yale University Press, 1976), 196.

9. The Akkadian version uses two terms that stand at the heart of both Jewish and Islamic depiction of man as in the image of God: *salmu*, which means "statue, image, likeness," and *uṣ-ṣir*, which means "fashion, form." As Chittick points out, the word "form" occurs three times in the Qur'ān: "*[God] created you, then proportioned you, then balanced you; in whatever form He willed He mounted you* (82:7–8). *He formed you, and He made your forms beautiful* (40:64, 64:3). God is the subject of the verb *to form (taṣwīr)* four times, and He is also called the "former," i.e., "form-Giver" (*muṣawwir*), once (59:24)." SD, 27. Chittick also indicates that in Islamic philosophy, the term "form" was used in the Aristotelian sense as the correlative of matter, whereas in ṣūfīsm, it was paired with "meaning" (*ma'nā*), a synonym of quiddity. Ibid., 27. Andrew George renders the text as: "What Anu thought of she fashioned within her." Andrew George, *The Epic of Gilgamesh: The Babylonian Epic Poem and Other Texts in Akkadian and Sumerian* (London: The Penguin Press, 1999), 5. What Anu thought of was a meaning (*ma'nā*), and it was this meaning that received a form (*ṣūra*) in Aruru's heart.

10. This is a reminder of the mother-doe which took care of *Ḥayy Ibn Yaqẓān*. See n.12.

11. G, 68:38–41.

12. "Mankind of that time (i.e., primordial times) knew not the eating of bread, knew not the wearing of garments. The people went around with skins on their bodies. They ate grass with their mouths like sheep, drank water from ditches." Jeffrey H. Tigay, *The Evolution of the Gilgamesh Epic* (Philadelphia: University of Pennsylvania Press, 1982), 203. Later in the story, when Enkidu is introduced to the human society and when people set bread before him, he gapes at it, not knowing what to do. See G, 92. Tigay draws our attention to the possible connection between the story of Enkidu and the reports about abandoned children who were raised in the wild by animals.

13. G, 71.

14. George, *Epic of Gilgamesh*, xxxiii.

15. Ibid., xxxiii–xxxiv.

16. G, 67:1. As George points out, the tradition that the first men roamed lawless and free of civilized conduct helped to give rise to the myth that kings were destined by the gods to be distinguished from the rest of mortals in appearance, as well as in capability. George, *Epic of Gilgamesh*, xli.

17. G, 68.

18. G, 72.

19. THA, 198.

20. G, 73.

21. The love-priestess belonged to those women who were in the service of the temple and who performed sacred prostitution related to the goddess Ishtar. See G, 76n.19.

22. G, 79.

23. George, *Epic of Gilgamesh*, 8. In a larger sense, the encounter with the priestess symbolizes the passage from *mythos* to *logos* in the early history of human intellectuality. Here, I wish to draw the reader's attention to an interesting account that Bruce Lincoln provides for the difference in meaning between *mythos* and *logos* as they are used by ancient texts to mark different sorts of discourse. In these texts, *mythoi* are spoken above

all in the battlefields as acts of speech that create power and dominance whereas *logoi* are acts of speech that women use to gain dominance by arousing desire. Lincoln quotes the following lines of poetry from the *Odyssey*:

Calypso restrained him from misery and lamentation;
Ever with soft and seductive *logoi*
She beguiled him in such a way he became forgetful of Ithaca.

Bruce Lincoln, "Gendered Discourses: The Early History of *Mythos and Logos*," *History of Religions* 36 (1996): 9. With seductive *logoi*, the priestess seduced Enkidu toward civilized Uruk and away from his natural dwelling.

24. *The Revised English Bible, Genesis*, 3:22.

25. Tigay, *Evolution of the Gilgamesh*, 207.

26. Ibid., 207n. 44.

27. Ibid., 208.

28. SD, 5. This applies also to fornication (*sifāḥ*) not only to lawful marriage (*nikāḥ*). See Sachiko Murata, *The Tao of Islam: A Sourcebook on Gender Relationships in Islamic Thought*, 152.

29. Claude Addas, "The Ship of Stone," *Journal of the Muḥyiddīn Ibn 'Arabī Society*, 19 (1996): 14.

30. Ibid., 8.

31. Ibid., 9.

32. SD, 334.

33. Murata, *Tao of Islam*, 152.

34. For more about the resemblance between the act of writing and sexual coupling according to Ibn al-'Arabī, see the discussion by Khālid Balqāsim, *al-Kitāba wa-al-Taṣawwuf 'inda Ibn 'Arabī* (al-Dār al-Bayḍā': Toubqāl, 2004), 40–47.

35. Ibid., 125.

36. FUT, 2, 466: 10–12.

37. There seem to be two accounts of the outcome of the fight: one makes Gilgamesh the winner and the other has Enkidu as the winner. The fact that Enkidu had the upper hand in the fight is confirmed by Jacobsen, *Treasures of Darkness*, 199.

38. G, 67.

39. G, 58.

40. "I was a Treasure but was not known, so I *loved* to be known; I created the creatures and made Myself known to them, so they came to know Me." SD, 21.

41. FUT, 2: 110. Ibn al-'Arabī often cites the following lines of poetry by Hārūn al-Rashīd: "The three ladies held me fast and penetrated each part of me. How is it that the whole world obeys me and I them and they disobey me? It is only because the power of love, which is what gives them strength, is above my power". FUT, 2, 113: 14–16.

42. FUT, 2, 665: 15–18.

43. According to Tigay, the priestess's conduct supports the folklore motif, according to which the woman plays the role of a "seducer toward civilization." Tigay, *Evolution of the Gilgamesh Epic*, 203.

44. G, 78.

45. G, 81.

46. G, 102.

47. G, 104.

48. Jacobsen, *Treasures of Darkness*, 199.

49. G, 108: 32.

50. As Tzvi Abusch explains, Gilgamesh's refusal to Ishtar's proposal was based on his recognition that whereas she attempted to present their marriage as this-worldly, it would only lead to his transferal to the netherworld—that is, to death. Tzvi Abusch, "Ishtar's Proposal and Gilgamesh's Refusal: An Interpretation of *The Gilgamesh Epic*, Tablet 6, Lines 1–79," *History of Religions* 26 (1986), 173.

51. G, 156: 103–4.

52. G, 162: 176–77.

53. See commentator's note, G, 167.

54. G, 175. Now that Enkidu is incapable of guarding the gazelles against the hunter, he implores the gods to do so. Enkidu was especially harsh toward the prostitute as he showered her with many curses; the most painful among them, in my opinion, is the decree that the road be her dwelling place. This is because it implies a total demeaning of her status as a priestess and dweller in the temple. That is why Shamash had to intervene and balance the curse. The curse, once uttered, cannot be cancelled, only balanced. See G, 175.

55. G, 183: 3–8.

56. G, 190: 6–7. As Abusch points out, Enkidu's death rendered human life unbearable for Gilgamesh. That is why he takes on the appearance of gods, for gods were often imaged as animals. See Abusch, "Ishtar's Proposal and Gilgamesh's Refusal," 181, and n.13.

57. G, 109.

58. G, 181.

59. G, 183.

60. G, 187.

61. Jacobsen, *Treasures of Darkness*, 203.

62. G, 187.

63. G, 212. Compare with THA, 139.

64. G, 188.

65. G, 196. The last sentence in this citation seems to be inconsistent with the contradistinction that George attempts to make between Gilgamesh, who does not show much respect for divine authority, and the hero of religious poetry, who "puts himself in the hands of his God." See George, *Epic of Gilgamesh*, xxxiv.

66. G, 210.

67. Jacobsen, *Treasures of Darkness*, 206. Jacobsen draws our attention to the relationship between the myth of the Flood and the creation story of *Enumma Elish*, which asserted that the whole world was once water. See the discussion in Julian Reade, "Sumerian Origins," in *Sumerian Gods and Their Representations*, eds. I. L. Finkel and M. J. Geller (Groningen: STYX, 1997), 225. As Abusch points out, the existence of antithesis and contradictions and the balancing of order and disorder are central to the Mesopotamian perspective. Abusch, "Ishtar's Proposal and Gilgamesh's Refusal ...,"

266. The notion of a devastating Flood is needed because it is against this notion that the notion of a totally new beginning (that is, creation) is measured and depicted as the paradigm of all new beginnings.

68. G, 200. *Uta* means "he found," and *napishtim* means "life." See Tigay, *Evolution of the Gilgamesh Epic*, 229. In the Qur'ān, al-Khaḍir is described as one of "our Good servants for whom God had granted mercy from himself and whom God had taught knowledge from his own presence." (Q 18:65)

69. G, 202. In the Qur'ān, this is the description of the state of unbelievers who find themselves lost in a sea of darkness (Q 24:40), as a bar is set in front of them and a bar behind them and they see not (Q 36:9). Rachel Milstein points out that in the poetry of Niẓāmī and Fīrdūsī, al-Khaḍir is depicted as joining Alexander, who searched for immortality, in the Land of Darkness. Rachel Milstein, "Light, Fire, and the Sun in Islamic Painting," in *Studies in Islamic History and Civilization*, ed. M. Sharon (Leiden: E. J. Brill, 1986), 541.

70. G, 205.

71. G, 209.

72. G, 212.

73. G, 221. Upon encountering Utnapishtim, Gilgamesh makes what proves to be a fatal mistake. He tells Utnapishtim that he has wearied himself out in sleeplessness. Utnapishtim will use this later to show Utnapishtim that as he is incapable of overcoming sleep, death's younger brother, he will be even less capable of overcoming death itself.

74. G, 224.

75. Like other Ṣūfīs, Ibn al-ʿArabī makes extensive use of this tradition. For him, sleep designates a *barzakh*, a liminal state that resembles the state in which the human being will be after death; that is, between death and resurrection. See also Chittick, *SD*, 339. FUT, 4, 99: 12–16.

76. G, 226.

77. G, 228.

78. See Tigay, *Evolution of the Gilgamesh Epic*, 216.

79. G, 240.

80. In the Babylonian epic of creation, *Enumma Elish*, the Apsū designates fresh water and Ti-āmat designates salt water:

When above the heaven had not (yet) been named,

(And) below the earth had not (yet) been called by a name;

(When) Apsū primeval, their begetter,

Mammu, (and) Ti-āmat, she who gave birth to them all,

(Still) mingled their waters together,

And no pasture land had been formed (and) not (even) a reed march was to be seen;

When none of the (other) gods had been brought into being;

(When) they had not (yet) been called by (their) name (s, and their) destinies had not (yet) been fixed,

(At that time) were the gods created within them.

Cited in Ewa Wasilewska, *Creation Stories of the Middle East* (London: Jessica Kingsley, 2000), 50.

81. G, 235. Gods are described as dogs curling up. Such depictions of gods as dogs and flies (G, 239) are used by Andrew George to support his view that the *Epic* is not a religious story. See George, *Epic of Gilgamesh*, xxxiii.

82. G, 212.

83. G, 240.

84. Ibid.

85. "Mouth" is the translation of *pi-i* rendered as "source" in G, 241. The words are a reminder of the dwelling place of al-Khaḍir at the Meeting-Place-Of-The-Two-Seas. Notice also that in the final stage of his mystical ascension (*mi'rāj*) Ibn al-'Arabī arrives at the Lotus-Tree-Of-The-Limit, from whose roots flow the four rivers, which symbolize the four kinds of knowledge. See James Winston Morris, "The Spiritual Ascension: Ibn 'Arabī and the Mi'rāj: Part 2," *Journal of the American Oriental Society*, 108 (1988): 70–71; FUT, 3, 350: 29–32.

86. G, 241.

87. G, 245.

88. Ibid.

89. Jacobsen, *Gilgamesh Epic*, 204.

90. G, 249.

91. Maureen Gallery Kovacs, *The Epic of Gilgamesh* (Stanford: Stanford University Press, 1985), 96.

92. Ibid., 106.

93. G, 250.

94. G, 213.

95. Abusch, "Ishtar's Proposal and Gilgamesh's Refusal," 181.

96. See the discussion in G, 256.

97. G, 253–54.

98. G, 263.

99. G, 265.

100. G, 172.

101. G, 265–66.

102. G, 177.

CHAPTER 10. THE *TALE OF BULŪQIYA*: BETWEEN IBN AL-'ARABĪ AND *GILGAMESH*

1. *Alf Layla wa-Layla*, 6 vols. (Beirut: Dar Ṣādir, 1999), 3: 737 (hereafter cited as A). Because I think that the *Tale of Bulūqiyā* is about a quest for knowledge, I find it appropriate to use Burton's "carnally knew" as a translation of *wāqa'a*. Richard Burton, *Arabian Nights*, 16 vols. (Beirūt: Khayāṭ, 1966), 5: 298. For a discussion of the *Tale of Bulūqiya* in relation to the *Gilgamesh Epic,* see Alison Salvesen, "The Legacy of Babylon and Nineveh in Aramaic Sources," in *The Legacy of Mesopotamia*, ed. Stephanie Dalley (Oxford: Oxford University Press, 1998), 150; Stephanie Dalley, "The Sassanian Period and Early Islam," in *The Legacy of Mesopotamia*, ed. Stephanie Dalley (Oxford: Oxford University Press, 1998), 171–72; Andrew George, *The Babylonian Gilgamesh Epic:*

Introduction, Critical Edition, and Cuneiform Texts, 2 vols. (Oxford: Oxford University Press, 2003), 1: 172.

2. Q 12:17.

3. As it turns out, the serpent does not keep her promise, for as she explains to him later, his leaving her place will cause her death. Careful readers can discern the resemblance to the storyteller Shehrezad's own story.

4. Consider what Gilgamesh says: "And after you, I [will cover my body with unshorn hair]: I will put on a dog-skin [and roam the wilderness]." G, 190: 6–7. For more about the significance of travel from a mystical point of view, see Michel Chodkiewicz, "The Endless Journey," in *Journal of the Muḥyiddīn Ibn ʿArabī Society* 19 (1996): 71–84.

5. Chittick, *Ṣūfī Path of Knowledge,* 379. FUT, 3, 105: 13–15, 19–21.

6. Humans alone can know God, and Muḥammad, who is the master of all humans, becomes the locus of the manifestation of God's love to be known.

7. Men are made of earth, the lowest element, and jin are made of fire, the highest. He who rules over earth and fire rules over all creatures.

8. A, 742.

9. Ibid.

10. In her speech to Gilgamesh, the Barmaid utters the following warning: "Gilgamesh, there has never been a crossing, and none from the beginning of days has been able to cross the sea…Even if you, Gilgamesh, cross the sea when you arrive at the waters of death, what would you do?" G, 212.

11. G, 219.

12. This seems to be a common motif in accounts of mystical encounters. A person is drawn away to witness what cannot be witnessed except in isolation. Consider, for example, the beginning of Ibn al-ʿArabī's encounter with Niẓām around the Kaʿba. This act of seclusion occurs in Bulūqiyā's case upon discovering the well of honey.

13. Claude Addas, *The Quest for the Red Sulphur. The Life of Ibn ʿArabī*, trans. Peter Kingsley (Cambridge UK: The Islamic Texts Society, 1993), 116.

14. In *Risālat al-Anwār*, Ibn al-ʿArabī mentions the plants that inform the possessor of revelation of their virtues. Ibn al-ʿArabī, *al-Anwār*, in *Majmūʿat Rasāʾil Ibn ʿArabī* (Beirūt: Dār al-Maḥaja al-Bayḍā,' 2000), 1: 276.

15. A, 742.

16. Compare with Procne's act of revenge upon her husband in Shelley D. Kauhod, "Ovid's Tereus: Fire, Birds, and the Reification of Figurative Language," *Classical Philology* 92 (1997), 69–71.

17. See FUT, 1, 127: 21.

18. FUT, 1, 127: 2.

19. See SD, 112; see also n. 36.

20. A, 743.

21. FUT, 1, 127: 35.

22. FUT, 1, 128: 20–22.

23. A, 746.

24. FUT, 1, 128: 1–7.

25. A, 746.

26. A, 747.

27. A, 751.

28. A, 753.

29. FUT, 1, 128: 24; 130: 32.

30. A, 750.

31. G, 241.

32. Moshe Hallamish, *An Introduction to The Kabbalah*, trans. Ruth Bar-Ilan and Ora Wiskind-Elper (Albany: State University of New York Press, 1999), 63.

33. Ibid.

34. SD, 112. Ibn al-ʿArabī mentions the heat following the mention of the revelation through striking or consideration. Also see Chittick, *Ṣūfī Path of Knowledge*, 262, for a translation of the passage in which Ibn al-ʿArabī discusses the heat of revelation.

35. G, 68.

36. Addas, *Quest for the Red Sulphur*, 116. In the Ṣūfī literature, the figure of al-Khaḍir was believed to be able to be present at the mosques of Syria, Jerusalem, Medina, and Mecca simultaneously and free of the constraints of time. See Jane Ackerman, "Stories of Elijah and Medieval Carmelite Identity," *History of Religions* (1995): 130.

CONCLUSION

1. TCD, xv. Compare this with what Michael Morgan says: "Platonic learning, then, is an ecstatic ritual process because it is precisely organized, religiously motivated by the desire to become divine, and facilitated by the assumption that the human soul, which is immortal, can become divine or nearly divine." Michael L. Morgan, "Plato and Greek Religion," in *The Cambridge Companion to Plato*, ed. Richard Kraut (Cambridge, Cambridge UK: University Press, 1992), 232.

2. TCD, *Letter 7*, 344: b 4–10. Thus, we must treat with caution statements such as the following: "Philosophy—as its very name, even in Arabic (*falsafa*), indicates—is the unique product of the Greek genius. What marked this product from the start was the relentless search for truth and the revolt against mythology and supernaturalism, all in the name of a rigorous rationalism...The chief outcome of this rationalism was the demand for strict logical coherence and unwavering compliance with its canons, in both the practical and the theoretical spheres of human activity." Majid Fakhry, "The Arabs and the Encounter with Philosophy," 1. One also has to be careful in relation to such statements that separate Plato's thought, for example, from the work of intuition and mystical inspiration. Richard Walzer, for example, says that the intuitive gifts of prophecy in Fārābī, as in Plato, "will be subordinated to his philosophical powers, instead of predominating as they do in the Athenian Neoplatonism in and after the time of Proclus." Richard Walzer, "The Rise of Islamic Philosophy," *Oriens* 3 (1950): 18–19. At the same time, I am aware of the distinction that must be drawn between the senses in which Plato's and Plotinus's philosophies are religious. See the discussion in ʿAbd al-Raḥmān Badawī, *Kharīf al-Fikr al-yūnānī* (Cairo: Maktabat al-Nahḍa al-Maṣriyya, 1970), 115.

3. TCD, *Letter 7*, 343: e 8–9.

4. THA, 144.

5. TCD, xv.

6. TCD, *Letter 7*, 344b 4–10.

7. Abū al-ʿAlāʿ Afīfī, *The Mystical Philosophy of Muḥyiddīn-IbnulʿArabī* (Lahore, Pakistan: Sh. Muḥammad Ashraf, 1964), xi.

8. Shams Inati introduces the following distinction between philosophical and nonphilosophical mysticism. Philosophical mystics, such as Ibn Sīnā, pursue the truth through theoretical intellect. Nonphilosophical mystics follow a spiritual shaykh and engage themselves in an act of purification to protect their heart. Shams Inati, *Ibn Sīnā and Mysticism: Remarks and Admonitions*, Part 4 (New York: Kegan Paul International, 1996), 62–63. In light of this distinction, Ibn al-ʿArabī can be identified with philosophical mysticism, although his philosophical mysticism is to be distinguished from that of the rest of Islamic philosopher-mystics.

9. Chittick, *Ṣūfī Path of Knowledge*, 159.

10. Ibid., 161. FUT 3, 333: 20.

11. As we have seen, certain scholars see in Ibn Ṭufayl's words a condemnation of the figure of Ibn Rushd.

12. Q 19:59; 25:43.

13. Chittick, *Ṣufi Path of Knowledge*, 160; also FUT, 2, 319: 13.

14. Ibid. The following words are brought by Sara Sviri from Tirmidhī's *Kitāb al-Riyāḍa*: "God fixed for Desire (*shahwa*) a gate [that opens] from its location [between the lung and the heart] onto the chest. [Through this opening] the smoke of desires, which Inclination (*hawā*) carries, flares up till it reaches the chest and encircles the *fu'ād* so that the eyes of the *fu'ād* are [covered] in smoke...and are hindered from beholding what the light of the intellect regulates." Sara Sviri, "Words of Power and the Power of Words," 225.

15. Ibid.

16. See the discussion in Bashier, *Ibn al-ʿArabī's Barzakh*, 86–88.

17. THA, 110.

18. THA, 124.

19. TCD, *Phaedrus*, 277: a.

20. In light of this reading, one should exercise caution about statements such as Badawi's that Plotinus's influence on Arabic thinkers was greater than Aristotle's because it extended not only to their philosophical work, but also to their spiritual and gnostic doctrines, to compare with "Aristotle's dry, outward, logical doctrine." ʿAbd al-Raḥmān Badawī, *Aflūṭīn ʿinda al-ʿArab* (Kuwait: Dār al-Maṭbūʿāt, 1977), 2. I tend to agree with Muḥsin Mahdī's statement that students of the history of Greek philosophy must be careful not to be misled by the dominant fashion of seeing Plato and Aristotle as opposed to each other and considering medieval attempts to establish agreement between them as an outcome of misunderstanding rather than legitimate interpretation. Muḥsin Mahdī, *Alfarabi and the Foundation of Islamic Political Philosophy* (Chicago: The University of Chicago Press, 2001), 31.

21. Ibn al-ʿArabī, *Dīwān*, 364.

22. Majid Fakhry, "The 'Antinomy' of the Eternity of the World in Averroes, Maimonides, and Aquinas," *Le Muséon* (1953): 143. See Ibn Rushd, *Faṣl al-Maqāl*, 104.

23. Alfred North Whitehead, *Modes of Thought* (New York: Free Press, 1968), 174.

Bibliography

ʿAbdul Ḥāmid, Khwāja. "The Philosophical Significance of Ibn Ṭufail's *Ḥaiy Ibn Yaqẓān*." *Islamic Culture* 22 (1948): 50–70.

Abusch, Tzvi. "Ishtar's Proposal and Gilgamesh's Refusal. An Interpretation of *The Gilgamesh Epic*, Tablet 6, Lines 1–79." *History of Religions* 26 (1986): 143–87.

Ackerman, Jane. "Stories of Elijah and Medieval Carmelite Identity." *History of Religions* (1995): 124–47.

Addas, Claude. *The Quest for the Red Sulphur: The Life of Ibn ʿArabī*. Trans. Peter Kingsley. Cambridge UK: Islamic Texts Society, 1993.

_____. "The Ship of Stone." *Journal of the Muḥyiddīn Ibn ʿArabī Society* 19 (1996): 5–24.

ʿAfīfī, Abū al-ʿAlā. *The Mystical Philosophy of Muhyiddīn Ibnul ʿArabī*. Lahore, Pakistan: Sh. Muḥammad Ashraf, 1964.

Aghatehrani, Morteza. *Khājah Naṣīr al-Din Ṭūsī on the Meta-Mysticism of Ibn Sīnā*. Ann Arbor, MI: UMI Dissertation Services, 1999

Akbarian, Reza. "The Fundamental Principles of Ibn Sina's Ontology." *Transcendent Philosophy* 2 (2001): 59–76.

Alf Layla wa-Layla, 6 vols. Beirut: Dār Ṣādir, 1999.

ʿAlī, ʿAbdullah Y. *The Meaning of the Holy Qur'ān*. Beltsville, MD: Amana Corporation, 1989.

Arias, Pablo B. "A Summary of the Life of the Prophet by Ibn ʿArabī and the Miracle of the Palm Tree of Seville." *Journal of the Muḥyiddīn Ibn ʿArabī Society* 30 (2001): 73–103.

Aristotle. *Basic Works of Aristotle*. Ed. Richard McKeon. New York: Random House, 1941.

_____. *Physics*. Trans. Hippocrates G. Apostle. Bloomington: Indiana University Press, 1973.

_____. *Al-Ṭabīʿa*. Ed. ʿAbd al-Raḥmān Badawī, 2 vols. Cairo: al-Dār al-Qawmiyya, 1965.

Austin, Ralph. "Ibn al-ʿArabī—Poet of Divine Realities." In *Muḥyiddīn Ibn ʿArabī: A Commemorative Volume*. Ed. Stephen Hirtenstein and Michael Tiernan, 181–89. Rockport, MA: Element, 1993.

Awin, Peter J. *Satan's Tragedy and Redemption: Iblīs in Ṣūfī Psychology*. Leiden: E. J. Brill, 1983.

Badawī, ʿAbd al-Raḥmān. *Al-Aflāṭūniyya al-Muḥdatha ʿInda al-ʿArab*. Kuwait: Wakālat al-Maṭbūʿāt, 1977.

_____. *Aflūṭīn ʿinda al-ʿArab*. Kuwait: Dār al-Maṭbūʿāt, 1977.

_____. *Aristū ʿinda al-ʿArab*. Kuwait: Wakālat al-Maṭbūʿāt, 1978.

_____. *Kharīf al-Fikr al-Yūnānī*. Cairo: Maktabat al-Nahḍa al-Maṣriyya, 1970.

_____. *Al-Muthul al-ʿAqliyya al-Aflāṭūniyya*. Cairo: Maṭbaʿat Dār al-Kutub al-Maṣriyya, 1947.

Balqāsim, Khālid. *al-Kitāba wa-al-Ṭaṣawwuf ʿinda Ibn ʿArabī*. Al-Dār al-Bayḍā': Toubqāl, 2004.

_____. *Ibn al-ʿArabī's Barzakh: The Concept of the Limit and the Relationship between God and the World*. Albany: State University of New York Press, 2004.

_____. "Plato and Ibn al-Arabī on Skepticism." *Journal of the Muḥyiddin Ibn ʿArabī Society* 30 (2001): 19–35.

Belo, Catarina. "Ibn Sīnā on Chance in the *Physics* of As-sifā'." In *Interpreting Avicenna: Science and Philosophy in Medieval Islam*. Ed. Jon McGinnis with the assistance of David C. Reisman, 25–41. Leiden: E. J. Brill, 2004.

Brann, Eva. *The Music of the Republic: Essays on Socrates's Conversations and Plato's Writings*. Philadelphia: Paul Dry Books, 2004.

Burgel, Christoph J. "Symbols and Hints: Some Considerations Concerning the Meaning of Ibn Ṭufayl's *Ḥayy Ibn Yaqẓān*." In *The World of Ibn Ṭufayl: Interdisciplinary Perspectives on Ḥayy Ibn Yaqẓān*, ed. Lawrence I. Conrad, 115–32. Leiden: E. J. Brill, 1996.

Burton, Richard. *Arabian Nights*. 16 vols. Beirut: Khayaṭ, 1966.

Capizzi, Antonio. *The Cosmic Republic: Notes for a Non-Peripatetic History of the Birth of Philosophy in Greece*. Amsterdam: J. C. Gieben, 1990.

Chittick, William C. "Ibn ʿArabī." In *Islamic Philosophy and Theology*, ed. Ian Richard Netton, vol. 4: 122–134. Routledge: London, 2007.

_____. *The Heart of Islamic Philosophy: The Quest for Self-Knowledge in the Teachings of Afḍal al-Dīn Kāshānī*. Oxford: Oxford University Press, 2001.

_____. *Imaginal Worlds: Ibn al-ʿArabī and the Problem of Religious Diversity*. Albany: State University of New York Press, 1994.

_____. *The Self-Disclosure of God*. Albany: State University of New York Press, 1998.

_____. *The Ṣūfī Path of Knowledge: Ibn al-ʿArabī's Metaphysics of Imagination*. Albany: State University of New York Press, 1989.

Chodkiewicz, Michel. "The Endless Journey." *Journal of the Muḥyiddīn Ibn ʿArabī Society* 19 (1996): 71–84.

Clark, Jane. "Universal Meanings in Ibn ʿArabī's *Fuṣūṣ al-Ḥikam*: Some Comments on the Chapter of Moses." *Journal of the Muḥyiddīn Ibn ʿArabī Society* 120 (2005): 105–29.

Classen, Albrecht. “Flowing Light of the Godhead: Binary Oppositions of Self and God in Mechthild von Magdeburg.” *Studies in Spirituality* 15 (2005): 79–97.

Coggan, Donald. *The Revised English Bible*. Oxford: Oxford University Press, 1989.

Conrad, Lawrence I. “Introduction: The World of Ibn Ṭufayl.” In *The World of Ibn Ṭufayl: Interdisciplinary Perspectives on Ḥayy Ibn Yaqẓān*, ed. Lawrence I. Conrad, 1–37. Leiden: E. J. Brill, 1996.

_____. “Through the Thin Veil: On the Question of Communication and the Socialization of Knowledge in *Ḥayy Ibn Yaqẓān*.” In *The World of Ibn Ṭufayl: Interdisciplinary Perspectives on Ḥayy Ibn Yaqẓān*, ed. Lawrence I. Conrad, 238–66. Leiden: E. J. Brill, 1996.

Corbin, Henry. *Avicenna and the Visionary Recital*. Trans. William R. Trask. London: Routledge and Kegan Paul, 1960.

_____. *Spiritual Body and Celestial Earth: From Mazdean Iran to Shi‘ite Iran*. Trans. Nancy Pearson. London: I. B. Tauris, 1990.

Dakake, M. Maria. “The Soul as *Barzakh*: Substantial Motion and Mullā Ṣadrā’s Theory of Human Becoming.” *Muslim World* 94 (2004): 107–30.

Dalley, Stephanie. *Myths from Mesopotamia: Creation, the Flood, Gilgamesh, and Others*. Oxford: Oxford University Press, 1989.

_____. The Sassanian Period and Early Islam.” In *The Legacy of Mesopotamia*, ed. Stephanie Dalley, 163–81. Oxford: Oxford University Press, 1998.

Damīrī, Kamāl al-Dīn. *Ḥayāt al-Ḥayawān al-Kubrā*. 2 vols. Beirut: Dār al-Fikr, n.d.

Davidson, Herbert A. *Alfarabi, Avicenna, and Averroes on Intellect: Their Cosmologies, Theories of the Active Intellect, and Theories of Human Intellect*. Oxford: Oxford University Press, 1992.

Druart, Therese-Anne. “Al-Fārābī, Emanation, and Metaphysics.” In *Neoplatonism and Islamic Thought*, ed. Parviz Morewedge, 127–48. Albany: State University of New York Press, 1992.

Fackenheim, Emil L. “The Possibility of the Universe in al-Fārābī, Ibn Sīnā, and Maimonides.” In *Islamic Philosophy*, 12 vols. Ed. Fuat Sezgin, 375–406. Frankfurt: Institute for the History of Arabic-Islamic Science, 1999.

Fakhry, Mājid. “The ‘Antinomy’ of the Eternity of the World in Averroes, Maimonides, and Aquinas.” *Le Muséon* (1953): 139–55.

_____. “The Arabs and the Encounter with Philosophy.” In *Philosophy, Dogma, and the Impact of Greek Thought in Islam*, 1–17. Brookfield, VT: Variorum, 1994.

Fārābī, Abū Naṣr. *Al-Jam‘bayna Ra’yay al-Ḥakīmayn*. Ed. Albīr Naṣrī Nādir. Beirut: Dār al-Mashriq, 1968.

_____. *Kitāb al-Ḥurūf*. Ed. Muḥsin Mahdī. Beirut: Dār al-Mashriq, 1970.

_____. *Taḥṣīl al-Sa‘āda*. Ed. Ja‘far Yāsīn. Beirut: Dār al-Andalus, 1981.

Fradkin, Hillel. “The Political Thought of Ibn Ṭufayl.” In *The Political Aspects of Islamic Philosophy: Essays in Honor of Muḥsin S. Mahdī*, ed. Charles E. Butterworth, 234–61. Cambridge, MA: Harvard University Press, 1992.

Galston, Miriam. A Re-examination of al-Fārābī’s Neoplatonism.” In *Islamic Philosophy and Theology*, ed. Ian Richard Netton, vol. 2, 126–49. Routledge: London, 2007.

_____. "The Theoretical and Practical Dimensions of Happiness as Portrayed in the Political Treatises of al-Fārābī." In *The Political Aspects of Islamic Philosophy: Essays in Honor of Muḥsin S. Mahdī*, ed. Charles E. Butterworth, 95–151. Cambridge, MA: Harvard University Press, 1992.

Gardner, John, and John Maier, with the assistance of Richard A. Henshaw. *Gilgamesh*. New York: Alred A. Knopf, 1984.

George, Andrew. *The Babylonian Gilgamesh Epic: Introduction, Critical Edition, and Cuneiform Texts*. Oxford: Oxford University Press, 2003.

_____. *The Epic of Gilgamesh: The Babylonian Epic Poem and Other Texts in Akkadian and Sumerian*. London: The Penguin Press, 1999.

Ghazālī, Abū Ḥamid. *Al-Munqidh min al-Ḍalāl*. Ed. ʿAlī Bū Milḥim. Beirut: Dār wa-Maktabat al-Hilāl, 1993.

_____. *Niche of Lights*. Trans. David Buchman. Provo, UT: Brigham Young University Press, 1998.

Goldziher, Ignaz. *Introduction to Islamic Theology and Law*. Trans. Andras and Ruth Hamori. Princeton: Princeton University Press, 1981.

Goodman, Lenn E. "Ibn Bājja." In *History of Islamic Philosophy*, eds. Seyyed Hossein Nasr and Oliver Leaman, vol. 1, 294–311. Routledge: New York, 2001.

_____. *Ibn Ṭufayl's Ḥayy Ibn Yaqẓān*. New York: Twayne, 1972.

_____. "Ibn Ṭufayl." In *History of Islamic Philosophy*, eds. Seyyed Hossein Nasr and Frances H. Simon. London: Routledge, 1955.

Hirtenstein, Stephen. "Aspects of Time and Light." In *Journal of the Muḥyiddīn Ibn al-ʿArabī Society* 6 (1987): 31–49.

_____. *The Unlimited Mercifier: The Spiritual Life and Thought of Ibn ʿArabī*. Oxford: Anqa Publishing, 1999.

Hourani, George. "The Principal Subject of Ibn Ṭufayl's *Ḥayy Ibn Yaqẓān*." *Journal of Near Eastern Studies* 15 (1956): 40–46.

Ibn al-ʿArabī, Muḥyiddīn. *Al-Anwār*. In *Rasāʾil Ibn al-ʿArabī*. 3 vols. Beirut: Dār al-Maḥaja al-Bayḍāʾ. 2000.

_____. *Bezels of Wisdom*. Trans. R. W. J. Austin. New York: Paulist Press, 1980.

_____. *Dīwān*. Ed. Nawāf al-Jarāḥ. Beirut: Dār Sādiq, 1999.

_____. *Fuṣūṣ al-Ḥikam*. Ed. Abū al-ʿAlāʿAfīfī. Beirut: Dār al-Kutub al-ʿArabī, 1946.

_____. *Al-Futūḥāt al-Makkiyya*. 4 vols. Beirut: Dār Ṣādir, 1968.

_____. *Al-Tadbīrāt al-ʾIlāhiyya fī ʾIṣlāḥ al-Mamlaka al-ʾInsāniyya*. In *Kleinere Schriften des Ibn al-ʿArabī*. Ed. H. S. Nyberg. Leiden: E. J. Brill, 1919.

_____. *Al-Tajalliyāt al-Ilāhiyya*. Ed. Osman Yahia. Tehran: Danshkahi, 1988.

_____. *Al-Tajalliyāt al-Ilāhiyya*. Ed. Muḥammad ʿAbd al-Karīm al-Nimrī. Beirut: Dār al-Kutub al-ʿIlmiyya, 2002.

_____. *ʿUqlat al-Mustawfiz*. In *Kleinere Schriften des Ibn al-ʿArabī*. Ed. H. S. Nyberg. Leiden: E. J. Brill, 1919.

Ibn Bājja, Abū Bakr. *Ittiṣāl al-ʿAql bi-al-Insān*. In *Rasāʾil Ibn Bājja al-Ilāhiyya*. Ed. Mājid Fakhry. Beirut: Dār al-Nahār, 1968.

_____. *Risālat al-Wadāʿ*. In *Rasāʾil Ibn Bājja al-Ilāhiyya*. Ed. Mājid Fakhry. Beirut: Dār al-Nahār, 1968.

_____. *Tadbīr al-Mutawaḥḥid*. In *Rasāʾil Ibn Bājja al-Ilāhiyya*. Ed. Mājid Fakhry. Beirut: Dār al-Nahār, 1968.

Ibn Khaldūn, ʿAbd al-Raḥmān. *Muqaddima*. Beirut: Dār al-Turāth al-ʿArabī, n.d.

Ibn Rushd Abū al-Walīd, *Faṣl al-Maqāl fī Taqrīr mā bayna al-Sharīʿa wa-al-Ḥikma min al-Ittiṣāl*. Ed. Muḥammad al-Jābirī. Beirut: Markiz Dirāsāt al-Waḥda al-ʿArabiyya, 2002.

_____. *Al-Kashf an Manāhij al-Adilla fī ʿAqāʾid al-Milla*. Ed. Muḥammad al-Jābirī. Beirut: Markiz Dirāsāt al-Waḥda al-ʿArabiyya, 1998.

_____. *Tahāfut al-Tahāfut*. Ed. Aḥmad Shams al-Dīn. Beirut: Dār al-Kutub al-ʿIlmiyya, 2001.

_____. *Talkhīs al-Āthār al-ʿUlwiyya*. Ed. Jamāl al-Dīn al-ʿUlwī. Beirut: Dār al-Gharb al-Islāmī li-al-Kitāb, 1994.

_____. *Talkhīs Kitāb al-Qiyās*. Ed. Muḥammad Qāsim. Cairo: al-Haiʾa al-Maṣriyya al-Āma li-al-Kitāb, 1983.

Ibn Sabʿīn, *Budd al-ʿĀrif*. Ed. George Katūra. Beirut: Dār al-Andalus, 1978.

Ibn Sīnā, Abū ʿAlī. *Al-Ishārāt wa-al-Tanbīhāt*. 4 vols. Ed. Sulaymān Dunyā. Cairo: Dār al-Maʿārif, 1957.

Ibn Ṭufayl, Abū Bakr. *Ḥayy Ibn Yaqẓān*. Ed. Farūk Saʿd. Beirut: Dār al Āfāq al-Jadīda, 1980.

Ikhwān al-Ṣafāʾ. *Rasāʾil Ikhwān al-Ṣafā*. Ed. Khair al-Dīn al-Zarkalī. Cairo: al-Maṭbaʿa al-ʿArabiyya, 1928.

Ivry, Alfred L. "The Utilization of Allegory in Islamic Philosophy." In *Interpretation and Allegory*, ed. Jon Whitman, 153–88. Leiden: E. J. Brill, 2000.

Jābirī, Muḥammad. *Naḥnu wa-al-Turāth*. al-Dār al-Baydāʾ: al-Markiz al-Thaqāfī al-ʿArabī. 1985.

_____. *Naqd al-ʿAql al-ʿArabī: Bunyat al-ʿAql al-ʿArabī*. Beirut: Markiz Dirāsāt al-Waḥda al-ʿArabiyya, 1990.

_____. *Naqd al-ʿAql al-ʿArabī: Takwīn al-ʿAql al-ʿArabī*. Beirut: Markiz Dirāsāt al-Waḥda al-ʿArabiyya, 2002.

Jacobsen, Thorkild. *The Treasures of Darkness: A History of Mesopotamian Religion*. New Haven, CT: Yale University Press, 1976.

Janssens, Jules. "Al-Ghazālī's *Tahāfut*: Is It Really a Rejection of Ibn Sīnā's Philosophy?" *Journal of Islamic Studies* 12 (2001): 1–17.

Jurjānī, ʿAlī. *Al-Taʿrīfāt*. Beirut: Maktabat Lubnān, 1969.

Kauhod, Shelley D. "Ovid's Tereus: Fire, Birds, and the Reification of Figurative Language." *Classical Philology* 92 (1997): 66–71.

Kennedy-Day, Kiki. *Books of Definition in Islamic Philosophy: The Limits of Words*. London and New York: Routledge Curzon, 2003.

Khālidī, Muḥammad A. "Al-Fārābī, *The Book of Letters*." In *Medieval Islamic Philosophical Writings*, ed. Muḥammad ʿAlī Khālidī, 1–26. Cambridge, UK: Cambridge University Press, 2005.

Kovacs, Maureen G. *The Epic of Gilgamesh.* Stanford, CA: Stanford University Press. 1985.

Kruk, Remke. "Ibn Ṭufayl: A Medieval Scholar's Views on Nature." In *The World of Ibn Ṭufayl: Interdisciplinary Perspectives on Ḥayy Ibn Yaqẓān*, ed. Lawrence I. Conrad, 69–89. Leiden: E. J. Brill, 1996.

Landolt, Herman. "Suhrawardī's 'Tales of Initiation.'" *Journal of the American Oriental Society* 107 (1987): 475–86.

Lane, Edward. *Arabic-English Lexicon,* 8 vols. Beirut: Librairie du Liban, 1980.

Lincoln, Bruce. "Gendered Discourses: The Early History of *Mythos* and *Logos*." *History of Religions* 36 (1996): 1–12.

López-Baralt, Luce. "Saint John of the Cross and Ibn ʿArabī: The Heart or Qalb as the Translucid and Ever-Changing Mirror of God." *Journal of the Muḥyiddīn Ibn al-ʿArabī Society*," 28 (2000): 57–90.

Lory, Pierre. "The Symbolism of Letters and Language in the Work of Ibn ʿArabī." *Journal of Muḥyiddīn Ibn ʿArabī Society* 23 (1998): 32–42.

Lucien, Malson, and Jean Itard. *Wolf Children: The Wild Boy of Aveyron.* Trans. Edmund Fawcett, Peter Ayrton, and Joan White. London: NLB, 1972.

Mahdi, Muhsin. *Alfarabi and the Foundation of Islamic Political Philosophy*. Chicago: University of Chicago Press, 2001.

_____. "Alfarabi on Philosophy and Religion." *Philosophical Forum* 4 (1972): 5–25.

Masri, Angelika. "Imagination and the Qur'ān in The Theology of 'Oneness of Being.'" *Arabica* 47 (2000): 523–35.

Meier, Fritz. "The Mystery of the Kaʿba: Symbol and Reality in Islamic Mysticism." In *The Mysteries: Papers From the Eranos Yearbooks*. Trans. Ralph Manheim, 149–68. New York: Pantheon Books, 1955.

Melamed, Abraham. *The Philosopher-King in Medieval and Renaissance Jewish Political Thought*. Ed. Lenn E. Goodman. Albany: State University of New York Press, 2003.

Milstein, Rachel. "Light, Fire, and the Sun in Islamic Painting." In *Studies in Islamic History and Civilization*, ed. M. Sharon, 533–53. Leiden: E. J. Brill, 1986.

Morgan, Michael L. "Plato and Greek Religion." In *The Cambridge Companion to Plato*, ed. Richard Kraut, 227–47. Cambridge, UK: Cambridge University Press, 1992.

Morris, James W. "Ibn ʿArabī and his Interpreters Part 2: Influences and Interpretations." *Journal of the American Oriental Society* 106 (1986): 733–56.

_____. "Ibn ʿArabī and his Interpreters Part 2: Influences and Interpretations (Conclusion)." *Journal of the American Oriental Society* 107 (1987): 101–14.

_____. *The Reflective Heart: Discovering Spiritual Intelligence in Ibn al-ʿArabī's Meccan Illuminations*. Louisville, KY: Fons Vitae, 2005.

_____. "The Spiritual Ascension: Ibn ʿArabī and the Miʿrāj: Part 2." *Journal of the American Oriental Society*, 108 (1988): 101–19.

Mubarrad, Abū al-ʿAbās. *Al-Kāmil fī al-Lugha wa-al-Adab*, 2 vols. Ed. Ḥanā al-Fākhūrī. Beirut: Dār al-Jīl, 1997.

Murata, Sachiko. *The Tao of Islam: A Source Book on Gender Relationships in Islamic Thought*. Albany: State University of New York Press, 1992.

Nakamura, Kojiro. "Imām Ghazālī's Cosmology Reconsidered with Special Reference to the Concept of *Jabarūt*." *Studia Islamica* 80 (1994): 29–46.

Naṣr, ʿĀtif. *al-Khayāl: Mafhūmuhu wa-Wadhā'ifuhu*. Cairo: al-Sharika al-Maṣriyya li-al-Nashr-Longman, 1997.

Nettler, Ronald L. *Ṣūfi Metaphysics and Qur'ānic Prophets: Ibn ʿArabī's Thought and Method in the Fuṣūṣ al-Ḥikam*. Cambridge UK: The Islamic Texts Society, 2003.

Netton, Ian R. "Theophany as Paradox: Ibn ʿArabī's Account of *al-Khaḍir* in His *Fuṣūṣ al-Ḥikam*." *Journal of the Muḥyiddīn Ibn ʿArabī Society* 11 (1992): 11–22.

_____. "Towards a Modern *Tafsīr* of *Sūrat al-Kahf*: Structure and Semiotics." *Journal of Qur'ānic Studies* 2 (2000): 67–87.

Ockley, Simon. *The Improvement of Human Reason Exhibited in the Life of Hai Ebn Yokdhan*. New York: Georg Olms Verlag, 1983.

Plato, *The Collected Dialogues*. Ed. Edith Hamilton and Huntington Cairns. Princeton, NJ: Princeton University Press, 1994.

Popper, Karl. *The Open Society and Its Enemies*. 2 vols. London: Routledge, 1966.

Qādī, ʿAbd al-Jabār. *Sharḥ al-Uṣūl al-Khamsa*. Ed. ʿAbd al-Karīm ʿUthmān. Cairo, 1965.

Qāshānī, ʿAbd al-Razzāq. *Sharḥ Fuṣūṣ al-Ḥikam*. Cairo: al-Maṭbaʿa al-Maymaniyya, n.d.

Qayṣarī, *Sharḥ Fuṣūṣ al-Ḥikam*, n.d.

Qazwīnī, Zakariyya. *ʿAjā'ib al-Makhlūqāt wa-Gharā'ib al-Mawjūdāt*. Ed. Fārūk Saʿd. Beirut: Dār al-Āfāq al-Jadīda, 1993.

_____. *Athār al-Bilād wa-Akhbār al-ʿIbād*. Beirut: Dār Ṣādiq, 1960.

Qushayrī, Abū al-Qāsim. *Al-Risāla al-Qushayriyya*. Cairo: Sharikat Maktabat wa-Maṭbaʿat Muṣṭafā al-Bābī al-Ḥalabī, 1940.

Radtke, Bernd. "How Can Man Reach the Mystical Union? Ibn Ṭufayl and the Divine Spark." In *The World of Ibn Ṭufayl: Interdisciplinary Perspectives on Ḥayy ibn Yaqẓān*, ed. Lawrence I. Conrad, 165–94. Leiden: E. J. Brill, 1996.

Ragai, Jehane. "The Philosopher Stone: Alchemy and Chemistry." *Alif* 12 (1992): 58–77.

Raska, Julius. "Alchemy in Islam." *Islamic Culture* 36 (1962): 30–36.

Reade, Julian. "Sumerian Origins." In *Sumerian Gods and Their Representations*. Eds. I. L. Finkel and M. J. Geller, 221–27. Groningen, the Netherlands: Styx publication, 1997.

Ridgeon, Lloyd. "ʿAzīz Nasafī's Six Ontological Faces." In *Islamic Philosophy and Theology*, ed. Ian Richard Netton, vol. 3, 359–89. Routledge: London, 2007.

Rosenthal, Erwin. "The Place of Politics in the Philosophy of al-Fārābī." *Islamic Culture* 29 (1955): 157–78.

Rosenthal, Franz. "Ibn ʿArabī Between 'Philosophy' and 'Mysticism.'" *Oriens* 31 (1988): 1–35.

Rustom, Mohammed. "Is Ibn al-ʿArabī's Ontology Pantheistic?." *Journal of Islamic Philosophy* 2 (2006): 53–67.

Saeed, Abdullah. "Rethinking 'Revelation' as a Precondition for Reinterpreting the Qur'ān: A Qur'ānic Perspective." *Journal of Qur'ānic Studies* 1 (1999): 93–114.

Salvesen, Alison. "The Legacy of Babylon and Nineveh in Aramaic Sources." In *The Legacy of Mesopotamia*, ed. Stephanie Dalley, 139–61. Oxford: Oxford University Press, 1998.

Santalana, David. *Al-Madhāhib al-Yūnāniyya fī al-ʿĀlam al-Islāmī*. Ed. Muḥammad Jalāl Sharaf. Beirut: Dār al-Nahḍa al-ʿArabiyya, 1981.

Sarton, George. *Introduction to the History of Science*. 2 vols. Baltimore, MD: Carnegie Institution of Washington, 1931.

Schäfer, Peter. *Mirror of His Beauty: Feminine Images of God from the Bible to the Early Kabbalah*. Princeton, NJ: Princeton University Press, 2002.

Smith, Norman. *Immanuel Kant's Critique of Pure Reason*. New York: St. Martin's Press, 1965.

Suhrawardī, Shihāb al-Dīn. *Book of Radiance: A Parallel English-Persian Text*. Ed. Hossein Ziai. California Costa Mesa: Mazda Publishers, 1998.

_____. *Al-Talwīḥāt al-Lawḥiyya wa-al-ʿArshiyya*. Ed. Henry Corbin. Istanbul: Maṭbaʿat al-Maʿārif, 1945.

Suyūṭī, Jalāl al-Dīn. *Al-Dur al-Manthūr fī al-Tafsīr al-Maʾthūr*. 8 vols. Beirut: Dār al-Kutub al-ʿIlmiyya, 1983.

_____. *Al-Muzhir fī ʿUlūm al-Lugha wa-Anwāʿiha*. Ed. Muḥammad al-Mawlā and Muḥammad Ibrāhīm. Cairo: Dār Iḥyāʾ al-Kutub al-ʿArabiyya, 1960.

Sviri, Sara. "Words of Power and the Power of Words." *Jerusalem Studies in Arabic and Islam* 27 (2002): 204–44.

Ṭabarī, Abū Jarīr. *Tafsīr al-Tabarī,* 12 vols. Beirut: Dār al-Kutub al-ʿIlmiyya, 1992.

Ṭarābīshī, George. *Naqd Naqd al-ʿAql al-ʿArabī: Waḥdat al-ʿAql al-ʿArabī al-Islāmī*, Beirut: al-Sāqī, 2002.

Tigay, Jeffrey H. *The Evolution of the Gilgamesh Epic*. Philadelphia: University of Pennsylvannia Press, 1982.

Van Den Bergh, Simon. *Averroes' Tahāfut al-Tahāfut (The Incoherence of the Incoherence)*, 2 vols. Oxford: Oxford University Press, 1954.

Voegelin, Eric. *Order and History,* 3 vols. Baton Rouge: Louisiana State University Press, 1957.

Walbridge, John. *The Leaven of the Ancients: Suhrawardī and the Heritage of the Greeks*. Albany: State University of New York Press, 2000.

_____. *The Wisdom of the Mystic East: Suhrawardī and Platonic Orientalism*. Albany: State University of New York Press, 2001.

Walker, Paul E. "Philosophy of Religion in al-Fārābī, Ibn Sīnā, and Ibn Ṭufayl." In *Reason and Inspiration in Islam: Theology, Philosophy, and Mysticism in Muslim Thought*, ed. Todd Lawson, 85–101. London: I. B. Tauris, 2005.

Walzer, Richard. "The Rise of Islamic Philosophy." *Oriens* 3 (1950): 1–19.

Wasilewska, Ewa. *Creation Stories of the Middle East*. London: Jessica Kingsley, 2000.

Watt, Montgomery W. "A Forgery in al-Ghazālī's *Mishkāt?*" *Journal of Royal Asiatic Society of Great Britain and Ireland* (1949): 5–22.

Index